America's
Unpatriotic
Acts

PETER LANG
New York • Washington, D.C./Baltimore • Bern
Frankfurt am Main • Berlin • Brussels • Vienna • Oxford

WALTER M. BRASCH

America's
Unpatriotic
Acts

The Federal Government's Violation
of Constitutional *and* Civil Rights

PETER LANG
New York • Washington, D.C./Baltimore • Bern
Frankfurt am Main • Berlin • Brussels • Vienna • Oxford

Library of Congress Cataloging-in-Publication Data

Brasch, Walter M.
America's unpatriotic acts: the Federal Government's violation
of constitutional and civil rights / Walter M. Brasch.
p. cm.
Includes bibliographical references and index.
1. Civil rights—United States. 2. Terrorism—United States—Prevention.
3. Internal security—United States. 4. Prisoners—Legal status,
laws, etc.—United States. I. Title.
JC599.U5B67   973.931—dc22   2004018808
ISBN 0-8204-7608-0

Bibliographic information published by **Die Deutsche Bibliothek**.
Die Deutsche Bibliothek lists this publication in the "Deutsche
Nationalbibliografie"; detailed bibliographic data is available
on the Internet at http://dnb.ddb.de/.

Cover design by Lisa Barfield

The paper in this book meets the guidelines for permanence and durability
of the Committee on Production Guidelines for Book Longevity
of the Council of Library Resources.

© 2005 Walter M. Brasch
Peter Lang Publishing, Inc., New York
275 Seventh Avenue, 28th Floor, New York, NY 10001
www.peterlangusa.com

Printed in the United States of America

For all persons who have sacrificed their personal comfort to speak out against injustice and for social change.

And, as always, to my parents, Milton and Helen Haskin Brasch, for providing the love and wisdom that helped shape what I am.

For my immediate family—Corey Ellen Brasch, Fannie Haskin Frieden, Morris Haskin, Samuel Frieden, Jeanette and Walter Haskin, Phil and Birdie Dworin, Leon Brasch, and Jeffrey and Matthew Gerber—who continue to provide a direction for my own life.

And, especially, to Rosemary R. Brasch for reasons far too numerous to be mentioned.

Contents

Acknowledgments

A project of this magnitude, under intense deadline pressures, could not be completed without the help of many others. More than three hundred persons provided information, sometimes a comment or an answer to a specific question, sometimes through extensive interviews, many on background or anonymously.

Several provided significant and substantial assistance. Judith F. Krug, director of the American Library Association's Office for Intellectual Freedom, and Chris Finan, president of the American Booksellers Foundation for Free Expression, have been active in First Amendment issues for several decades. They provided significant and substantial assistance.

Damon Zucca, an excellent and enthusiastic editor of the communications and media section at Peter Lang Publishing, believed in this project from the moment he heard about it, and was responsible for expertly bringing it to publication. Also providing significant support was Patricia Mulrane, marketing manager, who believed in this book and has done a fine job making sure the people are aware of its existence. Production coordinator was Sophie Appel. Proofreader was Joyce Li.

Stephen Goldstein and Oliver Witte read and evaluated the manuscript, and made several important suggestions. Mr. Goldstein, a former reporter and copyeditor for daily newspapers in New York, Michigan, and Virginia, is copyeditor at the *Washington Times*. Mr. Witte, a journalism professor, was a reporter, copyeditor, and section editor at the *Milwaukee Journal*, a professional writing coach and freelance writer for several newspapers and magazines. He is also coauthor of *Copyediting for Professionals* (2000).

Christine Varner and Jonathan Gass assisted in research and verification. Their work was efficient, accurate, and done with enthusiasm. Providing mental stimulation were Dr. Barbara S. Reed at Rutgers University, Dr. Ron Primeau at Central Michigan University, and Charles Levendosky (1937–2004), editorial page editor at the *Casper* (Wyoming) *Star-Tribune*, one of the nation's leading First Amendment advocates and writers.

MaryJayne Reibsome, against deadline pressures and within a set of unyielding constraints, did a solid job of typesetting. Her training as a journalist assured a meld of content and design. Providing additional technical assistance was Melanie Mills. Librarians Michael Coffta, Bill Frost, and Nancy Weyant also provided special assistance.

And, as always, to my wife, Rosemary Renn Brasch, who brought ideas to this study and read the manuscript several times, always providing valuable suggestions and intellectual stimulation.

Preface

Less than six weeks after terrorists attacked America on September 11, 2001, etched into the nation's memory as 9/11, the Department of Justice, under direction of the president of the United States, pushed onto a fearful nation and its Congress the USA PATRIOT Act. It was a 342-page bill, drafted in secret, which had minimal discussion, and which few members of Congress had read prior to its passage. The Act, which would modify almost twenty federal statutes, was designed to give the president and federal law enforcement sweeping powers. Only one of one hundred senators and sixty-six of 435 representatives voted against it.

A terrified nation, now seeking vengeance, justifiably demanded the Bush administration do something to avenge 9/11 and never to allow such an attack to again occur on American soil. Many appeared to be willing to sacrifice their constitutional freedoms for their safety. Most, however, had little knowledge of the USA PATRIOT Act or how the administration was planning to implement it. They just wanted to feel secure from terror.

Five weeks after President Bush signed the PATRIOT Act into law, John Ashcroft, testifying before the Senate Committee on the Judiciary, stated: "Since lives and liberties depend upon clarity, not obfuscation, and reason, not hyperbole, let me take this opportunity today to be clear: The Justice Department is working to protect American lives while preserving American liberties."[1]

About fifteen months later, again before the Senate Committee on the Judiciary, he reemphasized his earlier statements:

> I want to assure the Committee that . . . we have carefully crafted our post-September 11 policies to foster prevention while protecting the privacy and civil liberties of Americans. As I have often said, we at the Department [of Justice] must think outside the box, but inside the Constitution. I take seriously the concerns of civil libertarians, for I, too, believe that protecting America does not require the sacrifice of those very freedoms that make us Americans.[2]

Speaking to students and faculty of China's Tsinghua University on February 21, 2002, President George W. Bush stated:

> I am concerned that the Chinese people do not always see a clear picture of my country. . . . [S]ome Chinese textbooks talk of Americans bullying the weak and repressing the poor. Another Chinese textbook published just last year teaches that special agents of the FBI are used to repress the working people. Now, neither of these is true . . . [T]hey are misleading and they are harmful. Those who fear freedom

sometimes argue it could lead to chaos. But it does not. Liberty gives our citizens many rights.[3]

However, obstruction, a reduction of public information, distrust and resentment of the press, and a curtailment of civil liberties have been central to the philosophy of the Bush administration, which has been adept at spinning truth to its political agenda.

In Moscow, Idaho, about a hundred FBI and law enforcement agents swooped into town, interviewed all Muslims, arrested a doctoral candidate in computer science, claimed he aided terrorists by serving as a webmaster of an Islamic charity, held him in prison for sixteen months before trial, and wanted imprisonment of at least twenty-five years. Following a two-month trial, the jury said it found no basis for the prosecution.

In San Pedro, California, the federal government arrested and detained more than three years four Iranian businessmen, each of whom had been American residents between eight and twenty-two years. They were accused of minor visa violations and of attending rallies for a terrorist organization— one that Attorney General John Ashcroft himself had supported.

In Philadelphia, two air marshals grabbed a physician and retired Army officer, and then detained him for several hours because, as they told him, "We didn't like the way you looked."

Near Greeley, Colorado, the government arrested three antiwar nuns who had slipped past a chain-link fence, symbolically used a ball-peen hammer to tap the lid of a Minuteman silo, and held a peace vigil. Although the Air Force readily acknowledged they did nothing to compromise national security, the Department of Justice wanted to imprison each of them for up to thirty years.

In Miami, in an attempt to declare Greenpeace a terrorist organization, the Department of Justice used a federal law that had been dormant for more than a century to prosecute the world's leading environmental protection organization for unfurling a banner aboard a ship that carried illegal cargo. The jury disagreed with the government's claims.

In the Bush–Cheney era, dissent is not tolerated; jingoism is encouraged. In Des Moines, Iowa, the FBI ordered Drake University to identify the membership of an organization of law students who had organized a seminar about the war against Iraq, including a session on nonviolent protest. Before the national political conventions in summer 2004, police and FBI agents kept several peaceful antiwar activists under constant surveillance, and then interviewed them for no apparent reason other than to chill their free speech rights.

In Columbia, South Carolina, a fifty-four-year-old man was arrested for carrying a sign, "No More War for Oil." In Tampa, Florida, two grandmothers and a gay rights activist were arrested for peacefully holding protest signs. Near Pittsburgh, Pennsylvania, a sixty-five-year-old retired steel worker was arrested when he refused to go to a "free-speech zone." Under restrictive policies in violation of the First Amendment, anyone with a message not in agreement with the administration's beliefs had to be isolated, some as much as a half-mile away, during presidential and vice presidential public appearances.

At every Bush or Cheney appearance, official or political, persons are prescreened, allowed into rallies if they aren't vocal critics of the administration, and then expected to follow the Republican agenda. In Albuquerque, New Mexico, persons wanting to hear Dick Cheney had to sign loyalty oaths. In Saginaw, Michigan, a woman was thrown out of a Bush rally because she had a rolled-up pro-choice T-shirt. On Independence Day, 2004, at an official presidential appearance, two people were arrested when they refused to turn their T-shirts inside out so an anti-Bush message didn't appear. In Scranton, Pennsylvania, a woman was ordered to remove a small metal peace button from her lapel. In Hamilton, New Jersey, where Laura Bush was rallying the faithful to support the war in Iraq, a mother whose son was killed in Iraq was escorted out because she wore a T-shirt that declared, "President Bush You Killed My Son," and had the audacity to ask what the Republicans believed was a hostile question. Outside the auditorium, while talking with a reporter, she was ordered to leave, didn't do so, and then was handcuffed and arrested on defiant trespass charges. In Medford, Oregon, three peaceful women were thrown out of a campaign rally, and then threatened with arrests. Their offense? They wore T-shirts that said, "Protect Our Civil Liberties." Their cases are just a few of thousands throughout the country.

Reporters usually don't fare any better. In Tucson, Arizona, the Republicans demanded to know the race of some photojournalists before issuing them credentials. In Bloomsburg, Pennsylvania, two reporters were thrown out of a Dick Cheney rally; they were never told the reason, nor would the paid staffers identify themselves. At the Republican National Convention, paid staff, police, and Secret Service constantly harassed reporters, especially those who did not have a national audience, and who may have seemed to be the least bit noncompliant with the Bush–Cheney philosophy.

In Las Vegas, during a two week period before New Year's Day 2004, almost a hundred FBI agents moved into town and seized personal information about more than 350,000 tourists. None of them knew the government now had them in a database; under the PATRIOT Act, casinos, airlines, and car rental agencies were forbidden from even mentioning they had been contacted.

Throughout the country, libraries have put up signs warning that the FBI, under authority of the PATRIOT Act, may seize library records to determine reading habits of patrons. The congressional authority extends to bookstores, physicians' offices, grocery stores, Internet service providers, and virtually any business or organization that has personal data of customers.

Enforcement of the PATRIOT Act butts against the protections of six amendments to the Constitution: the First (freedom of religion, speech, press, and assembly, and the right to petition the government for a redress of grievances), Fourth (freedom from unreasonable searches), Fifth (right against self-incrimination and due process), Sixth (due process, the right to counsel, a speedy trial, and the right to a fair and public trial by an impartial jury), Eighth (reasonable bail and freedom from cruel and unusual punishment), and Fourteenth (equal protection guarantee for both citizens and non-citizens). How the federal government has implemented the PATRIOT Act also violates Article I, Section 9 of the Constitution which guarantees the right to petition the courts to issue a *writ of habeas corpus* to require the government to produce a prisoner or suspect in order to determine the legality of the detention. Only Congress may order a suspension of the right of the writ, and then only in "Cases of Rebellion or Invasion."[4] Congress did not act to suspended this right; nothing during or subsequent to the 9/11 attack indicated either a rebellion or invasion under terms of the Constitution.[5]

"It becomes increasingly difficult for the American government to look at its allies, or even enemies overseas, in the eye and defend human rights, when the U.S. government itself is engaging in efforts that erode personal privacy, that further racial profiling, that limit judicial review, that diminish due-process rights," said Anthony Romero of the American Civil Liberties Union (ACLU).[6]

The *New York Times* almost two years after the Act first passed, bluntly stated, "Rather than do the hard work of coming up with effective port security and air cargo checks, and other programs targeted to actual threats, the administration has taken aim at civil liberties."[7] Innumerable political leaders agreed. "The PATRIOT Act crossed the line on several key areas of civil liberties," Sen. Richard Durbin (D-Ill.), a member of the Senate's Committee on the Judiciary, stated later that year.[8] Al Gore, speaking to an audience in Washington, D.C., forcefully told the nation:

> The constant violations of civil liberties promote the false impression that these violations are necessary in order to take every precaution against another terrorist attack. But the simple truth is that the vast majority of the violations have not benefited our security at all; to the contrary, they hurt our security.[9]

Rep. Dennis Kucinich (D-Ohio), one of the strongest civil liberties proponents in the House of Representatives, and one of the few who had voted against the PATRIOT Act, summed up the feeling of those opposed: "This administration has over-reached in the area of civil liberties. Government shouldn't have that power. It's not consistent with what we are as a nation."[10]

Among dozens of national organizations that uncover abuses and fight for the preservation of American constitutional and civil rights are the American Booksellers Foundation for Free Expression, American Civil Liberties Union, American Library Association, Bill of Rights Defense Committee, Center for Constitutional Rights, Center for Democracy and Technology, Electronic Frontier Foundation, Electronic Privacy Information Center, Free Congress Foundation, Free Expression Policy Project, National Coalition to Repeal the Patriot Act, Open the Government, and People for the American Way, all of which have challenged how the PATRIOT Act is being enforced.

Vanity Fair, the *Sacramento* (Calif.) *Bee, Las Vegas Review-Journal, American Reporter, Bushwatch, Counterbias, Counterpunch, Democratic Underground, Dissident Voice, Liberal Opinion Week, Liberal Slant, Smirking Chimp, The Dubya Chronicles, The Dubya Report,* and several other newspapers, magazines, and alternative publications have been at the forefront of coverage of the effects of the PATRIOT Act. But most media, like most of society, were late in recognizing and reporting the critical issues. Even worse, many were far too deferential to the Bush administration following 9/11, perhaps believing that it would be unpatriotic to oppose the tools the president said he needed to fight the war on terrorism. Many didn't even publish much about the issues, pro or con, perhaps incorrectly believing they were being "journalistically objective."

Almost three years after its passage, two-thirds of Americans believed the USA PATRIOT Act either didn't go far enough (21 percent) or was "about right" (46 percent) in protecting Americans' civil liberties and free-dom. The groups that are "least likely to say the Act goes too far," according to the Gallup Poll, which conducted the survey on behalf of CNN and *USA Today,* are "women . . . Republicans, conservatives, people from rural areas, and those with no college education."[11]

That same CNN/*USA Today*/Gallup poll also revealed that most Ameri-cans aren't familiar with the PATRIOT Act, with 41 percent saying they either are "not too" or "not at all" familiar with the provisions of the Act, while 46 percent claim to be "somewhat" familiar with it.[12] It is for this reason, combined with the general lack of knowledge about the reach of the Act, why *America's Unpatriotic Acts* was written.

This book isn't meant to be a comprehensive analysis of all 150 sections of the USA PATRIOT Act, nor is it meant to be a legal analysis of the Act and the six constitutional amendments it violates. Because of methods of enforcement of the PATRIOT Act and opposition to it, this book can never be current. But, this book *is* meant to be an overview of a number of areas, both of the Act itself and of related actions that help explain a part of the Bush administration's political philosophy and how the administration has dealt with civil rights, including fair and humane treatment of American citizens, immigrants, and prisoners. More importantly, it looks at the rights of privacy, free speech, and due process, as well as related rights, including access to public records for American citizens. Perhaps this book might answer PATRIOT Act supporters who believe, "if you're innocent, you have nothing to fear."

Although the PATRIOT Act forms the base for this book, violations of constitutional and civil liberties aren't confined to one political administration, or to one piece of legislation; all governments and all leaders—some more so than others—develop policies that threaten Americans' rights. When the people allow intrusions upon the Bill of Rights, they effectively destroy the foundation that Jefferson, Madison, Franklin, and the other Revolutionaries fought so hard to build.

The "war on terrorism," like Lyndon Johnson's "war on poverty" and Ronald Reagan's "war on drugs," may never end. But Americans must ask themselves if the *way* America has chosen to fight this war is worth the cost to their Constitutional rights and if the greatest subversion to our country may not be foreign terrorists but our own fears.

CHAPTER 1

'The System Was Blinking Red'

In February 1993, a car packed with more than a thousand pounds of explosives blew up in a garage beneath the World Trade Center. Six were killed, about a thousand wounded.

In November 1995, a bomb near an American military training center in Saudi Arabia killed seven. Seven months later, a truck with five thousand pounds of explosives near a housing complex in Saudi Arabia killed nineteen Americans and injured about 300 others. In August 1998, suicide bombers killed about 250 and injured more than five thousand in the area of the American embassy in Nairobi, Kenya. About the same time, a suicide bomber killed ten and injured seventy at the American embassy in Dar es Salaam, Tanzania.

American intelligence identified the attacks as having been launched by al-Qaeda (in Arabic, "the base"), under command of Osama bin Laden. Bin Laden, the multimillionaire leader of the terrorist organization, had received funding and training from the United States during the Reagan–Bush years of the 1980s while Afghanistan was occupied by the Soviet Union. Untouched while planning terroristic attacks from Saudi Arabia, bin Laden had declared a worldwide terror campaign against America, Israel, Jews, and their allies.

In November 1998, a federal grand jury in Manhattan indicted bin Laden for the bombing at the World Trade Center in February 1993; five others had previously been convicted. The Saudis, refusing to allow Americans to interview suspects in the bombings in 1993 and 1995, executed persons they claimed were involved. Following the attack on the American embassies, and after consultation with congressional leaders of both major political parties, President Bill Clinton ordered cruise missiles into a chemical weapons factory in the Sudan known to have significant ties to al-Qaeda. Simultaneously, the U.S. fired cruise missiles into the al-Qaeda base camp, a weapons and storage facility, and four other al-Qaeda training camps in Afghanistan. President Clinton identified bin Laden as "perhaps the pre-eminent organizer and financier of international terrorism in the world today." He said there was "compelling" evidence that al-Qaeda was planning further attacks.[1] The president ordered American financial institutions to freeze the assets of bin Laden and two of his top lieutenants. In October 2000, suicide bombers attacked the U.S.S. Cole, a guided missile destroyer, off the coast of Yemen; seventeen

1

sailors were killed, thirty-seven wounded. Yemeni authorities blocked the U.S. from sending the FBI and other investigators into the country.[2]

Then, on September 11, 2001, terrorists under bin Laden's direction attacked the United States, leaving about three thousand dead, and several thousand more injured.

Before 9/11, the Bush administration had been staring into headlights. During the transition of power, the incoming Bush administration had discounted the Clinton administration's severe and substantial warnings about terrorist activities. During the first months after the inaugural, Attorney General John Ashcroft himself opposed an FBI proposal to add more counterterrorism agents. Numerous memos by the CIA, backed by data from foreign intelligence agencies, were shuffled into a bureaucratic limbo by the Bush administration. More significant, the Bush administration in the months leading up to the 9/11 murders had substantial warnings about the probability that al-Qaeda would use commercial airplanes to conduct terrorist activities.[3]

The National Commission on Terrorist Attacks Upon the United States (commonly known as the 9/11 commission), an independent commission reluctantly appointed by President Bush, and then only after sustained lobbying by the families of 9/11 victims, reported in December 2003 that the 9/11 attacks could have been prevented. "As you read the report, you're going to have a pretty clear idea of what wasn't done and what should have been done; this was not something that had to happen," Thomas H. Keane, commission chair and a former Republican governor of New Jersey, told CBS News.[4] CIA Director George Tenet told the commission "the system was blinking red,"[5] and that two months before 9/11 it was obvious an imminent threat to the country existed.[6]

In his book, *Against All Enemies: Inside America's War on Terrorism*, and again in testimony before a congressional committee in March 2004, Richard Clarke charged that the Bush administration had not placed terrorism as a priority. Clarke, who had served as antiterrorism director under Presidents George H. W. Bush, Bill Clinton, and George W. Bush, said George W. Bush prior to 9/11 had "ignored terrorism, for months" and refused to heed significant and almost daily warnings from the CIA and Clarke's staff about the imminent threats posed by al-Qaeda. One week before 9/11, Clarke had sent an urgent memo to Condoleezza Rice, the president's national security advisor, informing her that the Department of Defense had done little against al-Qaeda and Osama bin Laden, and for the administration to "imagine a day after hundreds of Americans lay dead at home or abroad after a terrorist attack." One day before 9/11, John Ashcroft had rejected an FBI request for additional funds and personnel to enhance its counterterrorism programs.

The 9/11 commission, in its final report, concluded there were substantial errors made by the Federal Aviation Administration, the Department of

Defense, and the Bush administration the day of the attacks, and that much of the delay in response was because of long-standing bureaucratic structures.[7]

A month after 9/11, after ordering the Taliban regime in Afghanistan to surrender bin Laden, President Bush ordered an aerial attack upon Afghanistan, and then sent in ground forces by the end of November. The Taliban regime surrendered in mid-December 2001. A joint resolution of Congress authorized the president, in his role as commander-in-chief, to use "all necessary and appropriate force against those nations, organizations, or persons he determines planned, authorized, committed, or aided the terrorist attacks . . . or harbored such organizations or persons."[8] The president would use a broad interpretation of that authorization for military force to eventually restrict some American civil liberties, apparently in the mistaken belief that a commander-in-chief was not just a commander-in-chief of the military but of the entire country as well.

The 9/11 commission in April 2004, following several months of depositions and testimony, determined, "[W]hile there were many reports on bin Laden and his growing al Qaeda organization, there was no comprehensive estimate of the enemy, either to build consensus or clarify differences . . . [T]he methods developed for decades to warn of surprise attacks were not applied to the problem of warning against terrorist attacks." The Commission also determined not only did Iraq not have weapons of mass destruction, but there was absolutely "no credible evidence that Iraq and al-Qaeda cooperated on attacks against the United States," and that no "collaborative relationship" between Iraq and al-Qaeda ever existed, arguments the Bush administration advanced as reasons to go to war in Iraq, and continued to maintain even after the Commission report. The 9/11 Commission, however, did conclude there was significant collusion between al-Qaeda and the governments of Pakistan, Iran, and Saudi Arabia.[9]

From being caught unaware, from fear, and from trying to show a nation that it was doing all it could to seek out and destroy the perpetrators of 9/11, combined with a political agenda, came the USA PATRIOT Act, the subsequent invasion of Iraq, and significant civil rights violations, all in the guise of defeating terrorists.

CHAPTER 2

Drafted Under a Cloak of Secrecy

Cicero, writing in the first century B.C., had stated, *"Silent enim leges inter arma"* (roughly: "For laws are silent when arms are raised" or "In time of war, the laws fall silent").[1] His words, both historic and prophetic, would influence governments, totalitarian and republic, for centuries.

Following 9/11, the nation first went into panic and then revenge. President George W. Bush told Attorney General John Ashcroft, "Make sure this can't happen again."[2] At the top of the Department's website is the statement, "The Department of Justice's first priority is to prevent future terrorist attacks."[3]

Congress and the American public gave the government wide latitude to seek out and destroy those responsible. The nation had been attacked; Americans were rightfully frightened. The people believed they may have had to temporarily yield some of their own civil liberties to gain their permanent security. Although understandable in the horror of the events of 9/11, the willing sacrifice of civil liberties would probably have shocked and saddened the nation's founders who wrote our keystone documents under terrors we can't imagine.

Within a week of 9/11, John Ashcroft and his assistants drafted in secret under a cloak of "national security" the Anti-Terrorism Act of 2001.[4] It would soon be renamed the Uniting and Strengthening America by Providing Appropriate Tools Required to Intercept and Obstruct Terrorism Act, better known by the clever acronym, USA PATRIOT Act.[5] The base of the USA PATRIOT Act is three separate acts—the Foreign Intelligence Surveillance Act of 1978 (FISA),[6] passed during the Cold War at a time when there had been increased worldwide terrorism, especially in the Middle East; the Antiterrorism and Effective Death Penalty Act, passed in 1996; and a massive overreaching bill that same year that did not meet Congressional approval. Much of FISA was noncontroversial, its provisions written to assist law enforcement without violating civil liberties. Much of the PATRIOT Act also is noncontroversial. Some of it is purely administrative. It allows expenditure of funds for government offices involved in pursuing terrorists, permits federal law enforcement to hire more translators, and reinforces federal law against discrimination.

John Ashcroft had said numerous times the Department of Justice needed the new laws to deal with terrorism. However, prosecutors, from small towns to the federal government, already had legal and constitutional authority to

4

pursue anyone they believed was either knowledgeable about a crime or had committed a crime. The new laws were merely ways for the federal government to shortcut innumerous constitutional guarantees, including the rights of due process.

Many of the changes incorporated into the PATRIOT Act had previously been rejected by Congress. "The government was seeking a lot of these powers before 9-11," said Steve Lilienthal of the conservative Free Congress Foundation, "but after the attacks, they seized upon terrorism as a way to get what they had always wanted."[7] The Bush administration saw the confusion after the attacks as political convenience. Karl Rove, the president's leading political advisor, would even state in January 2002 that the events of 9/11 and Bush's anti-terrorism position would help elect more Republicans in the fall elections. "We can go to the country on this issue," Rove told the Republican National Committee.[8]

The legislation to create the PATRIOT Act was sent first to the Senate. Sen. Patrick Leahy (D-Vt.), chair of the Committee on the Judiciary, reluctantly agreed to negotiate the proposed bill with the Bush administration rather than to send it through the committee structure for passage. However, after the senators and the various administration officials reached a tentative agreement, John Ashcroft brazenly announced he wouldn't accept it. About a week later, the Senate voted on the bill, with Leahy telling the Senate he had "deep concerns," although he and the Democratic leadership, knowing all Republican senators would vote for the bill, reluctantly urged all Democrats to do the same. Attempts by Sen. Russell Feingold (D-Wisc.), chair of the Constitution, Civil Rights, and Property Rights subcommittee of the Committee on the Judiciary, to introduce amendments were shot down by the Democratic leadership.

In the House of Representatives, James Sensenbrenner Jr. (R-Wisc.) announced he intended to follow all House rules and regular committee procedures. Hearings in the House Judiciary Committee led to a compromise bill with more constitutional protections. Apparently, that didn't meet with the president's or attorney general's approval. Hours before the vote, they persuaded the Republican leadership to rewrite the bill to restore much of the original language. To those who raised any opposition, John Ashcroft roared: "Your tactics aid terrorists."[9] Rep. Lynn Woosley (D-Calif.) recalled that Ashcroft, in demanding passage of the Act in three days, "implied that Congress would have blood on its hands if there was another terrorist attack while we deliberated."[10] Possibly influencing the Congress may have been the reality that less than six weeks after 9/11, five persons had been killed and seventeen had become ill from anthrax hidden within envelopes. Both Sens. Tom Daschle and Patrick Leahy received envelopes with anthrax, but didn't open them; Congress was forced to work in temporary quarters. None of the guilty parties, whether individuals or a large terrorist operation, ever were identified, but the terror of a biological attack underlined the nation's justifiable fear after 9/11.

The House leadership pushed the bill to a vote. There was little time to read or analyze the bill, and only one hour of debate on the floor of the House. "This was the least democratic process for debating questions fundamental to democracy I have ever seen," said Rep. Barney Frank (D-Mass.), who explained the bill was "drafted by a handful of people in secret, subject to no committee process, [and which came] before us immune from amendment."[11] Most members admitted they read only a few paragraphs, if any at all, of the 150-section 342-page document.[12] That was the intent of the Bush administration. Rep. John Conyers Jr. (D-Mich.) later said the Republican leadership provided only two copies of the bill to the Democrats.[13] Rep. Peter DeFazio (D-Ore.) remembers, "It was a time to be stampeded, and who wanted to be against the USA Patriot Act at a time like that?"[14]

In *Losing America* (2004), Sen. Robert C. Byrd (D-W.Va.), first elected to the Senate in 1958, and one of those who had voted for the PATRIOT Act, boldly declared the PATRIOT Act is "a case in the perils of speed, herd instinct and lack of vigilance when it comes to legislating in the face of crisis." The Congress, wrote Byrd, "basically got stampeded by Attorney General John Ashcroft[,] and the values of freedom, justice and equality received a trampling in the headlong rush."[15]

The House of Representatives passed the bill, 357–66; the Senate passed it 98–1. To critics who would later oppose many of the pro-visions of the PATRIOT Act, the Department of Justice righteously pointed to the overwhelming vote by Congress to justify the Act—it never referred to the arm-twisting done by the Bush administration, the deferential attitudes of Congress to presidential authority following 9/11, and the procedures that led to passage of the Act.

Sen. Orrin Hatch (R-Utah), one of the bill's strongest advocates, claimed it passed "because the American people and extraordinary circumstances demanded it."[16]

President Bush enthusiastically signed the bill on October 26, 2001, commenting that his administration took "an essential step in defeating terrorism, while protecting the constitutional rights of all Americans. . . . [It] upholds and respects the civil liberties guaranteed by our Constitution."[17]

The president undoubtedly believed what he was saying, but his subsequent actions belied that belief. Of those who voted against the bill, Rep. Earl Blumenauer (D-Ore.) said he had opposed it because of "problems regarding freedom of speech,"[18] and Rep. Carolyn Kilpatrick (D-Mich.) said, "vigilance must abide to ensure that our nation does not succumb to terrorism from beyond, but also to ensure that we do not succumb to tyranny from within as well."[19] The only senator to vote against the bill was Russell

Feingold. The nation must "be sure we are not rewarding these terrorists and weakening ourselves by giving up the cherished freedoms that they seek to destroy," Feingold said the day of the vote, emphasizing, "We must redouble our vigilance to ensure our security and to prevent further acts of terror. But we must also redouble our vigilance to preserve our values and the basic rights that make us who we are."[20] Almost every one of the cautions and problems Feingold pointed out in his 5,200-word speech in the Senate were prophetic.

The federal government claims parts of the PATRIOT Act have been successful in giving federal law enforcement the tools it needs to bring about arrests of several persons loyal to al-Qaeda or other terrorists who were in "sleeper cells" in Buffalo, Detroit, Portland, and Seattle.

Without the PATRIOT Act, according to Sen. Lindsey Graham (R-S.C.), it would not have been possible for federal law enforcement to have "gained important information on terrorist safe houses, training camps and recruitment efforts in the United States."[21] Robert J. Cleary, U.S. Attorney for New Jersey at the time of 9/11, believes that prior to the PATRIOT Act, "our laws providing investigative tools to law enforcement did not keep pace with the development of new technologies."[22] Before the Senate Committee on the Judiciary, Cleary argued that "to increase the odds of bringing terrorists to justice, investigators and prosecutors must be able to operate with enhanced efficiency. In the Patriot Act, Congress has given them the tools to do so."[23]

The conviction of three persons in the Detroit "sleeper cell" was the first major conviction of terrorism following 9/11, and was widely flaunted by John Ashcroft and the Bush administration for almost three years as a major success of the PATRIOT Act. However, by direction of U.S. District Judge Gerald E. Rosen, the Department of Justice initiated a vigorous nine-month posttrial investigation of prosecutorial misconduct, as well as an intense investigation of the original evidence, much of it withheld by the Department of Justice. In September 2004, the Department of Justice asked for a dismissal of all charges of terrorism against two of the four who were convicted; a third was convicted only of document fraud; a fourth had been acquitted. In dismissing the charges, Judge Rosen said the federal prosecutors not only acted outside the limits of the Constitution, but "simply ignored or avoided any evidence or information which contradicted or undermined" their opinion that the four Moroccans were guilty of plotting acts of terrorism. The judge praised the work of the new prosecutors who conducted the investigation.[24]

Nevertheless, others believe the mechanisms and procedures from FISA and other criminal codes, which were enhanced in 1998, and which help assure protection of civil liberties, were already sufficient in the post-9/11 era. Nevertheless, certain sections threaten Americans' civil liberties while doing little to protect the safety of the nation.[25]

The PATRIOT Act gave legal authority for the FBI and CIA to share information and evidence (sections 201, 901). Implicit in the intent was that the FBI and CIA, by maintaining their own territorial imperatives, may not have been as efficient in monitoring terrorism as they should have been. Innumerable members of the Bush administration and federal law enforcement agencies have argued that the "wall" between the FBI and CIA, initiated during the 1970s to restrain significant civil liberties violations that arose from domestic spying during the Vietnam era, also allowed significant lapses of intelligence and law enforcement. They argue that the PATRIOT Act has torn down this wall.

In testimony before the National Commission on Terrorist Attacks Upon the United States, John Ashcroft claimed that the "single greatest structural cause for the September 11th problem was the wall that segregated or separated criminal investigators and intelligence agents."[26] The attorney general then attacked 9/11 commission member Jamie Gorelick, deputy attorney general under President Clinton. Ashcroft told the commission that Gorelick was the architect of a memo in 1995 that established that wall; conveniently, he had just declassified that memo in time for the hearings. However, that memo was merely a clarification to continue separation of intelligence and law enforcement functions. The policy, which Ashcroft knew was formulated well before the Clinton administration, was continued during the Bush administration prior to 9/11.

Kate Martin, executive director of the Center for National Security Studies, points out:

> This "wall" metaphor is inaccurate and the existence of legal barriers to sharing information is highly exaggerated. Such talk is used to obscure bureaucratic failures of coordination and communication between the FBI and CIA, as well as inside each agency. . . .
>
> Indeed, to protect civil liberties and guard against the creation of a Gestapo-like agency, the CIA's original charter, the 1947 National Security Act, prohibited the agency from exercising any "police, subpoena, law-enforcement powers, or internal security functions." . . . But this early attempt to prevent the CIA from spying on Americans was not enforced through any law or oversight mechanism, and in fact the intelligence agencies did engage in widespread political spying. . . .
>
> The reforms undertaken since the 1970s to prevent such abuses have been misunderstood as creating a so-called "wall" between law enforcement and intelligence.[27]

The legal mechanisms for coordination between agencies were in place prior to 9/11. The Foreign Intelligence Surveillance Act of 1978, as Gorelick noted, allowed intelligence investigators to "conduct electronic surveillance in the United States against foreign targets under a more lenient standard than is required in ordinary criminal cases, but only if the 'primary purpose' of the surveillance were foreign intelligence rather than criminal prosecution."[28] Gorelick also pointed out it was the Department of Justice under

Presidents Ronald Reagan and George H. W. Bush "that began to read the statute as limiting the department's ability to obtain FISA orders," that the current administration one month before 9/11 "formally reaffirmed the 1995 guidelines," and that "nothing in the 1995 guidelines prevented the sharing of information between criminal and intelligence investigators."[29] What the PATRIOT Act did was to reduce judicial oversight.

Within days of Ashcroft's attack upon Gorelick, the Department of Justice website revealed more memos,[30] which Ashcroft declassified, but which didn't give the complete picture of the history of the "wall." President Bush, the day after the documents appeared on Justice's website, said he was "disappointed" in Ashcroft's attacks upon Gorelick, and asked him to remove the offending language and documents from the website.[31] The documents remained on the site for months after the president's strong request.

The PATRIOT Act also expanded the government's surveillance powers to permit almost unrestricted information-gathering while reducing the oversight function of the courts, but did nothing to break down the non-existent "wall." Under FISA, the government could conduct covert surveillance of individuals but only after seeking an order from a secret court created by the federal government. The court consists of eleven federal district court judges from throughout the country, appointed by the chief justice of the United States, and who serve in addition to their other duties.[32] The court meets at least twice a month behind locked doors on the top floor of the Department of Justice building. If that court denies a request for surveillance, the government may appeal to the three-member Court of Review, its members appointed by the Chief Justice of the United States. However, that appeals court had only one case; the lower court between its creation in 1978 and mid-2004, granted all but one of the government's more than fifteen thousand requests. The court essentially had become a puppet of the executive branch since FISA court judges, under both the original law and its subsequent broadening by the PATRIOT Act, are required to grant FBI surveillance requests if the FBI claims its actions are in accordance with the law. In state actions, individuals have the right to ask local and state courts to quash subpoenas for records. If denied, they may appeal to state supreme courts. No such protection exists under FISA. Individuals and businesses may not be represented in that secret court. The only appeal allowed is one initiated by the government, and all parties are bound by a federal gag order prohibiting any disclosure of such an order even being issued. There is no recourse.

On the floor of the House, during the brief time permitted to discuss the pending PATRIOT Act bill, Rep. Jerry Nadler (D-N.Y.) not only argued against passage of the bill, but specifically the extension of the secret courts; his argument showed the hypocrisy in the current administration:

[L]ast year candidate George Bush pledged to seek repeal of the secret courts provision of the 1996 antiterrorism bill because he claimed to understand that the law was passed hastily and that this provision at least endangered civil liberties without contributing to national security. Now the president, the same George Bush, and the leadership of this House is insisting that we again enact hastily, and again in the name of national security and antiterrorism, act so hastily as probably to endanger our civil liberties without necessarily helping our security.[33]

FBI Director Robert Mueller III, who had once stated that his agency "has been the agency to protect the rights of others," admitted that it had lied in at least seventy-five instances when it applied for wiretap authorization from the Foreign Intelligence Surveillance Court.[34]

Nevertheless, civil libertarians didn't object to the PATRIOT Act extending the use of roving wiretaps. Under FISA, the federal government already was authorized to use such wiretaps in criminal investigations related to terrorism or drug dealing.[35] However, they did object to some of the re-duction of procedural safeguards following 9/11. According to Kate Martin, "In the Patriot Act, Congress and the Bush administration first re-pealed the most important check against abuse of FISA surveillance. And then required wholesale sharing of information on Americans with the CIA with virtually no safeguards."[36]

The USA PATRIOT Act reduces judicial oversight of telephone and Internet surveillance. Under the PATRIOT Act, federal law enforcement agencies aren't required to determine if a suspect uses or is likely to use a phone before planting a "bug." Under Sections 214 and 216, the federal government is also authorized to sweep the records of Internet Service Pro-viders (ISPs) and network administrators in both private and public sectors, and may monitor and intercept e-mail and cell phone usage without first being required either to have a court order or to report such activities to judicial oversight. The federal government only has to believe that the information is "relevant," and does not need to show there is a "probable cause," as required under the Fourth Amendment. More important, the fede-ral government can receive such warrants without the courts being allowed to determine if the allegations are truthful. Because the United States is essentially a "wired nation," with almost as many families having access to computers as they do to televisions, the problem of databases and possible privacy intrusions becomes even more severe. America Online (AOL), for instance, has a database of over ninety-two million names, with several identifying characteristics per name, all accessible under the PATRIOT Act.

Subsequent modifications to the Act now allow the government to obtain blanket warrants without identifying who is being monitored or which phones or computers are the target. The Department of Justice says the Act only allows the devices to "reveal the electronic addresses of the users of these media; they do not give law enforcement agents access to the contents of communications that are transmitted over them."[37] However, by knowing each page a person accesses by computer, even if for reasons of curiosity, a person's rights of privacy are violated. Even if a person chooses to purchase an item online, such as a box of dog treats, an electronic address of a specific page will reveal that information.

According to the Center for Constitutional Rights:

> Section 216 gives the government wide latitude to decide what constitutes "content." Of special concern is the fact that Section 216 authorizes the government to install its new Carnivore or DCS1000 system, a formidable tracking device that is capable of intercepting all forms of Internet activity, including email messages, web page activity, and Internet telephone communications. Once installed on an Internet Service Provider (ISP), Carnivore devours *all* of the communications flowing through the ISP's network—not just those of the target of surveillance but those of all users—and not just tracking information but content as well. The FBI claims that through the use of filters, Carnivore "limits the messages viewable by human eyes to those which are strictly included within the court order." However, neither the accuracy of Carnivore's filtering system, nor the infallibility of its human pro-grammers [*sic*], has been demonstrated. While Section 216 requires the government to maintain a record when it utilizes Carnivore, this record need not be provided to the court until 30 days after the termination of the order, including any extensions of time. Section 216 is not scheduled to expire.[38]

The Carnivore system, according to documents obtained by the Electronic Privacy Information Center through a court order in May 2002,[39] had signifi-cant problems that caused "the improper capture of data," which resulted in "unauthorized interceptions [that] not only can violate a citizen's privacy, but also can seriously 'contaminate' ongoing investigations."[40]

In March 2004, the Department of Justice petitioned the Federal Com-munications Commission to allow even greater access for FBI wiretaps and other electronic surveillance. The department proposed that the cost of the technology to establish and maintain increased surveillance be borne by those who are connected to the Internet.[41]

Amazingly, Ashcroft's attitude about the government's spying upon American electronic communication was in direct conflict with his political statement about privacy and national security, written in 1997 for the *USIA Electronic Journal*. As a conservative Republican senator from Missouri, Ashcroft unleashed an attack upon President Clinton for requesting the government's right to monitor e-mail:

> The Clinton administration would like the Federal government to have the capability to read any international or domestic computer communications. The FBI wants access to decode, digest, and discuss financial transactions, personal e-mail, and proprietary information sent abroad—all in the name of national security. To accomplish this, President Clinton would like government agencies to have the keys

for decoding all exported U.S. software and Internet communications.

This proposed policy raises obvious concerns about Americans' privacy, in addition to tampering with the competitive advantage that our U.S. software companies currently enjoy in the field of encryption technology. Not only would Big Brother be looming over the shoulders of international cyber-surfers, but the administration threatens to render our state-of-the-art computer software engineers obsolete and unemployed.

There is a concern that the Internet could be used to commit crimes and that advanced encryption could disguise such activity. However, we do not provide the government with phone jacks outside our homes for unlimited wiretaps. Why, then, should we grant government the Orwellian capability to listen at will and in real time to our communications across the Web?

The protections of the Fourth Amendment are clear. The right to protection from unlawful searches is an indivisible American value. Two hundred years of court decisions have stood in defense of this fundamental right. The state's interest in effective crime-fighting should never vitiate the citizens' Bill of Rights.[42]

Heavy political pressure from Congress forced the Clinton administration to abandon its proposals.

The PATRIOT Act lowers the standard of proof for a warrant from "probable cause" to the nebulous "reasonable cause," significantly reducing the standard of what is required to obtain a search warrant (Section 218). Senior officials of the Department of Justice had claimed the PATRIOT Act doesn't violate the constitutional guarantees that law enforcement will detain and arrest individuals only for "probable cause." More than a year after the PATRIOT Act had become law, LaRae Quy, FBI spokesperson in San Francisco, said, "We still have to show probable cause for any actions we take. It's not just an agent descending and saying, 'Hey, I want to go in and see what this person is doing.'"[43] Within a month, Mark Corallo of the Department of Justice told the media that not only must there be a "probable cause that the person you are seeking the information for is a terrorist or a foreign spy,"[44] but that law enforcement officials had "to convince a judge that the person for whom you're seeking a warrant is a spy or a member of a terrorist organization."[45]

They were wrong. According to Jameel Jaffer, staff attorney with the American Civil Liberties Union (ACLU):

[T]he FBI can obtain records . . . merely by specifying to a court that the records are 'sought for' an ongoing investigation. . . . That standard . . . is much lower than the standard required by the Fourth Amendment, which ordinarily prohibits the government from conducting intrusive searches unless it has probable cause to believe that the target of the investigation is engaged in criminal activity.[46]

Before the House Judiciary Committee, John Ashcroft finally admitted that the standard under the PATRIOT Act was "lower than probable cause," and that federal officials could go after citizens who were neither spies nor members of terrorist organizations.[47]

The PATRIOT Act, extending FISA, also allows secret searches to seize an individual's property without notifying that person even after the seizure (Section 806); and "sneak-and-peek" searches (Section 213) without notifying the citizen, to allow a search the premises while the subjects are away, not just for investigation of potential terrorism cases but also for "any criminal investigation." For almost the entire history of the United States, a legal principle, based upon the Fourth Amendment, demanded that law enforcement, with a few exceptions, "knock and announce" their presence to execute a warrant. Part of that reason is to allow citizens to notify their attorneys, point out irregularities in the warrants (such as a wrong address), or to oversee that the limits of the warrant are not exceeded.

In May 2004, the FBI, with a court warrant obtained through regular procedures, searched the home and office of Brandon Mayfield, a family and immigration lawyer from Oregon. The government seized innumerable "tangible items," including "Spanish documents," which proved to be homework by one of his children. The FBI placed Mayfield into prison as a "material witness," which could have resulted in an indefinite detention with no charges ever being filed, monitored his every move, and announced with "nearly 100 percent certainty" that he was involved in a terrorist attack in Madrid two months earlier that killed almost two hundred and injured about two thousand. The court order was issued on the basis of an FBI claim that a partial fingerprint found on a package of detonator caps was Mayfield's. The Spanish authorities, who provided the fingerprint to the FBI by fax, weren't so sure. Subsequent analysis revealed the Spanish authorities were correct— the fingerprint was that of an Algerian national.

After two weeks in prison, Mayfield, a Muslim and former Army officer, was released. The FBI, which acknowledged it did a sloppy job of processing the print and investigating the case, publicly apologized; John Ashcroft called it "an unfortunate incident." The announced search of Mayfield's home may have been the second search. Steven T. Wax, a federal public defender, and one of Mayfield's attorneys, believes the FBI may have conducted an even more secret search under authority of the PATRIOT Act. The Department of Justice, claiming national security concerns, refused to acknowledge the previous search.

"We need to be safe and secure in our homes, not just from the bad guys but from the government as well," Mayfield told the Portland City Club following his release.[48] A subsequent investigation initiated by the Department of Justice's inspector general, following a complaint by Mayfield, revealed that the FBI may have improperly used the PATRIOT Act to search Mayfield's home without his knowledge.[49]

According to documents filed in *North Jersey Media Group v. Ashcroft,* almost all delays to notify citizens that warrants were executed upon their property were at least ninety days.[50] The Department of Justice claims: "Delayed notification search warrants are a long-existing, crime-fighting tool upheld by courts nationwide for decades in organized crime, drug cases and child pornography."[51] However, according to the Center for Democracy and Technology (CDT):

> Contrary to the Justice Department's assertion, the Supreme Court has never ruled that delayed notification is permissible for execution of a warrant to physically search someone's home or office. The case cited by the Justice Department, *Dalia v. United States*, 441 U.S. 238 (1979), held that a covert entry was permitted to install a bug because there was no other way to effectively execute the order authorizing the bug. In the context of wiretaps and bugs, it would be nonsensical to notify someone that you are planning to monitor their communications. That rationale simply does not apply in the context of physical searches. The Supreme Court has never ruled on the constitutionality of sneak and peek searches.
>
> While courts had previously held that this delay in notification [excluding wiretaps] is permissible in limited circumstances, the PATRIOT Act provided statutory authority with entirely inadequate standards. The PATRIOT Act allows these extraordinary searches to be used in all criminal cases, not just terrorism cases, and the standard is so loose that it could arguably be used in almost every criminal case. The presumption has long been that law enforcement officers have to knock and announce themselves when they execute a search warrant, and an exception to that rule should be made only in limited circumstances with strict guidelines—which the PATRIOT Act does not contain.[52]

"In addition to ignoring fundamental Fourth Amendment privacy rights, it also greases the slippery slope that was clearly anticipated, but specifically addressed and avoided by the drafters of our Constitution in the threefold separation-of-powers system of government they crafted so magnificently," says Bob Barr, a former CIA intelligence official, U.S. attorney, and conservative congressman who had been a vigorous opponent of the Clinton administration.[53] Barr has repeatedly stated that innumerable provisions of the USA PATRIOT Act "undercut basic conceptions of due process and privacy [and] their effectiveness is questionable."

The PATRIOT Act further gives the government the authority to indefinitely imprison legal immigrants and noncitizens without showing any court probable cause that they are terrorists or suspected of aiding others who are terrorists, and doesn't give the accused the right to challenge the government's assertions (Section 412); and expands the definition of terrorism to allow labeling dissenters as terrorists (Sections 411 and 802).

The PATRIOT Act also grants the FBI almost unlimited and unchecked access to "any tangible things (including books, records, papers, documents, and other items)" from individuals or companies without requiring them to show even minimal evidence of a crime, and places a "chilling effect" upon free speech (Section 215). The Act's sweeping provisions apply not only to homes, businesses, and newsrooms, but also to synagogues, churches, mosques, and other places of religious worship. Under provisions of the PATRIOT Act, the federal government can require libraries to divulge who uses public computers or what books they check out, video stores to reveal what tapes and DVDs customers bought or rented, even grocery and drug stores to disclose what paperbacks or magazines shoppers bought. Before the House Judiciary Committee, John Ashcroft even acknowledged that the federal government could obtain an individual's medical and educational records, and possibly DNA information as well, all without needing a court's determination there was "probable cause" for such a search.[54]

Under provisions of Section 505, the Department of Justice has the authority to use National Security Letters, essentially administrative sub-poenas without judicial oversight. The U.S. Code (18 U.S.C. § 2709) had permitted use of such letters, but the PATRIOT Act significantly expanded and loosened the requirements. National Security Letters may be issued against "electronic communication service providers" to disclose information about individuals, including content of their communications. The National Security Letters, as defined within the PATRIOT Act, don't require the show of "probable cause" nor a "compelling need" for access to the information. The FBI no longer needs to have the name of an individual or even specific facts of a case. There is no judicial oversight; there is no provision for any challenge, and the persons who are served such letters are forbidden by law from disclosing that they were served such letters or even discussing such issuance with an attorney. Under the PATRIOT Act, the government may require companies to surrender confidential information about their employ-ees or customers, even if they are not suspected of any crime.

"Before the Patriot Act, the FBI could use this invasive authority only against suspected terrorists and spies," pointed out ACLU attorney Jameel Jaffer, "[and] now it can issue National Security Letters to obtain information about anyone at all."[55] Several hundred may have been filed between October 2001 and February 2003, according to U.S. District Judge Victor Marrero.

In a suit filed in the U.S. District Court for the Southern District of New York in April 2004, the ACLU charged: "[T]he gag provision is uncon-stitutionally vague, overbroad, and imposes an unlawful prior restraint on speech." The ACLU sought a declaration that Section 2709 of FISA, as amended by Section 505 of the PATRIOT Act, violated the First, Fourth, and Fifth Amendments."[56]

Under the "gag rule" of the PATRIOT Act, however, the court sealed that suit. None of the parties were allowed to disclose that a suit even was filed, nor could they even consult with an attorney. No record appeared on a public docket. A heavily redacted version, which deleted the names of one of the plaintiffs, was finally released after three weeks of intense negotiations.

Subsequently, the court issued guidelines to allow public disclosure.[57]

"It is remarkable that a gag provision in the Patriot Act kept the public in the dark about the mere fact that a constitutional challenge had been filed in court," said Ann Beesen, ACLU associate legal director. She observed that "President Bush can talk about extending the life of the Patriot Act, but the ACLU is still gagged from discussing details of our challenge to it."[58]

In a comprehensive 120-page opinion issued in September 2004, Judge Marrero declared NSLs to be unconstitutional. In ruling against the perpetual "gag" provisions, Judge Marrero determined:

> Public knowledge ensures freedom. Under the mantle of secrecy, the self-preservation that ordinarily impels our government to censorship and secrecy may potentially be turned on ourselves as a weapon of self-destruction. At that point, secrecy's protective shield may not serve as much to secure a safe country as simply to save face. . . .
>
> [A]s our sunshine laws and judicial doctrine attest, democracy abhors undue secrecy, in recognition that public knowledge secures freedom [and, thus, NSLs have] no place in our open society.[59]

Judge Marrero determined that FBI-issued NSLs have "the effect of authorizing coercive searches effectively immune from any judicial process," and, as such, violate Fourth Amendment protections against unreasonable searches and seizures.

In ruling that NSLs violate the First Amendment, Judge Marrero determined:

> [The NSL] works as both a prior restraint on speech and as a content-based restriction, and hence, is subject to strict scrutiny. . . .
>
> The FBI theoretically could . . . issue an NSL under § 2709 to discern the identity of someone whose anonymous online web log, or "blog," is critical of the government. Such inquiries might go beyond the permissible scope of the FBI's power under § 2709 because targeted information might not be relevant to the authorized investigation to protect against international terrorism or clandestine intelligence activities, or because the inquiry might be conducted solely on the basis of activities protected by the First Amendment. These prospects only highlight the potential danger of the FBI's self-certification process and the absence of judicial oversight.[60]

Judge Marrero, however, stayed the ruling ninety days to give the government time to appeal.

At first, only a few opposed the USA PATRIOT Act. For the same reason Congress passed the bill, the public, politicians, local and state officials, and the media were afraid that by speaking against the Act, or the administration, they would be perceived as being not only unpatriotic but treasonous in the newly declared war on terrorism. It was certainly an impression the Bush administration pushed. Within months, however, some of the public began speaking out. And as the excesses of the PATRIOT Act became known, others began to question its effectiveness in the post-9/11 era.

"Our legislators get carried away sometimes, and go to extremes," said Al Fratzke, a resident of Sun City West, Arizona, and a prisoner of war during World War II; the PATRIOT Act is an extreme reaction to 9/11, he said.[61] Dr. Harry Kraus, Queens College professor emeritus of history, said the PATRIOT Act "is an invasion of our civil rights, our constitutional rights."[62] Former CBS News anchor Walter Cronkite, interviewed by CNN's Larry King, called the USA PATRIOT Act "disastrously severe."[63]

Rep. Don Young (R-Alaska), who had voted for the PATRIOT Act, agrees. Young, in his sixteenth term in the House and that body's ninth ranking member, told a news conference that not only was the Act "not really thought out," but that he was "very concerned that, in our desire for security and our enthusiasm for pursuing supposedly [*sic*] terrorists, that sometimes we might be on the verge of giving up the freedoms which we are trying to protect."[64]

Before a cheering audience of more than three thousand people in Washington, D.C., slightly more than two years after passage of the PATRIOT Act, former Vice President Al Gore ripped the Bush administration's failure to defend civil liberties:

> I want to challenge the Bush Administration's implicit assumption that we have to give up many of our traditional freedoms in order to be safe from terrorists. Because it is simply not true.
>
> In fact, in my opinion, it makes no more sense to launch an assault on our civil liberties as the best way to get at terrorists than it did to launch an invasion of Iraq as the best way to get at Osama Bin Laden. In both cases, the administration has attacked the wrong target.
>
> In both cases they have recklessly put our country in grave and unnecessary danger, while avoiding and neglecting obvious and much more important challenges that would actually help to protect the country.
>
> In both cases, the administration has fostered false impressions and misled the nation with superficial, emotional and manipulative presentations that are not worthy of American Democracy.
>
> In both cases they have exploited public fears for partisan political gain and postured themselves as bold defenders of our country while actually weakening not strengthening America.[65]

It was a speech that should have been given more than a year earlier, but would now serve as a focal point for opposition to the Bush administration policies.

CHAPTER 3

'A Monstrous Failure of Justice'

In January 2002, the first nineteen hundred Joint Task Force personnel, civilian and military, arrived at the U.S. Naval Base, Guantánamo Bay, Cuba, to prepare for the imprisonment of persons captured in combat in Afghanistan. One week later, the Department of Defense moved the first of several hundred prisoners from Afghanistan into the temporary facility known as Camp X-Ray. At the end of April, prisoners were moved into the more permanent Camp Delta.

Because the president declared this to be a "war on terrorism," he believed he was justified to use certain executive privileges not available to him otherwise. He claimed because those sent to Guantánamo Bay were "enemy combatants" and not American citizens the Constitution didn't apply. Until formally used by the Bush administration, "the term 'enemy combatant' appeared nowhere in U.S. criminal law, international law or in the law of war," according to Gary D. Solis, a former Marine combat officer who has taught military law at both the U.S. Military Academy and Georgetown University.[1]

Under presidential directive, those detained at Guantánamo Bay were to be held indefinitely, even if no charges ever were filed; they were denied access to legal counsel and any right to review evidence against them, or to know even if charges were filed. They were also denied any right to visit with their families. If, and when, the government decided, they would be brought before a secret military tribunal; they would not be allowed to face their accusers, nor would they be allowed to cross-examine witnesses. They could be executed, all without review by the judiciary. Apparently, the Bush administration had no plans to release the prisoners under any conditions. Brig. Janis L. Karpinski, a Reservist commanding a military police bri-gade in Iraq, says she asked a lieutenant colonel and lawyer assigned to Guantánamo Bay about procedures for release of prisoners. According to Karpinski, she was told:

> We're not releasing anybody. . . . Most of these prisoners will never leave Guantánamo Bay. They'll spend the rest of their lives in detention.[2]

When Karpinski asked about visits from family, she was told, "These are terrorists, ma'am. They're not entitled to visitors from home."[3]

Under government rules, which mimicked those in the PATRIOT Act, anyone revealing information about any prisoner, or even if someone was a

18

prisoner, could be subjected to prison and a fine. In a concurring opinion, written during the Korean War, Justice Robert Jackson had pointed out that although a president should be given the "widest latitude" during times of war:

> Loose and irresponsible invocation of war as an excuse for discharging the Executive Branch from the rules of law that govern our Republic in times of peace [is not acceptable]. . . . No penance would ever expiate the sin against free government of holding that a President can escape control of executive powers by law through assuming his military role. . . . Our government has ample authority under the Constitution to take those steps that are genuinely necessary for our security. At the same time, our system demands that government act only on the basis of measures that have been the subject of open and thoughtful debate in Congress and among the American people, and that invasions of the liberty or equal dignity of any individual are subject to review by courts which are open to those affected and independent of the government which is curtailing their freedom.[4]

White House counsel Alberto R. Gonzales had once stated that proposed tribunals against noncitizens detained at Guantánamo Bay, Cuba, "will be as open as possible."[5] However, for more than two-and-a-half years, there had been no trials, and President Bush had signed an executive order that allows closed proceedings.

With increased public pressure, and mounting congressional concern about the status and rights of prisoners, the Bush administration in July 2003 decided to bring six prisoners before tribunals, which would be conducted without the presence of the defendants, with the possibility that evidence would be withheld from the defendants and their counsels, and with hearsay and unsubstantiated evidence allowed.

In an unusual move that could shake apart the entire concept of tribunals, the government-appointed military lawyer representing one of the six defendants who were facing tribunals, charged that the tribunals were illegal under both U.S. and international law, violating American military laws as well as the Geneva Conventions.[6] The tribunals, said Navy Lt. Cdr. Charles Swift, a Naval Academy graduate, did not have the "necessary congressional approval," violated constitutional requirements of "separation of powers and equal protection principles of the U.S. Constitution, and constitutes an illegal suspension of the writ of habeas corpus." The president's actions are "an unprecedented, unconstitutional, and dangerously unchecked expansion of executive authority," Swift charged in the suit filed in April 2004 in the U.S. District Court for the Western District of Washington on behalf of his client Salim Ahmed Hamdan, a Yemeni laborer.[7]

Hamdan was captured in November 2001 in Afghanistan during a sweep by mercenaries whose intent was to sell Arabs to the Americans as prisoners of war. He freely admitted he had been a driver for workers on a farm owned by Osama bin Laden. According to the suit:

Mr. Hamdan is not, and never has been, an enemy alien or unlawful combatant of the United States. He has never been a member of Al Qaida or any other organization recognized as a terrorist group by the United States. He has never taken up arms against the United States, or knowingly participated in any way in any plan to kill or injure Americans, or to damage American property, and he has not knowingly assisted anyone in such efforts. Furthermore, Mr. Hamdan did not plan, authorize, commit, or aid in the terrorist attacks against the United States that occurred on September 11, 2001, and he has not "harbored" anyone who had done so.[8]

Hamdan, like others categorized as "enemy combatants," could "serve a potential life sentence without ever being charged with a crime and without being afforded a chance to prove his innocence," according to the suit.[9] He had been in U.S. custody more than two years before being allowed to see an attorney. In demanding the court issue a *writ of mandamus* to the executive branch, Swift asked the court to "determine that Mr. Hamdan has been denied a speedy trial; that his incarceration violates the Constitution, laws, treaties and regulations of the United States; that the Military Order is unconstitutional; and that Respondents have no jurisdiction over Mr. Hamdan."[10]

In a procedural ruling shortly after the suit was filed, District Judge Robert Lasnik said the case had "monumental significance" on several constitutional issues, but delayed Swift's request pending a Supreme Court decision that could decide a related constitutional and jurisdictional issue.[11]

Capt. Kevin Barry (USCG-Ret.), a specialist on military law, told the *Washington Post* he believed "it's the first time a military defense counsel has filed suit in federal court on a case to which he's been assigned."[12]

About three months after Swift filed his suit, the federal government decided to try Hamdan in a military tribunal on one count of terrorism, conspiracy to commit murder, and attacks upon civilians. The government claimed Hamdan delivered weapons for al-Qaeda, but did not give any specifics if he killed anyone or committed any act of violence. He became the fourth prisoner to be held for the tribunal, still under legal question.

In two separate and independent decisions, federal district courts had agreed with the administration's claims that prisoners held at Guantánamo Bay Naval Base were not under jurisdiction of the U.S. courts because the U.S. leases the military base from Cuba, which has "complete sovereignty"; thus, the base is not on American soil.[13]

In *Gherebi v. Bush*, the U.S. Court of Appeals for the Ninth Circuit (Alaska, Arizona, California, Hawaii, Idaho, Montana, Nevada, Oregon, Washington, Guam, and Northern Mariana Islands), however, ruled in December 2003 that the Bush administration wrongly asserted that U.S. courts held no jurisdiction and that prisoners were not entitled to legal counsel. In a stinging attack upon the Bush administration's refusal to acknowledge judicial oversight, the court ruled:

[E]ven in times of national emergency—indeed particularly in such times—it is the obligation of the Judicial branch to ensure preservation of our constitutional values and to prevent the Executive Branch from running roughshod over the rights of citizens and aliens alike. Here, we cannot accept the government's position that the Executive Branch possesses the unchecked authority to imprison indefinitely any persons, foreign citizens included, on territory under the sole jurisdiction and control of the United States without permitting such prisoners recourse of any kind to any judicial forum, or even access to counsel, regardless of the length or matter of their confinement. We hold that no lawful policy or precedent supports such a counter-intuitive and undemocratic procedure. .... In our view, the government's position is inconsistent with fundamental tenets of American jurisprudence and raises most serious concerns under international law.[14]

However, the U.S. Court of Appeals for the District of Columbia Circuit agreed with the administration's claims that the federal courts have no jurisdiction.[15] More than two years after Camp Delta was opened, about six hundred prisoners from forty-four countries remained in U.S. custody at Guantánamo Bay or at the Naval brig in Charleston, South Carolina. Their detention, without due process and rights to counsel, as well as the refusal by the Bush administration to allow judicial overview, according to dozens of international organizations, including the Center for Constitutional Rights, violated the Geneva Conventions and the Universal Declaration of Human Rights, as well as due process provisions of the Uniform Code of Military Justice, which the federal government continued to believe didn't apply to "enemy combatants."

Fred Koramatsu, whose case against the government in 1942 for unconstitutionally detaining Japanese–Americans led to a major Supreme Court error and a lingering blemish upon the nation, now spoke out on behalf of those held without due process during the "war on terror":

It is only natural that in times of crisis our government should tighten the measures it ordinarily takes to preserve our security. But we know from long experience that we often react too harshly in circumstances of felt necessity and underestimate the damage to civil liberties. Typically, we come later to regret our excesses, but for many that recognition comes too late. The challenge is to identify excess when it occurs and to protect constitutional rights before they are compromised unneces-sarily. These cases provide the court with the opportunity to protect constitutional liberties when they matter most rather than belatedly, after the fact.[16]

In his oral argument before the Supreme Court of the United States, which had consolidated two cases,[17] U.S. Solicitor General Theodore B. Olson charged that the country "is at war" and faces an "extraordinary threat."[18] He claimed the Supreme Court was being asked "to assert juris-diction that is not authorized by Congress, does not arise from the Con-stitution, has never been exercised by this court."[19] In response to a question by Justice John Paul Stevens, a decorated veteran of World War II, Olson claimed he would be making the same argument whether or not the country was at war. "So the existence of the war is really irrelevant to the legal issue," Stevens noted.[20]

Defense Attorney John J. Gibbons argued if the administration's opinion was accurate about incarceration during what it claimed was a war:

> [N]either the length of the detention, the conditions of their confinement, nor the fact that they have been wrongfully detained makes the slightest difference. Respondents would create a lawless enclave, insulating the executive branch from any judicial scrutiny, now or in the future. . . . What's at stake in this case is the authority of the federal courts to uphold the rule of law.[21]

Two months later, the Supreme Court agreed. In a 6–3 decision, the Court reversed the decision of the Court of Appeals and remanded the case to the original district court for further action.[22] Essentially, the Supreme Court had determined that the American-run prison at Guantánamo Bay, although leased from Cuba, was under the complete control of the United States and that federal courts held jurisdiction. It was a major blow to the Bush administration's belief that the base was not on American soil and, thus, the executive branch held legal control of the prisoners. In delivering the opinion of the Court, Justice John Paul Stevens dismissed the government's position that the laws of the United States don't apply to foreign nationals—"United States courts have traditionally been open to nonresident aliens"—and quoted Justice Robert Jackson from a 1953 case:

> Executive imprisonment has been considered oppressive and lawless since John, at Runnymede, pledged that no free man should be imprisoned, dispossessed, outlawed, or exiled save by the judgment of his peers or by the law of the land. The judges of England developed the writ of habeas corpus largely to preserve these immunities from executive restraint.[23]

Michael Ratner, president of the Center for Constitutional Rights which had brought the case into the court system, summarized the impact of the Supreme Court decision:

> This is a major victory for the rule of law and affirms the right of every person, citizen or non-citizen, detained by the United States to test the legality of his or her detention in a U.S. Court. The Center for Constitutional Rights has long believed that even in a time of danger, executive detentions have no place in a democracy.[24]

However, three justices disagreed. In his dissent, Justice Antonin Scalia, joined by Chief Justice William Rehnquist and Justice Clarence Thomas, complained, "the court boldly extends the scope of the habeas statute to the four corners of the earth." In a shocking disregard for the rule of law and due process of all persons, Scalia, with Rehnquist and Thomas, determined, "The commander in chief and his subordinates had every reason to expect that the internment of combatants at Guantánamo Bay would not have the consequence of bringing the cumbersome machinery of our domestic courts into military affairs." It is precisely that "cumbersome machinery" the nation's Founding Fathers determined was necessary to protect the rights of all people.

CHAPTER 4

'Treated in a Cruel, Inhumane and Degrading Manner'

Not long after 9/11, President Bush and his senior advisors began to think about extending the war from Afghanistan to Iraq. Richard Clarke, who had been the nation's counterterrorism director under two Republican and one Democratic president, told Congress the president "made the whole war on terrorism so much worse by invading Iraq." He further claimed that Defense Secretary Donald Rumsfeld wanted a strike against Iraq because "there aren't any good targets in Afghanistan and there are lots of good targets in Iraq." Within weeks of 9/11, President Bush signed a national security directive to the Defense Department to begin preparing for an invasion of Iraq—"even though they knew at the time from me, from the FBI, from the CIA that Iraq had nothing to do with 9/11."[1]

The White House attacked Clarke's statements as inaccurate and unleashed a barrage of invective, saying he was a "disgruntled" former staffer and questioned his political allegiances; Clarke is a registered Republican. Vice President Dick Cheney had said that Clarke didn't have access to the facts since he "wasn't in the loop," leading the nation to wonder why the head of anti-terrorism activities wasn't "in the loop." Those "in the loop" led the nation to believe that the war needed to be extended because there were links to al-Qaeda, that Iraq, under Saddam Hussein had weapons of mass destruction and that the United States faced an imminent threat. The drumbeating for war continued for more than a year while the president told the nation he had not made any decisions about Iraq. Former four-star generals, including Colin Powell who had been chair of the Joint Chiefs of Staff during the first Gulf War, opposed the impending war. Millions around the world and in the United States protested. Most of the media, however, devoted significantly more space and air time to the administration's statements than to the antiwar demonstrations. They either took no editorial position or, if they did, it was usually to support the administration; few wanted to be seen as "unpatriotic." Both the *New York Times* and the *Washington Post* would later publicly acknowledge they were not as rigorous as they should have been in challenging the Bush administration statements or of claims by Iraqi defectors, and delayed or buried stories that had questioned such arguments and claims.[2]

In March 2003, the United States invaded Iraq. Against only light resistance, the "coalition," consisting primarily of American and United

Kingdom forces, overthrew the regime of Saddam Hussein. More than one thousand American soldiers would die, more than seven thousand would be wounded—most by insurgents after the president declared "Mission Accomplished." A 22,000-word special investigation by *Vanity Fair*, published a year after the initial invasion against Iraq, concluded, "America went to war on flawed or exaggerated intelligence."[3]

Joseph C. Wilson IV, former *chargé d'affairs* at the U.S. embassy in Iraq for George H. W. Bush prior to the first Gulf War and a career diplomatic officer, charged George W. Bush with lying to the people in order to attack Iraq to create the second Gulf War. In an opinion column for the *San Jose Mercury News* a year after the United States unleashed what Rumsfeld called a "shock and awe" strategy that led to Hussein's overthrow and essentially destroyed Iraq's infrastructure, Wilson charged:

> The Bush administration lied to get us into war, and it lied when it said the war in Iraq was part of the struggle against terrorism.
>
> The invasion of Iraq may have been about other things: among them, the president's otherworldly vision of bringing what he calls the Almighty's gift of freedom to the Middle East, at the barrel of a gun. But it was not about weapons of mass destruction, and it was not about terrorism. At least not until we attacked and gave al-Qaeda the best recruitment tool it ever had.
>
> Americans have been bombarded in recent weeks with overwhelming evidence that our government has bungled its way into the desert equivalent of a quagmire. Former administration loyalists Paul O'Neill [former secretary of the Treasury] and Richard Clarke essentially said so, arguing that the White House was so focused on overthrowing Saddam Hussein that it pushed aside other priorities, including fighting al-Qaeda.[4]

But the United States, as Colin Powell once warned, now owned the country. In Guantánamo Bay, it held persons who may have been in al-Qaeda, although later evidence showed that few had been active terrorists. In Iraq, it held prisoners who were primarily soldiers and non-military citizens, with a few petty criminals, almost none of whom could have been linked to any terrorist plots against the United States. The rules for treatment of prisoners in Iraq were similar to those of treatment of prisoners at Guantánamo Bay.

In response to questions about how seemingly abusive the treatment of prisoners could be condoned under Geneva Conventions rules, the Bush administration decided such rules didn't apply. Alberto Gonzales, the president's counsel, stated in January 2002:

> The nature of the new war places a high premium on other factors, such as the ability to quickly obtain information from captured terrorists and their sponsors in order to avoid further atrocities against American civilians. . . . In my judgment, this new paradigm renders obsolete Geneva's strict limitations on questioning of enemy prisoners and renders quaint some of its provisions.[5]

That same month, Defense Secretary Donald Rumsfeld declared those detained by U.S. forces in Afghanistan "do not have any rights" under the Geneva Conventions. John C. Yoo, who had been the primary analyst of Geneva Conventions rules while at the Department of Justice between 2001 and 2003, claimed the Geneva Conventions "do not apply to the war on terrorism [because] it applies only to conflicts between signatory nations." Yoo said that al-Qaeda isn't a nation and has not signed onto the rules for prisoners.[6] However, even if we agree with Yoo's assumption that it isn't necessary to follow Geneva Conventions rules because al-Qaeda isn't a signatory nation, there is no evidence that any or all of the prisoners held at Guantánamo Bay were leaders of al-Qaeda; only a couple of dozen were even members.[7] Most, if not all, of those held in Iraq and Afghanistan, were not al-Qaeda members. Yoo also claimed that any prisoners who were militia members of the Taliban, the ruling authority in Afghanistan, also weren't subject to Geneva Conventions rules because they "did not wear uniforms, did not operate under responsible commanders, and systematically violated the rules of war."[8] If we accepted such reasoning, the rules for prisoners would not have applied to the pro-American Philippine guerillas during World War II, the Montagnards of South Vietnam, the Viet Cong in North Vietnam, the Contras in Nicaragua—or the American colonial Revolutionary War soldiers.

The opinions of the White House, Department of Justice, and Department of Defense would also influence conditions at Guantánamo Bay. When others pointed out that Geneva Conventions rules for treatment of prisoners did apply, Rumsfeld arrogantly declared not only was the U.S. acceptance of those rules optional, but that any concern about mistreatment of prisoners was nothing more than "isolated pockets of international hyperventilation."[9]

"The US administration has shown a consistent disregard of the Geneva Conventions and basic principles of law, human rights and decency," said Irene Khan, secretary general of Amnesty International. She said that this violation of international law "has created a climate in which US soldiers feel they can dehumanize and degrade prisoners with impunity."[10]

In response to increasing public concern about the treatment of prisoners detained at Guantánamo Bay and Afghanistan, or in military prisons in the United States, Defense Secretary Donald Rumsfeld said in January 2002:

No detainee has been harmed. No detainee has been mistreated in any way. . . .

The detainees are being treated humanely. They have been, they are being treated humanely today, and they will be in the future. . . .

And the numerous articles, statements, questions, allegations, and breathless reports on television are undoubtedly by people who are either uninformed, misinformed or poorly informed.[11]

The website for the Joint Task Force Guantánamo Bay claims:

Enemy combatants detained at Camp Delta are always treated humanely and in a manner consistent with the principles of the Third Geneva Convention of 1949.

Furnishings inside each cell consist of a metal bed raised off the floor, sink with running water and a floor-style toilet. Each detainee is issued a set of comfort items which include an orange jump suit, prayer cap, thong-style shoes, foam sleeping mattress, a sheet, a blanket, a 1/2 inch thick prayer mat, soap, wash cloth, and towel. Detainees are also given a copy of the Koran.

Detainees are given three culturally appropriate meals a day and are allowed to pray as desired. They are allowed to take showers and are given exercise breaks each week. They are also allowed to freely converse with detainees in adjacent cells as well as send and receive mail. . . .

A new Medium Security Facility was built inside Camp Delta and become fully operational on April 2, 2003. This facility is used for detaining enemy combatants who are considered less of a security risk to guards and other detainees, and who have been cooperative in the interrogation process. The total capacity of this camp is approximately 160.

The Medium Security Facility differs substantially from the other detention units inside Camp Delta. In this facility, detainees are housed in building complexes where each unit consists of a communal living area, with a private toilet and sink, and a larger shower and toilet room that serves the entire complex. A complex consists of four communal living rooms that can house up to 10 enemy combatants each. Detainees have a bed with a mattress, locker for storing personal items and material such as writing paper and books. Each complex also has a recreational area for playing games and team sports.

The Detention Hospital is located inside Camp Delta and is dedicated to providing expert medical care to the detainees. The hospital is comparable to a full-service medical facility used by U.S. military forces when deployed anywhere in the world, with state-of-the-art equipment and professional medical staff.[12]

On June 26, 2003, United Nations International Day in Support of Victims of Torture, President Bush declared: "The United States is committed to the worldwide elimination of torture and we are leading this fight by example." He called upon nations to prohibit, investigate, and prosecute "all acts of torture and . . . to prevent other cruel and unusual punishment."[13] The president promised that the United States would not torture prisoners nor use "cruel and unusual" methods of interrogation. However, the actions of the Bush administration in Guantánamo Bay, Afghanistan, and Iraq showed not the example the president wished, but one of cruelty, torture, and significant human rights violations, all approved at the highest levels of the government.

Lord Justice Johan Steyn, senior judge in England's House of Lords, and one of that nation's most respected judges, said that conditions imposed by the Department of Defense at Guantánamo Bay were of "utter lawlessness," a "monstrous failure of justice," and "not quite torture, but as close as you can get."[14] BBC diplomatic correspondent Barnaby Mason pointed out, "It is rare for British judges to speak on contentious political issues and almost unheard of for them to attack a foreign government."[15]

In January 2004, Jakob Kellenberger, president of the International

Committee of the Red Cross, met with Secretary of State Colin Powell, Deputy Defense Secretary Paul Wolfowitz, and National Security Advisor Condoleezza Rice to discuss conditions at Guantánamo Bay. Although Red Cross investigations are confidential, it issued a rare public statement questioning treatment of prisoners:

> Mr Kellenberger, while appreciating the frankness of the dialogue with the US authorities, lamented the fact that two years after the first detainees arrived at Guantanamo, and despite repeated pleas, they are still facing seemingly indefinite detention beyond the reach of the law. He also noted that the ICRC's concerns regarding certain aspects of the conditions and treatment in Guantanamo have not yet been adequately addressed. . . .
> Beyond Guantanamo, the ICRC is increasingly concerned about the fate of an unknown number of people captured as part of the so-called global war on terrorism and held in undisclosed locations. Mr Kellenberger echoed previous official requests from the ICRC for information on these detainees and for eventual access to them, as an important humanitarian priority and as a logical continuation of the organization's current detention work in Guantanamo and Afghanistan.[16]

About a week later, based upon twenty-nine specific concerns the Red Cross had, the Army reduced a number of restrictions, allowing detainees to have cloth upon which to place their Korans and providing shorts so they could use the common showers and meet the modesty requirements of their religion.[17]

In March 2004, the United States sent five British nationals back to England after more than two years' imprisonment at Guantánamo Bay. After interrogation by British police, they were released. Reuters reported that "Procedures at Guantánamo, where captives are not given lawyers, make it difficult to try the men in Britain because the courts here do not accept evidence gathered in the absence of a lawyer."[18] Their repatriation followed several months of increased public comments by senior British judges and by government officials about the legality of the United States holding prisoners at Guantánamo Bay, combined with negotiations between the governments of Great Britain and the United States. Robert Lizar, an attorney for one of those released, told Agence France Presse that his client "has been detained as an innocent for a period of two years. He has been treated in a cruel, inhumane and degrading manner."[19] In an extremely rare public announcement, the International Committee of the Red Cross, almost five months after the prisoners' release, declared, "Some of the abuses alleged by the detainees would indeed constitute inhumane treatment" and, if proven, could constitute war crimes.[20]

Four months after the United States released the British prisoners, it released four French detainees who had also been held two years. The release came after what French President Jacques Chirac called "long and intense negotiations" with the Bush administration. Three other French citizens were not sent to France. With the release of the four French citizens, the United

States had released 129 prisoners; most of them had been imprisoned for two years, none of them were charged with any act of terrorism or of aiding forces opposed to the United States.[21]

A *New York Times* investigation by Tim Golden and Don Van Natta Jr. revealed "government and military officials have repeatedly exaggerated both the danger the detainees posed and the intelligence they have provided." That same investigation also revealed a CIA report in September 2002 that questioned the arrests. Most of those picked up in Afghanistan and transferred to Guantánamo Bay, according to the CIA investigation, were low-level recruits or innocent men.[22]

Abuse and illegal detention of prisoners wasn't confined to Guantánamo Bay. In Afghanistan, the military regularly violated the Geneva Conventions, according to Human Rights Watch (HRW). A fifty-nine page report in March 2004 detailed innumerable human rights violations:

> There are . . . credible reports that U.S. forces have beaten and abused persons during arrest operations, and that Afghan troops accompanying U.S. forces have abused local residents and looted the homes of those detained. . . .
> Bright lights were set up outside [prisoners'] cells, shining in, and U.S. military personnel took shifts, keeping the detainees awake by banging on the metal walls of their cells with batons. The detainees said they were terrified and disoriented by sleep deprivation, which they said lasted for several weeks. During interrogations, they said, they were made to stand upright for lengthy periods of time with a bright spotlight shining directly into their eyes. They were told that they would not be questioned until they remained motionless for one hour, and that they were not entitled even to turn their heads. If they did move, the interrogators said the "clock was reset." U.S. personnel, through interpreters, yelled at the detainees from behind the light, asking questions. . . .
> According to detainees who have been released, U.S. personnel punish detainees at Bagram when they break rules—for instance, talking to another prisoner or yelling at guards. Detainees are taken, in shackles, and made to hold their arms over their heads; their shackles are then draped over the top of a door, so that they can not lower their arms. They are ordered to stand with their hands up, in this manner, for two-hour intervals.[23]

The international agency, which has the respect of most countries, even those with totalitarian governments, also detailed instances of beatings and the subjugation of prisoners to freezing temperatures, all in violation of the Geneva Conventions. In opposition to observations by HRW personnel and statements from prisoners, the military denied there was mistreatment. However, Roger King, military spokesman at the Bagram prison did tell the Associated Press:

> We do force people to stand for an extended period of time. . . . Disruption of sleep has been reported as an effective way of reducing people's inhibition about talking or their resistance to questioning.[24]

He also acknowledged that interrogation tactics permitted stripping the prisoners for extended time, again in violation of the Geneva Conventions.

In Iraq, according to a confidential report by the International Committee of the Red Cross (ICRC):

> Arresting authorities entered houses usually after dark, breaking down doors, waking up residents roughly, yelling orders, forcing family members into one room under military guard while searching the rest of the house and further breaking doors, cabinets and other property. . . .
> Sometimes they arrested all adult males present in a house, including the elderly, handicapped or sick people. . . . Treatment often included pushing people around, insulting, taking aim with rifles, punching and kicking and striking with rifles.[25]

The Army had initiated investigations in about fifty separate cases during 2003 and the first half of 2004 involving assaults on detainees before being processed for imprisonment. Ten of those cases may have been homicides, according to Army records.[26] Military intelligence officers, according to the ICRC, "attributed the brutality of some arrests to the lack of proper supervision of battle group units."[27] In May 2003, four soldiers had received "dishonorable" or "other-than-honorable" discharges for what the Army claimed was abuse of Iraqi prisoners at Camp Bucca near Umm Qasr in southern Iraq. But no further actions apparently were taken to investigate if wider problems existed.

The International Committee of the Red Cross had been granted, by its own account, "unimpeded access to all detainees and all sections of the prison."[28] The Red Cross stated it had made several trips into Abu Ghraib and other prisons, and interviewed thousands of prisoners. Many of the prisoners were common criminals, others may have been terrorists, but most of them were detained solely because the military thought they might be able to provide information. The Red Cross sent several reports to officials in the Bush administration, which seemed to ignore or downplay most of the reports.

In May 2003, the Red Cross strongly objected to the military's practice of putting a wristband, with the word "terrorist" imprinted, on every prisoner. The military subsequently removed the wristbands from non-Iraqi prisoners.[29] The Red Cross continued to visit the prisons; it continued to issue reports of conditions, which military officials treated in "a light-hearted manner," according to a senior commander in Iraq.[30]

An Army investigation subsequently revealed that CIA and military interrogators, apparently operating under direct authority of Donald Rumsfeld and the military chain of command, deliberately hid certain prisoners in Iraqi prisons from the Red Cross. An Army investigation said the actions were "deceptive, contrary to Army doctrine, and in violation of international law."[31] Janis Karpinski, who had been in charge of the seventeen prisons and 3,400 reservists, says she vigorously disagreed with the policy to create certain "ghost prisoners," but was overruled by military intelligence and senior officers.[32] The International Committee of the Red Cross believes the United States hid additional "ghost" prisoners outside of Guantánamo Bay, Iraq, or Afghanistan and for which the United States did not provide "notification or access," a violation of the Geneva Conventions and international law.[33] Gen. Paul J. Kern told the Senate Armed Service Committee in August 2004 there may have been as many as one hundred detainees kept off of all official records.[34] A dozen or more were taken out of Iraq for CIA interrogation, a violation of the Geneva Conventions.[35]

Even with access denied to certain prisoners, the Red Cross, which observed conditions during most of 2003, reports it was "aware of the situation in Abu Ghraib, and on the basis of its findings, has repeatedly requested the US authorities to take corrective action."[36] Red Cross policies don't permit public disclosure of its findings, which the ICRC says are confidential "so as to prevent humanitarian issues from be-coming politicized."[37]

The *Wall Street Journal*, however, after the scandal broke, released information from the twenty-four page summary report, issued on February 4, 2004, without Red Cross approval. In that report, the Red Cross had concluded that military intelligence used "physical and psychological coercion that in some cases might amount to torture" in a systematic way to gain confessions and extract information and other forms of cooperation and that the "ill-treatment against persons deprived of their liberty went beyond exceptional cases and might be considered a practice tolerated" by the occupying forces.[38]

The Red Cross also charged that more than a hundred prisoners were held in "strict solitary confinement in small concrete cells devoid of daylight," and allowed only twenty minutes a day of physical exercise. Their treatment, reported the Red Cross, violated both the third and fourth Geneva Conventions. The report also documented deaths of unarmed prisoners from shootings and beatings. Some of the deaths resulted from uprisings. Although the military claimed each killing was justified, the Red Cross stated that "less extreme measures could have been used to quell the demonstrations." The killing of a prisoner who was throwing rocks "showed a clear disregard for human life and security" of the prisoners.

Upon publication of the *Journal*'s report, the ICRC operations director confirmed the abuse was not only "tantamount to torture" and that there were "clearly incidents of degrading and inhuman treatment," but that the problem was widespread and not "isolated acts" as President Bush claimed.[39]

Amnesty International had also brought the conditions in Iraq's prisons to the attention of President Bush. In a letter to the president, Secretary

General Irene Khan pointed out:

> In July 2003 [nine months earlier], Amnesty International sent your government a *Memorandum on Concerns Relating to Law and Order in Iraq*. The Memorandum included allegations of torture and ill-treatment of Iraqi detainees by US and Coalition forces. (1) The allegations included beatings, electric shocks, sleep deprivation, hooding, and prolonged forced standing and kneeling. We have never received a response or any indication from the administration or the Coalition Provisional Authority that an investigation took place. Likewise, we have never received a response to the *Memorandum to the US Government on the rights of people in US custody in Afghanistan and Guantánamo Bay* which we sent to you in April 2002, and which also raised concerns about questions and allegations of torture and ill-treatment.[40]

Alex Arriaga, Amnesty International's government relations director, says Bush administration officials "listened and never disputed any of the facts" her agency brought to their attention, "but we have never received any written response."[41]

Among others who had earlier pressed the Bush administration for an investigation into abuse and torture of Iraqi prisoners were Paul Bremer, U.S. administrator in Iraq, and Secretary of State Colin Powell. According to senior administration officials, in anonymous conversations with the *Washington Post*, "Bremer pressed the military to improve conditions and later made the issue a regular talking point in discussions with Rumsfeld, Vice President Cheney and National Security Advisor Condoleezza Rice,"[42] A senior State Department official said: "It's something Powell has raised repeatedly—to release as many detainees as possible—and, second, to ensure that those in custody are properly cared for and treated."[43]

In contrast to the American government's unwillingness to make significant changes in how it handled and interrogated prisoners, the British government, upon notification by the Red Cross that it might have violated Geneva Conventions at its prison at Umm Qasr, ceased such practices.[44]

General public outrage against abuse and torture didn't occur until pictures taken in American-controlled prisons in Iraq were made public in May 2004. In January 2004, Spec. Joseph M. Darby had received from a fellow soldier a CD-ROM of still photos of the abuse and notified his superiors, at first anonymously, then under oath. Soldiers had been taking souvenir photos and trading them. Those photos showed beatings and American soldiers celebrating after having ordered the prisoners to commit lewd acts while naked. Some of the photos revealed slurs written on the prisoners' bodies. One photo showed a hooded prisoner standing on a box, wires attached to his hands; subsequent testimony revealed that the prisoner was told he would be electrocuted if he fell from that box.

There may have even been a sinister reason for the photographs. Investigative reporter Seymour M. Hersh says he was told:

[T]here may have been a serious goal, in the beginning, behind the sexual humiliation and the posed photographs. It was thought that some prisoners would do anything—including spying on their associates—to avoid dissemination of the shameful photos to family and friends. [A high-level] government consultant said, "I was told that the purpose of the photographs was to create an Army of informants, people you could insert back in the population." The idea was that they would be motivated by fear of exposure, and gather information about pending insurgency action, the consultant said. If so, it wasn't effective; the insurgency continued to grow.[45]

Janis Karpinski, agrees. In an interview with the *Santa Clarita* (Calif.) *Signal*, she said she believed:

[T]hose pictures were planned, were programmed, that they used the MPs to get the detainees out of their cells, and that there was an official set of photographs being taken. . . .   I see an opportunity for an interrogation team to exploit those photographs.[46]

About six days after Spec. Darby first gave the Army's Criminal Investigation Division (CID) the photos, Lt. Gen. Ricardo Sanchez, military commander in Iraq, ordered an investigation into prisoner conditions. A scathing fifty-three page summary report[47] by Maj. Gen. Antonio M. Taguba, classified "secret" in late February 2004[48] but leaked to Hersh about two months later, revealed that the Army in Iraq had committed numerous instances of "sadistic, blatant, and wanton criminal abuses,"[49] primarily during the last three months of 2003.

The Taguba report documented some of the abuses at the 280-acre Abu Ghraib prison camp, about twenty miles west of Baghdad:

Punching, slapping, and kicking detainees; jumping on their naked feet; Videotaping and photographing naked male and female detainees; Forcibly arranging detainees in various sexually explicit positions for photographing; Forcing detainees to remove their clothing and keeping them naked for several days at a time; Forcing naked male detainees to wear women's underwear; Forcing groups of male detainees to masturbate themselves while being photographed and videotaped; Arranging naked male detainees in a pile and then jumping on them; Positioning a naked detainee on a MRE Box, with a sandbag on his head, and attaching wires to his fingers, toes, and penis to simulate electric torture; Writing "I am a Rapest" (sic) on the leg of a detainee alleged to have forcibly raped a 15-year old fellow detainee, and then photographing him naked; Placing a dog chain or strap around a naked detainee's neck and having a female Soldier pose for a picture; A male MP guard having sex with a female detainee; Using military working dogs (without muzzles) to intimidate and frighten detainees, and in at least one case biting and severely injuring a detainee. . . . Breaking chemical lights and pouring the phosphoric liquid on detainees; pouring cold water on naked detainees; beating detainees with a broom handle and a chair; threatening male detainees with rape; allowing a military police guard to stitch the wound of a detainee who was injured after being slammed against the wall in his cell; sodomizing a detainee with a chemical light and perhaps a broom stick, and using military working dogs to frighten and intimidate detainees with threats of attack, and in one instance actually biting a detainee.[50]

Subsequent information revealed there were about thirty-five suspicious deaths of prisoners in Iraq and Afghanistan, including several first marked as deaths from "natural causes," but which medical examiners later ruled to be homicides.[51] In May 2004, the Department of Defense finally acknowledged that two guards at Guantánamo Bay were disciplined for using excessive force. In Afghanistan, two civilians died while in American custody; the Department of Defense classified both deaths as homicides.[52] The *Denver Post* reported that autopsies, required under the Geneva Conventions for suspicious deaths, may not have been done; the *Post* also revealed that the death of former Iraqi Maj. Gen. Abed Hamed Mowhoush, originally reported as from "natural causes," was caused by being shoved into a sleeping bag and then suffocated.[53] In September 2004, the Army finally brought charges of negligent homicide, assault, maltreatment of prisoners, and dereliction of duty against two dozen soldiers for what the Army called "blunt-force" injuries.

Several months after Taguba released his report, the Army acknowledged it was also investigating murders of civilians. In one instance, an Army officer apparently shot the driver of a car, which he believed to have contained insurgents. Then, according to an Army report, "the wounded driver was shot and killed at close range."[54] In another incident, four Army soldiers pushed two Iraqi civilians from a bridge about twelve feet over the Tigris River— their offense was staying out past curfew.[55] One of the civilians apparently drowned. In a subsequent hearing against the soldiers, who were charged with involuntary manslaughter, three Army officers, who had received nonjudicial reprimands for the incident but were not at the site, testified under immunity they directed their soldiers to corroborate each others' stories and to cover up the incident. The Army acknowledged that the battalion had been under intense combat pressure from insurgents, and had undertaken thirty-six individual combat operations in less than forty-eight hours.[56]

Spec. Sabrina D. Harman, an MP accused of some of the crimes, confirmed that prisoners were stripped, then "made to stand or kneel for hours."[57] She told the *Washington Post*, "They would bring in one to several prisoners at a time already hooded and handcuffed. The job of the MP was to keep them awake, make it hell so they would talk."[58] She said soldiers took their orders from Army military intelligence and CIA officers, and from civilians contracted by the Department of Defense. Military intelligence officers "took over the whole base; it was their show," Sgt. First Class Joseph Mood said, explaining, "They would try to get us to keep prisoners up all night, make them stand outside, have them stand up all the time—sometimes they asked the guards to do something that was totally against what you believed in doing."[59] Karpinski also blamed military intelligence, which had been given control of Abu Ghraib interrogation, and outside her immediate chain of command, for the abuses that occurred. According to the *Washington Post*, Karpinski said, "I think the MI people were in this all the way. I think they were up to their ears in it. . . . I don't believe that the MPs, two weeks onto the job, would have been such willing participants, even with instructions, unless someone had told them it was all okay."[60] A lawyer assigned to one of the defendants rhetorically asked Seymour Hersh, "Do you really think a group of kids from rural Virginia decided to do this on their own? Decided the best way to embarrass Arabs and make them talk was to have them walk around nude?"[61]

The intense questioning may have had a political motive. The *Wall Street Journal* reported:

> Mr. [Guy] Womack [a civilian attorney representing one of the MPs] says he has been told that [his client's] cohorts didn't make a move in the Iraqi prison without the approval of military intelligence officers. Those intelligence officers, he says, were under intense pressure from superiors in Iraq and Washington to find evidence of weapons of mass destruction.[62]

Statements from prisoners interviewed by military investigators also revealed the wanton abuse and failure to observe even the basic human rights. "They forced us to walk like dogs on our hands and knees, and we had to bark like a dog, and if we didn't do that they started hitting us hard on our face and chest with no mercy," one prisoner told investigators.[63] Other prisoners independently said the MPs demanded they denounce Islam, force-fed them pork and liquor, and threw food into toilets, and then made them eat it. One prisoner said that when soldiers began hitting his broken leg, "I cursed my religion. They ordered me to thank Jesus that I'm alive."[64]

Taguba's report condemned more than the enlisted soldiers. According to the *New York Times*, the report revealed "a much broader pattern of command failures than initially acknowledged by the Pentagon and the Bush administration in responding to outrage over the abuse."[65] Taguba blamed interrogators, military intelligence officers, and civilians of CACI International, hired by the Department of Defense, for not only allowing but also encouraging the prison guards to "soften up" the prisoners.[66]

Some of the abuse occurred in retaliation for a series of offenses by prisoners, some just for the amusement of the guards.[67] Gen. Taguba concluded that Col. Thomas M. Pappas, in charge of military intelligence, was "either directly or indirectly responsible for the actions of those who mistreated and humiliated Iraqi prisoners." Army documents obtained by the *Washington Post* revealed that Sanchez had given military intelligence officers "wide latitude in handling detainees" following a visit in September

2003 to Iraq by Maj. Gen. Geoffrey D. Miller, commander of detention facilities at Guantánamo Bay, who was in Iraq with a seventeen-member team to brief military intelligence officers on interrogation tactics and limits.[68] A report by a thirty-member investigative team, headed by Maj. Gen. George W. Fay, documented that the interrogative techniques conducted at Guantánamo Bay and Afghanistan to "enemy combatants" were applied in Iraq to those who probably had never fired at the occupying forces.[69] Sanchez, according to a subsequent investigation by an independent commission appointed by the secretary of defense, blamed Sanchez for "lacking specific authorization to operate beyond the confines of the Geneva Convention" by broadening interrogation tactics in Iraq.[70]

Miller, said Karpinski, said prisoners "are like dogs, and if you allow them to believe at any point that they are more than a dog, then you've lost control of them."[71] The Army's own policy guidelines specifically forbid "the use of physical or mental torture or any coercion to compel prisoners to provide information . . ."[72] The policy also directs that "Prisoners may not be threatened, insulted, or exposed to unpleasant or disparate treatment of any kind because of their refusal to answer questions."[73] Karpinski said she told Miller that the situation of prisoners in Iraq was different from that at Guantánamo Bay, and that what may have worked there wasn't appropriate in Iraq. Karpinski said that Miller essentially brushed her off—"What I was telling him was inconsequential to his plan to 'Gitmoize' the interrogation operation. . . . [H]e was not listening to anything I was saying."[74]

An investigation by Lt. Gen. Paul T. Mikolashek, the Army's inspector general, concluded that not only was there poor training, a failure to plan for massive prisoner detention, and a confusing command structure, but because the command structure "encourages behavior at the harsher end of the acceptable range of behavior toward detainees, [it] may unintentionally increase the likelihood of abuse."[75] His report also documented inadequate health care, tainted meals, and improper sanitation and sewage control.

Implicated in the abuse of prisoners was the military medical community. According to an investigation by Steven H. Miles, professor of bioethics at the University of Minnesosta, writing in *Lancet*, one of the world's most respected medical journals:

> The complicity of US military medical personnel during abuses of detainees in Iraq, Afghanistan, and Guantanamo Bay is of great importance to human rights, medical ethics, and military medicine. Government documents show that the US military medical system failed to protect detainees' human rights, sometimes collaborated with interrogators or abusive guards, and failed to properly report injuries or deaths caused by beatings. . . .
>
> US Army investigators concluded that Abu Ghraib's medical system for detainees was inadequately staffed and equipped. . . . The International Committee of the Red

Cross (ICRC) found that the medical system failed to maintain internment cards with medical information necessary to protect the detainees' health as required by the Geneva Convention; this reportedly was due to a policy of not officially processing (ie, recording their presence in the prison) new detainees. . . . Few units in Iraq and Afghanistan complied with the Geneva obligation to provide monthly health inspections. . . . The medical system also failed to assure that prisoners could request proper medical care as required by the Geneva Convention. For example, an Abu Ghraib detainee's sworn document says that a purulent hand injury caused by torture went untreated. The individual was also told by an Iraqi physician working for the US that bleeding of his ear (from a separate beating) could not be treated in a clinic; he was treated instead in a prison hallway. . . .

The medical system failed to establish procedures, as called for by Article 30 of the Geneva Convention, to ensure proper treatment of prisoners with disabilities. An Abu Ghraib prisoner's deposition reports the crutch that he used because of a broken leg was taken from him and his leg was beaten as he was ordered to renounce Islam. The same detainee told a guard that the prison doctor had told him to immobilise a badly injured shoulder; the guard's response was to suspend him from the shoulder. . . .

The medical system failed to accurately report illnesses and injuries. . . . Abu Ghraib authorities did not notify families of deaths, sicknesses, or transfers to medical facilities as required by the Convention. . . . A medic inserted an intravenous catheter into the corpse of a detainee who died under torture in order to create evidence that he was alive at the hospital. . . . In another case, an Iraqi man, taken into custody by US soldiers was found months later by his family in an Iraqi hospital. He was comatose, had three skull fractures, a severe thumb fracture, and burns on the bottoms of his feet. An accompanying US medical report stated that heat stroke had triggered a heart attack that put him in a coma; it did not mention the injuries.

Death certificates of detainees in Afghanistan and Iraq were falsified or their release or completion was delayed for months. . . . Medical investigators either failed to investigate unexpected deaths of detainees in Iraq and Afghanistan or performed cursory evaluations and physicians routinely attributed detainee deaths on death certificates to heart attacks, heat stroke, or natural causes without noting the unnatural aetiology of the death. . . . In one example, soldiers tied a beaten detainee to the top of his cell door and gagged him. The death certificate indicated that he died of "natural causes . . . during his sleep." After news media coverage, the Pentagon revised the certificate to say that the death was a "homicide' caused by "blunt force injuries and asphyxia."[76]

Ricardo Sanchez, as military commander of all forces in Iraq, had issued several guidelines during September and October 2003 to conduct inter-rogations in a "lawful and humane manner with command oversight."[77] However, there may have been a special set of instructions for interrogations requiring Sanchez's formal approval. Sanchez went to Abu Ghraib three times in October 2003. "Why was he going out there so often? Did he know something was going on?" asked Karpinski.[78]

Army documents revealed that Sanchez approved "high-pressure options" that included maintaining "stress positions" for as long as forty-five minutes every four hours, heat and air conditioning deprivation,[79] isolation for more than thirty days, and "sensory assault," including the blaring of loud music and exposure to bright lights.[80] Many of the techniques were not acceptable under the Geneva Conventions rules, which covered prisoners in Iraq and Afghanistan but, by the Bush administration's interpretations, did not cover those designated as "enemy combatants" in Guantánamo Bay. Some of the techniques, including the use of dogs, stress positions, extended interrogations, and stripping the prisoners, approved by Donald Rumseld in December 2002 for use at Guantánamo Bay and to be applied against Taliban and al-Qaeda suspects, were phased out about five months later. However, they were still used in Iraq against probable noncombatants by military intelligence, possibly without Rumsfeld's direct knowledge.

Taguba singled out three persons who refused to accept duties that would have been in violation of the Geneva Conventions. In addition to Joseph Darby, who first reported the abuse to the CID, Taguba also cited First Lt. David O. Sutton who, he said, "took immediate action and stopped an abuse, then reported the incident to the chain of command,"[81] and Master-at-Arms First Class William J. Kimbro, a Navy dog handler, for refusing "to participate in improper interrogations despite significant pressure from MI [military intelligence] personnel."[82]

Army reports indicate that Pappas approved the use of unmuzzled dogs to intimidate the prisoners, although the Army *Field Manual* specifically forbids such use.[83] In January 2002, according to the *Washington Post*, Donald Rumsfeld approved the use of dogs to intimidate prisoners at Guantánamo Bay. Although dogs were not used there, they were used at Abu Ghraib. Sanchez apparently approved the use of dogs after the visit by Geoffrey Miller and his senior staff from Guantánamo Bay.[84] Dog handlers gave Army investigators sworn statements they were directed to bring their dogs to frighten or intimidate prisoners, occasionally bringing a snarling dog within inches of a prisoner's face. At least one incident involved a dog that was allowed to chase a frightened prisoner and then bite him on both legs.[85]

Maj. Gen. Charles Hines, who had commanded the Army's military police school prior to retirement, told Seymour Hersh that the use of dogs to intimidate prisoners "would never have been tolerated" during his command, and that he would "never have authorized it for interrogating or coercing prisoners." During his tour of duty, had he authorized such use of guard dogs, he says, he would have "been put in jail or kicked out of the Army."[86]

The atrocities at Abu Ghraib apparently had been known for more than a year. The justification for torture apparently had its authorization almost two years before.

A Department of Justice memo sent to the White House in January 2003 outlined ways that administration officials could not be charged with war crimes for how they established policy to detain and interrogate prisoners.[87] In August 2002, the Department of Justice prepared a searing fifty page legal analysis that apparently justified the use of torture and near-torture interrogation. The report, prepared at the request of the CIA for legal guidance on interrogations, was transmitted to the White House. In that report, the Department of Justice advised the president that "certain acts may be cruel, inhuman, or degrading, but still not produce pain and suffering of the required intensity to fall within . . . proscription against torture," and that "for purely mental pain or suffering to amount to torture . . . it must result in significant psychological harm of significant duration, e.g., lasting for months or even years."[88] Torture, suggested the Department of Justice, which may have written the report to justify previous acts of torture conducted by the CIA against suspected terrorists, "is not the mere infliction of pain or suffering on another, but is instead a step well removed. The victim must experience intense pain or suffering of the kind that is equivalent to the pain that would be associated with serious physical injury so severe that death, organ failure, or permanent damage resulting in a loss of significant body function will likely result."[89] It was an interpretation that far exceeded the parameters of the Geneva Conventions. The Department of Justice also suggested that torturing al-Qaeda suspects "may be justified," and that international laws prohibiting torture of prisoners "may be unconstitutional if applied to interrogations" during the president's "war on terrorism."[90] If the military were to employ methods of torture, soldiers "would be doing so in order to prevent further attacks on the United States" and under authority of the highest levels of government would be immune from prosecution, according to the Department of Justice.[91]

In June 2004, the still-classified memo first became public. Within a day, the *Wall Street Journal*, *Washington Post*, and *New York Times* each revealed new details about the Bush administration's plans to justify the use of torture. In March 2003, the Department of Defense, basing much of its interpretation and analysis upon the Department of Justice memo seven months earlier, advised the military that the president, in his role as commander-in-chief, wasn't bound by treaties or American domestic law. The contents of that memo, first released by the *Wall Street Journal*, laid out the arguments for absolute authority:

> In order to respect the president's inherent constitutional authority to manage a military campaign . . . the prohibition against torture . . . must be construed as inapplicable to interrogations undertaken pursuant to his commander-in-chief authority. . . .
> National security decisions require the unity in purpose and energy in action that characterize the presidency rather than Congress. . . .
> Any effort by Congress to regulate the interrogation of unlawful combatants would violate the Constitution's sole vesting of the commander-in-chief authority in the president.[92]

Thus, the Department of Justice and Department of Defense were not only justifying the use of torture, they were also arguing that the authority of the president was absolute, unchecked by Congress, the courts, or standard military procedures. More importantly, the memos from the two departments asserted that any person committing torture was untouchable by the judicial system since that person needed only to claim he or she was following orders of a superior. Civilian lawyers from the Justice and Defense departments, and counsels to both the president and the vice president, approved the memo; opposing it was William H. Taft IV, counsel for the Department of State.[93]

"It appears that what they were contemplating was the commission of war crimes and looking for ways to avoid legal accountability," Tom Malinowski of Human Rights Watch told the *Washington Post*. "The effect," said Malinowski, "is to throw out years of military doctrine and standards on interrogations."[94] The Department of Justice arguments, as well as subsequent reinterpretation by the Department of Defense, were in conflict with the Army *Field Manual* which has significant restrictions more in line with Geneva Conventions rules.

"Every flag JAG lodged complaints," a senior Pentagon official told the *Washington Post*.[95] However, although the judge advocate generals (JAGs) of the Army, Navy, and Air Force opposed the memo, they reluctantly signed off on it, after having reined in some of the more odious language. In May 2003, eight senior military lawyers, frustrated with civilian leadership at the Pentagon they believed encouraged prisoner abuse, but unable to get that civilian leadership to respect military law, secretly complained to the New York City Bar Association about human rights abuses. The senior officers of both the Army's and the Navy's Judge Advocate General Corps called the interrogation of prisoners "frightening," and stated such practices could "reverse 50 years of a proud tradition of compliance with the Geneva Conventions."[96] Scott Horton of the Bar Association said the officers "wanted us to challenge the Bush administration about its standards for detentions and interrogations. They were urging us to get involved and speak in a very loud voice."[97] The JAG lawyers went to the Bar Association "out of a sense of desperation and frustration" at the civilian leadership's failure to respect the rules of the Geneva Conventions, according to Rear Adm. John Hutson (USN-Ret.), the Navy's judge advocate general from 1997 to 2000.[98] Several other high-ranking military officers also questioned civilian political policies. Donald Rumsfeld would later claim that the interrogation procedures were authorized by Department of Defense lawyers, but wouldn't confirm if they were civilian-appointed lawyers or military lawyers.[99] Sen. Patrick Leahy had even written to both the White House and the Department of Defense about prisoners subjected to beatings and Geneva Conventions abuses. The reply from both the Pentagon and the CIA was that prisoners were not tortured.[100]

Before the Senate Committee on the Judiciary, two days after the media revealed the existence of the memos suggesting torture was acceptable, John Ashcroft denied that the Bush administration condoned torture—and also refused to provide the Senate with copies of the memo or to discuss specific instances where the memo may have led to abuse. "There are certain things that, in the interest of the executive branch operating effectively, that I think it is inappropriate for the attorney general to say," said Ashcroft.[101] Within a week, the *Washington Post* put the entire memo on its website. A few days later, the Department of Justice, apparently to quench the firestorm that it helped create, disavowed the memo and told the public that a new memo was being prepared.[102]

Based primarily upon Taguba's investigation and analysis, the Army initially suspended seventeen soldiers from duties, pending a final investigation. Subsequent charges would include aggravated assault, battery, maltreatment, conspiracy, cruelty, and dereliction of duty. Seven soldiers were held for courts martial. The Army informed an additional seven officers and sergeants they would receive letters of reprimand.

After holding the story for two weeks at the personal request of Gen. Richard B. Myers, chairman of the Joint Chiefs of Staff, CBS-TV finally released some of the still photos in a "60 Minutes II" report at the end of April 2004. Donald Rumsfeld would later state that the "60 Minutes II" report did not "break" news; his own Central Command issued a news release three days after Spec. Darby brought the photos to CID, leading to the investigation. The release was seven lines, and glossed over all significant information. Most media ignored the information or failed to follow up on an issue that should have been a "red flag" to even the most junior reporters. However, Karpinski believes that command officers didn't fully brief Rumsfeld for three months, and speculates it might be because they might have been trying to cover-up the extent of the abuse.[103]

Following the "60 Minutes II" report, the first public notice that Americans were abusing prisoners in Iraq, Gen. Myers at first said that the incidents were caused by "just a handful" of soldiers, but later admitted he hadn't read Taguba's report, filed almost two months earlier. Rumsfeld later said there were even more photos and videos of prisoner abuse, perhaps hundreds taken by soldiers and unavailable to the military, but "if these are released to the public, obviously, it's going to make the matter worse."[104] These photos, said Rumsfeld, depicted "acts that can only be described as blatantly sadistic, cruel, and inhuman."[105] Eventually, a videotape, that included scenes of Iraqi guards raping boys, as well as group sex by American soldiers, would surface.

Some of the abuse was undoubtedly endemic to how the Bush administration failed to handle a postwar occupation. There was significant understaffing—a half dozens MPs often guarded five hundred or more prisoners in a prison that was filled to more than twice its capacity—and a breakdown of military discipline and morale, some of it because of problems from failure to provide essentials to both the military and prison population, some of it because the administration had called upon the Army reserve and national guard to conduct most of the missions in Iraq, took them from their jobs and families for a year, extended their tours of duty after promising them they would return home to resume their civilian jobs, and did not assure adequate training and oversight.[106]

Karpinski, who had been in charge of Iraqi prisons only three months before military intelligence took over all interrogation and used her MPs, received a letter of admonishment and was suspended from her command. However, the abuses occurred not under her command but by MPs, military intelligence, and civilian contractors in a twisted chain of command that had placed military intelligence in charge of the prison. Her superiors had believed she was doing a strong job under difficult circumstances. According to Karpinski:

> Never once did [Sanchez] ever mention to me his concerns about my leadership ability. He never mentored me, he never suggested that I try something differently, he never criticized me, not once. Gen. Wodjakowski, the deputy, who I briefed every other night, never mentioned any concerns.[107]

Although trained in operations and military intelligence, and having previously served several years in the Middle East, like almost every one of her soldiers she had minimal experience in a prison environment nor had she been formally trained in criminology or penology when the Army assigned her first to a battalion command then to command the 800th Military Police Brigade.

Sgt. First Class Paul Shaffer told *The New York Times*, "You're a person who works at McDonald's one day; the next day you're standing in front of hundreds of prisoners, and half are saying they're sick and half are saying they're hungry. We were hit with so much so fast, I don't think we were prepared."[108]

"We were supposed to be the experts on this," said Sgt. 1st Class Scott McKenzie, "[but] we never learned how to deal with a riot, what to do when we were being assaulted."[109]

The United States is a signatory to all the rules of the Geneva Conventions, among them:

> Persons taking no active part in the hostilities . . . shall in all circumstances be treated humanely, without any adverse distinction founded on race, colour, religion or faith, sex, birth or wealth, or any other similar criteria.
>   To this end, the following acts are and shall remain prohibited at any time and in any place whatsoever with respect to the above-mentioned persons:
>   (a) Violence to life and person, in particular murder of all kinds, mutilation, cruel treatment and torture;
>   (b) Taking of hostages;
>   (c) Outrages upon personal dignity, in particular humiliating and degrading

treatment;

(d) The passing of sentences and the carrying out of executions without previous judgment pronounced by a regularly constituted court, affording all the judicial guarantees which are recognized as indispensable by civilized peoples.[110]

According to CBS, "The Army investigation confirms that soldiers at Abu Ghraib were not trained at all in the Geneva Conventions rules. And most were reservists, part-time soldiers who didn't get the kind of specialized prisoner of war training given to regular Army members."[111] Spec. Harman told the *Washington Post*:

> The Geneva Convention was never posted, and none of us remember taking a class to review it. The first time reading it was two months after being charged. I read the entire thing highlighting everything the prison is in violation of. There's a lot.[112]

However, Karpinski disputes that. "They're trained throughout the year and it's part of qualifications," she told the *Santa Clarita* (Calif.) *Signal*. She said that her JAG officers "would routinely do refresher training" with the MPs, that every prisoner was provided a copy of the Geneva Conventions rules in their own language, and that copies were posted throughout the prison system.[113] The investigation by the Army's inspector general, however, revealed that only four of the prisons in Iraq, and none of the prisons in Afghanistan, had provided prisoners copies of the Geneva Conventions in their own languages.[114]

Innumerable times, President Bush had told the nation he was giving the military in Iraq and Afghanistan all the resources they needed. Karpinski says she didn't have enough troops or resources, that the military chain refused to replace troops who were sent home or rotated out of her command, that her brigade wasn't properly trained, and that when she complained to her superiors, they ignored her. "They just wanted it to go away," she said.[115]

"I never saw a set of rules of SOP [Standard Operation Procedures] . . . just word of mouth," said Sgt. Javal S. Davis, one of the MPs accused of prisoner abuse.[116]

Staff Sgt. Ivan "Chip" Frederick, one of the soldiers charged with the crimes, and in civilian life a prison guard in Virginia, said the MPs "had no support, no training whatsoever. And I kept asking my chain of command for certain things . . . like rules and regulations. And it just wasn't happening."[117] His words echoed sentiments he had expressed in letters he had sent home in January 2004:

> I questioned some of the things that I saw . . . such things as leaving inmates in their cells with no clothes or in female underpants, handcuffing them to the door of their cell—and the answer I got was, "This is how military intelligence [MI] wants it done." . . . MI has also instructed us to place a prisoner in an isolated cell with little

or no clothes, no toilet or running water, no ventilation or window, for as much as three days. . . . [MI] encouraged and told us, "Great job," they were now getting positive results and information.[118]

At a Senate/House Armed Service Committee hearing, Rep. Gene Taylor (D-Miss.) told Donald Rumsfeld, "Moms and dads . . . had to write me and tell me that their kids weren't getting the proper body armor." He said a National Guard unit "showed me proudly their efforts to make their own up-armored Humvee, because apparently no one above was bothering to tell Congress, which writes the checks for these things, that they needed to be protected."[119] His words gave credence to similar statements by Karpinski and the MPs at Abu Ghraib.

Sen. Carl Levin (D-Mich.), ranking member of the Senate Armed Forces Committee, outlined some of the conditions that led to abuse:

> [S]ome of the environment here was actually set at the White House when they said it was a bunch of legalisms to discuss whether or not the Geneva Conventions would apply to prisoners directly or whether they would be treated with the Geneva Conventions or in the same way but not precisely. . . .
> [That policy was] splitting legal hairs about the application of Geneva Conventions, and it seems to me that sent exactly the wrong message to the intelligence people and to the guards themselves.[120]

Now, in the glare of public outrage, both the Department of Defense and the White House contradicted their earlier statements about why the Geneva Conventions didn't apply to prisoners. Before the combined Senate/House Armed Forces Committee hearing, Donald Rumsfeld testified that the soldiers were required to follow the Geneva Conventions rules,[121] contradicting statements made during the previous two years in which he had called the rules optional and not applicable. Also contradicting earlier statements was White House counsel Alberto Gonzales, the former Texas Supreme Court judge, who two years earlier had signed the controversial memo that declared many of the provisions of the Geneva Conventions were "quaint" and weren't applicable. Ironically, although Gonzales would take the heat for those comments, almost the entire memo was written by David Addington, senior counsel to Vice President Dick Cheney, probably the administration's leading proponent for attacking Iraq.[122] In an Op-Ed article in the *New York Times*, Gonzales implied the Bush administration always followed the Geneva Conventions:

> President Bush recognized that our nation will continue to be a strong supporter of the Geneva treaties. The president also reaffirmed our policy in the United States armed forces to treat Al Qaeda and Taliban detainees at Guantánamo Bay humanely and, to the extent appropriate and consistent with military necessity, in

keeping with the principles of the Third Geneva Convention.[123]

Under intense condemnation by world public opinion, President Bush and Condoleezza Rice went on Arab television to say they regretted the treatment of the prisoners and the humiliation they suffered, but never formally apologized, nor did they address the issue of torture. At a public meeting with Jordanian King Abdullah II, President Bush revealed an earlier conversation, but he didn't acknowledge any wider responsibility than those who personally committed the atrocities against the prisoners:

> I told him I was sorry for the humiliation suffered by the Iraqi prisoners, and the humiliation suffered by their families. I told him I was equally sorry that people who have been seeing those pictures didn't understand the true nature and heart of America. I assured him Americans, like me, didn't appreciate what we saw, that it made us sick to our stomachs. I also made it clear to His Majesty that the troops we have in Iraq, who are there for security and peace and freedom, are the finest of the fine, fantastic United States citizens, who represent the very best qualities of America: courage, love of freedom, compassion, and decency.[124]

Leaders of both major political parties condemned not only the atrocities but also the failure of the Department of Defense first to investigate the abuse in a timely manner, then apparent attempts to cover it up and not keep the president or a congressional oversight committee informed. The president later issued a public apology and acknowledged he had admonished Donald Rumsfeld for conditions at Abu Ghraib and for not informing him sooner;[125] however, Donald Rumsfeld testified that in late January or early February he had made the president aware of the prisoner abuse. Before a combined Senate/ House Armed Forces committee hearing, a contrite Rumsfeld, under pressure from the White House to quell a political firestorm, said, "These events occurred on my watch . . . I am accountable for them. I take full responsibility."[126] He offered his "deepest apology," and said the United States would give "appropriate [financial] compensation" to those who were subjected to "grievous and brutal abuse and cruelty."[127] But he and Gen. Myers, reflecting President Bush's statements, both seemed to place the blame on individual soldiers rather than on the system that they had helped to create that led to the abuse. Sen. Lindsey O. Graham (R-S.C.), a former Air Force chief prosecutor, later said, "We just don't want a bunch of privates and sergeants to be the scapegoats here. It's clear to me that we had [a] system failure."[128] A month after the hearings, President Bush continued to blame "a few American troops"[129] for the abuse, although evidence was mounting there were massive violations not just at Abu Ghraib, but in both Afghanistan and throughout Iraq almost from the time of the American invasion in May 2003, as documented by continued Army investigations.[130]

Part of the "system failure" was created at the highest levels of government. Combining the missions of the military police and military intelligence, with military intelligence taking a commanding role, violated long-established military policies that kept the two operations independent. There were several critical reasons for that independence, but with MPs now taking orders from military intelligence officers, the role of the MPs was compromised. As Janis Karpinski many times tried to tell her superiors, such a fusion led to a "dysfunctional" chain of command.

Further, an investigation by Seymour Hersh, published in *The New Yorker*, revealed that Donald Rumsfeld had authorized the expansion of a secret operation that "embittered the American intelligence community, damaged the elite combat units, and hurt America's prospects in the war on terrorism."[131] Known as Copper Green, among other code words, the special-access program (SAP) was a clandestine operation originally designed to "respond immediately to time-sensitive intelligence," says Hersh. The SAP would "recruit operatives and acquire the necessary equipment, including aircraft," with funding and traceability that congressional oversight committees would not know about. The president and his national security advisor both had given their approval for the program; fewer than two hundred people knew about the program. One of the missions of the SAP, says Hersh, "encouraged physical coercion and sexual humiliation of Iraqi prisoners."[132] Both the CIA and military intelligence communities opposed the tactics of this special SAP.

Rumsfeld, in his testimony before the Armed Forces committee, never acknowledged the SAP. The Department of Defense called Hersh's reporting "outlandish, conspiratorial, and filled with error and anonymous conjecture."[133]

Dozens of members of Congress, political leaders, and leading public figures, outraged by revelations of the Defense Department's handling of prisoners, questioned Rumsfeld's and Myers' ability to continue to lead. As evidence mounted against the way the Department of Defense conducted the war in Iraq and the treatment of prisoners, several Republican members of Congress called for an end to the hearings, some even attacking Sen. John Warner (R-Va.), the committee's chair and a former secretary of the Navy, for continuing the Senate investigation.[134] A combative Dick Cheney, a long-time personal and political friend of Rumsfeld's, said people should "get off his case," a statement that infuriated several members of the Armed Forces committees who had initiated the hearings into prisoner abuse and the Defense Department's role. President Bush emphasized that Rumsfeld was "doing a superb job,"[135] and "is an important part of my cabinet." The president emphasized he had no intention of replacing him.[136]

In a subsequent hearing, in response to a question asking how specific abuses happened, Taguba summarized his observations: "Failure in leadership, sir, from the brigade commander on down. Lack of discipline, no training whatsoever and no supervision. Supervisory omission was rampant."[137] Others would address problems of critical understaffing, and the government's failure to adequately plan for or properly execute postwar occupation. The Bush administration had failed to understand, or accept, Colin Powell's advice that once the United States destroyed Iraq, "you own it."

The *Army Times*, a private newspaper with significant and substantial influence in the military and civilian leadership, suggested that removing those at the top of the chain of command would be reasonable:

> Around the halls of the Pentagon, a term of caustic derision has emerged for the enlisted soldiers at the heart of the furor over the Abu Ghraib prison scandal: the six morons who lost the war. . . .
>
> But the folks in the Pentagon are talking about the wrong morons. . . .
>
> [W]hile responsibility begins with the six soldiers facing criminal charges, it extends all the way up the chain of command to the highest reaches of the military hierarchy and its civilian leadership. . . .
>
> The entire affair is a failure of leadership from start to finish. . . .
>
> Army commanders in Iraq bear responsibility for running a prison where there was no legal adviser to the commander, and no ultimate responsibility taken for the care and treatment of the prisoners. . . . .
>
> Gen. Richard Myers, chairman of the Joint Chiefs, also shares in the shame. Myers asked "60 Minutes II" to hold off reporting news of the scandal because it could put U.S. troops at risk. But when the report was aired, a week later, Myers still hadn't read Taguba's report . . . Defense Secretary Donald Rumsfeld also failed to read the report until after the scandal broke in the media. . . .
>
> By then, of course, it was too late. . . .
>
> Myers, Rumsfeld and their staffs failed to recognize the impact the scandal would have not only in the United States, but around the world. . . .
>
> On the battlefield, Myers' and Rumsfeld's errors would be called a lack of situational awareness—a failure that amounts to professional negligence. . . .
>
> This was not just a failure of leadership at the local command level. This was a failure that ran straight to the top. Accountability here is essential—even if that means relieving top leaders from duty in a time of war.[138]

"It should now be evident that the monitoring of detention facilities by the armed forces has been insufficient to ensure compliance with U.S. obligations under international human rights and humanitarian law, particularly the Geneva Conventions," observed Kenneth Roth, executive director of Human Rights Watch,[139] which had pleaded with the Bush administration for several months to allow better access to the prisons and to improve conditions for all prisoners.

About the time that Rumsfeld testified before Congress, the Department of Defense announced it was suspending all "stress and duress" interrogation techniques in Iraq. It did not address use of those techniques in Afghanistan and Guantánamo Bay. A few weeks later, the Department of Defense announced all Red Cross reports in Iraq would go to a single commander who would now be required to bring the reports to the attention of senior commanders in Iraq and the Pentagon. Gen. John Abizaid, commander of the U.S. Central Command, acknowledged that the Pentagon had "a real problem [with] the way" Red Cross reports had been previously handled.[140]

Another problem, not unlike one at Guantánamo Bay and in the prisons in Afghanistan, was apparent in Iraq. According to Seymour Hersh:

> A lack of proper screening also meant that many innocent Iraqis were wrongly being detained—indefinitely, it seemed, in some cases. The Taguba study noted that more than sixty per cent of the civilian inmates at Abu Ghraib were deemed not to be a threat to society, which should have enabled them to be released. Karpinski's defense, Taguba said, was that her superior officers [as well as military intelligence officers] "routinely" rejected her recommendations regarding the release of such prisoners. . . .
>
> Under the fourth Geneva convention, an occupying power can jail civilians who pose an "imperative" security threat, but it must establish a regular procedure for insuring that only civilians who remain a genuine security threat be kept imprisoned. Prisoners have the right to appeal any internment decision and have their cases reviewed. Human Rights Watch complained to Secretary of Defense Donald Rumsfeld that civilians in Iraq remained in custody month after month with no charges brought against them. Abu Ghraib had become, in effect, another Guantánamo.[141]

A Red Cross investigation had placed the number of innocent persons more at 70–90 percent.[142] An Army investigation conducted the previous November revealed not only was Karpinski correct in her assertions about senior military commanders who refused to release prisoners that posed no security threat, but that many of the prisoners were held by the Army solely because they opposed the American occupation.[143] Following disclosures of prisoner abuse, the military began releasing hundreds of prisoners—but had also kept the prisoners to overcrowded capacity by additional arrests. Ironically, the interrogations at Abu Ghraib produced almost no information of value to the United States. According to Army documents, almost all information about the insurgency movement or location of former Iraqi officials was done in the field before prisoners were taken to Abu Ghraib.[144]

In May 2004, in a speech at the Army War College in Carlisle, Pennsylvania, President Bush pledged to tear down the Abu Ghraib prison and build a new one. However, the $200–$300 million cost was not in the budget, and Congress had earlier rejected an administration request for $400 million to build two maximum-security prisons, approving $100 million for a medium-security prison. "For all intents and purposes, the money is not there" for a new maximum security prison, said Tim Rieser, staff assistant on the Senate Appropriations Committee.[145] Even if Congress were to approve a new prison, it would take at least two years, based upon construction of similar prisons. The president's pledge also ran into opposition from both

Iraqis and the Army. The Iraqis wanted the prison to remain as a museum. The Army wanted it to be preserved as evidence in subsequent trials. About a month after the president's attempt to "spin" a disaster into a public relations coup, Col. James Pohl, an Army military judge, ruled that the Abu Ghraib prison is a crime scene and evidence had to be preserved during all trials. Pohl also ordered that the defendants had a right to call senior officers to testify about their own actions.[146]

In response to continued attacks upon his leadership, Rumsfeld appointed an independent panel to conduct its own investigation into causes for the abuses at Abu Ghraib. That panel—two former secretaries of defense, a retired Air Force general who had been in charge of the air war against Iraq in 1991, and a former congresswoman who had chaired an investigation into sexual harassment at the Air Force Academy—had Rumsfeld's complete support, and focused upon senior levels of the chain of command. Their conclusion, in contradiction to the president's belief that the problem was confined to "rogue" soldiers, was there were significant leadership failures in organization, command structures, training, and detention, extending into the top levels of both civilian and military components of the Department of Defense.

The panel, although finding that Rumsfeld had made extensive efforts to establish clear guidelines for the treatment of prisoners and for trying to avoid abuse, found senior commanders in Iraq and in the Pentagon command structure failed to provide "clear, consistent guidance" in the handling of prisoners.[147] According to Tillie K. Fowler, one of the four panel members:

> We found a string of failures that go well beyond an isolated cell block in Iraq. . . . We found fundamental failures throughout all levels of command, from soldiers on the ground to the Central Command and to the Pentagon. These failures of leadership helped to set the conditions which allowed for the abusive practice to take place.[148]

The effect of the separate internal Army investigations and the special Department of Defense independent panel was, said Sen. Lindsey Graham, a "clear message . . . that the system failed in a widespread manner."[149] However, it was the enlisted soldiers, not the military intelligence officers, not the CIA agents at the prison, not the civilian leadership, who were the first ones brought to courts martial. In May 2004, Spec. Jeremy C. Sivits was sentenced to one year imprisonment after pleading guilty. In September 2004, Spec. Armin Cruz, a soldier in a military intelligence unit, was sentenced to eight months imprisonment. The following month, Staff Sgt. Ivan "Chip" Frederick, the highest ranked soldier brought to court martial, on a plea bargain and an agreement to testify against others, was sentenced to eight years imprisonment. All three were reduced in rank and received bad conduct discharges.

CHAPTER 5

'A Perilous New Course'

The Supreme Court of the United States has ruled several times that fear and even terrorism might be a dominating concern at various times in the American experience, but that under the Constitution preservation of rights and of law are the best ways to preserve the democracy.

A year after the Civil War, the Supreme Court, in *Ex parte Milligan*, ruled:

> The Constitution of the United States is a law for rulers and people, equally in war and in peace, and covers with the shield of its protection all classes of men, at all times . . . and under all circumstances. No doctrine, involving more pernicious consequences, was ever invented by the wit of man than that any of its provisions can be suspended during any of the great exigencies of government. Such a doctrine leads directly to anarchy or despotism, but the theory of necessity on which it is based is false; for the government, within the Constitution, has all the powers granted to it, which are necessary to preserve its existence; as has been happily proved by the result of the great effort [the Civil War] to throw off its just authority.[1]

Reaffirming the principles of the *Milligan* decision, in 1934 the Supreme Court ruled that "even the war power of the Federal Government is not without limitations, and that such an emergency does not suspend constitutional limitations and guaranties."[2]

In a case brought into the federal courts during World War II, the Supreme Court ruled, "We must be on constant guard against an excessive use of any power, military or otherwise, that results in the needless destruction of our rights and liberties. There must be a careful balancing of interests."[3]

In April 2003, Justice Stephen Breyer, possibly signaling future Supreme Court decisions arising from the PATRIOT Act, explained the balancing interests of safety and freedom:

> Courts, as well as lawyers, ask this question ["Why is this restriction necessary?"] of government officials. Those officials can explain the special need, backing up the explanations with relevant supporting material. Courts can examine that material, *in camera* if necessary, even *ex parte*, say, with counsels' permission. Courts can give weight, leeway, or deference to the Government's explanation insofar as it reflects underlying expertise. But deference is not abdication. And ultimately the courts must determine not only the absolute importance of the security interest, but also, and more importantly, its relative importance, *i.e.,* its importance when examined through the Constitution's own legal lens—a lens that emphasizes the values that a democratic society places upon individual human liberty.[4]

And now, in the "war on terrorism," the judicial system would be required to affirm or redefine not only the precedents that put the interests of what the executive branch called a necessity for the national security opposite the need to protect constitutional guarantees, but also the limits of executive authority.

In the interest of "national security," John Ashcroft declared Yaser Esam Hamdi, a twenty-one-year-old American citizen, to be an "enemy combatant" and, thus, not entitled to legal representation, that he could be held indefinitely in secret without charges being filed, and that even *if* a lawyer were to be present, all conversations had to be recorded, a violation of the Fourth Amendment. The Department of Justice claimed the PATRIOT Act allowed the conversations to be recorded to eliminate collusion between the attorney and client that could lead to further criminal acts. However, there had always been a remedy to such possible abuse of the attorney-client privilege since law enforcement could obtain court orders after showing probable cause; what the PATRIOT Act did was to remove this constitutional protection.

Under the same "gag order" governing the noncitizens held prisoner at Guantánamo Bay, any reporter who revealed information about Hamdi's detention could be charged under the PATRIOT Act. "That sounds idiotic, doesn't it?" asked Judge Robert G. Doumar of the U.S. District Court for the Eastern District of Virginia.[5]

The government couldn't provide any evidence that Hamdi had any links to terrorists,[6] although the government claimed not only was Hamdi captured in Afghanistan, he was a combatant with the Taliban government. The Taliban government, of course, had ties to al-Qaeda but was not involved in the 9/11 killings.

The U.S. Court of Appeals for the Fourth Circuit (Maryland, North and South Carolina, Virginia, and West Virginia), widely accepted in the legal community as one of the more conservative courts, reversed Judge Doumar's ruling, and accepted the Department of Defense designation of Hamdi as an "enemy combatant" since he was found in a "zone of armed conflict."[7] In her dissent, Judge Diana Gribbon Motz, noted:

> [T]he panel embarks on a perilous new course—approving the Executive's designation of enemy combatant status not on the basis of facts stipulated or proven, but solely on the basis of an unknown Executive advisor's declaration, which the panel itself concedes is subject to challenge as "incomplete" . . . and "inconsistent" hearsay.[8]

With mounting public pressure, and facing additional legal challenges, after more than two years the government allowed Hamdi to talk with his lawyer but with the military monitoring all conversations.[9]

José Padilla, an American citizen who the government believed knew something about the al-Qaeda network, but which had no documented evidence, was arrested by FBI agents in May 2002 after landing at O'Hare Airport, Chicago, on a flight from Pakistan.

Padilla, who had a criminal background as a juvenile, was first held as a material witness and assigned a public defender. However, a month later President Bush declared him to be an enemy combatant, believing he had worked with al-Qaeda on a "dirty bomb," and sent him to a Navy prison in Charleston, South Carolina. The only evidence was a brief written statement by a government agent; there was no supporting evidence. For eighteen months, he wasn't permitted contact with his counsel, his family, or any other nonmilitary personnel. The Bush administration argued that to allow Padilla legal counsel would undermine its interrogation and national security. The government failed to produce any evidence that Padilla worked with al-Qaeda or even that he was involved with building a "dirty bomb."

Ironically, Viet Dinh, who left the Department of Justice to become a professor at Georgetown University, told *Vanity Fair* in November 2003 he didn't "necessarily agree with the position the president and the U.S. government is adopting with respect to military detention" of citizens.[10]

Gary Solis, law professor and former combat Marine officer, further posed the question:

> [W]hy is Padilla in a military brig? Is his military custody a violation of the Posse Comitatus Act, the federal law that prohibits the military from executing civilian law? The military did not investigate or seek Padilla. He is a civilian, not a prisoner of war and, enemy combatant or not, he is outside the jurisdiction of the Uniform Code of Military Justice. Nor is he in pretrial confinement, because no military trial is envisioned. What is the military supposed to do with him—and when? Unfortunately for the image of U.S. military justice, many will presume the military can hold anyone for an indefinite period without charges; after all, isn't that what they do to soldiers, sailors and Marines?
>
> That is not what the military does, and years have been spent trying to erase that outdated image. Thanks to the Justice Department, the military is positioned to appear fast and loose with service personnel's rights. Justice has done the military no favors by saddling it with Padilla. Nor do the Justice Department's actions serve the Constitution.[11]

Padilla's attorneys, hired by relatives and denied the right to talk with their client, argued that Bush's actions against a U.S. citizen violated the 1971 Non-Detention Act, part of which forbids the government from holding American citizens without due process except by an act of Congress. In December 2002, U.S. District Judge Michael Mukasey ruled that Padilla had a right to confer with a lawyer.[12]

"We recognize the government's responsibility to do everything possible to prevent another attack on our nation, but we also worry that the methods employed in the Hamdi and Padilla cases risk the use of excessive government power and threaten the checks and balances necessary in our federal system," argued the American Bar Association (ABA) Task Force on Treatment of Enemy Combatants.[13] According to the ABA report, which covered the detention of citizens in Naval brigs in the continental United States and of noncitizens at Guantánamo Bay:

> The government's concerns that access to counsel may impede the collection of intelligence, or that counsel might facilitate communications with others, do not justify denial of access to counsel. These concerns are frequently overcome in sensitive criminal prosecutions, as in the case of the 1993 World Trade Center bombers and the current Moussaoui prosecution, where defense attorneys (or standby attorneys) were required to submit to security clearance background checks and the courts have not hesitated to place sensitive pleadings and documents under seal. Lawyers can provide effective representation—and have, in numerous cases–without threatening the nation's security. . . .
>
> While the Sixth Amendment does not technically attach to uncharged "enemy combatants," there is no dispute that individuals who have been criminally charged do have a Sixth Amendment **right** to counsel, and it is both paradoxical and unsatisfactory that uncharged U.S. citizen detainees have fewer rights and protections than those who have been charged with serious criminal offenses. . . .
>
> International agreements recognized by the United States also suggest a detainee's right to judicial review and access to counsel. They include Articles 8 and 9 of the Universal Declaration of Human Rights and the International Covenant on Civil and Political Rights . . . which attempt to protect individuals from arbitrary detention, and guarantee a meaningful review of a detainee's status.[14]

At its mid-season meeting, the ABA House of Delegates urged the executive branch and Congress to consider:

> U.S. citizens and residents who are detained within the United States based on their designation as "enemy combatants" be afforded the opportunity for meaningful judicial review of their status under a standard according such deference to the designation as the reviewing court determines to be appropriate to accommodate the needs of the detainee and the requirements of national security; and [that they] not be denied access to counsel in connection with the opportunity for such review. . . [that] Congress, in coordination with the Executive Branch, [establishes] clear standards and procedures governing the designation and treatment of U.S. citizens, residents, or others who are detained within the United States as "enemy combatants;" and . . . [I]n setting and executing national policy regarding detention of "enemy combatants," Congress and the Executive Branch should consider how the policy adopted by the United States may affect the response of other nations to future acts of terrorism.[15]

In December 2003, following an appeal by the Department of Justice, the U.S. Court of Appeals for the Second Circuit (Connecticut, New York, and Vermont) declared the government doesn't have the right to declare a U.S. citizen seized on American soil away from any combat as an "enemy combatant," that it doesn't have the right to deny counsel to that person, and that the Bush administration has no judicial or congressional authority to keep American citizens *incommunicado*. It ordered the government to release

Padilla. In a sharp rebuke to the Bush administration, the court ruled:

> As this Court sits only a short distance from where the World Trade Center once stood, we are as keenly aware as anyone of the threat al Qaeda poses to our country and of the responsibilities the president and law enforcement officials bear for protecting the nation. But presidential authority does not exist in a vacuum . . . and this case involves not whether those responsibilities should be aggressively pursued, but whether the president is obligated, in the circumstances presented here, to share them with Congress. . . .
>
>   Where . . . the president's power as Commander-in-Chief of the armed forces and the domestic rule of law intersect, we conclude that clear congressional authorization is required for detentions of American citizens on American soil because 18 U.S.C. § 4001(a) (2000) (the "Non-Detention Act") prohibits such detentions absent specific congressional authorization. Congress's Authorization for Use of Military Force Joint Resolution, Pub. L. No. 107-40, 115 Stat. 224 (2001) ("Joint Resolution"), passed shortly after the attacks of September 11, 2001, is not such an authorization, and no exception to section 4001(a) otherwise exists.[16]

The Bush administration declared the court's opinion to be "troubling and flawed," and declared it would delay and appeal. The nation was now faced with two conflicting views about the detention of American citizens. In *Hamdi v. Rumsfeld*, the Fourth Circuit agreed with the government's position; in *Padilla v. Rumsfeld*, the Second Circuit disagreed. In February 2004, the Supreme Court of the United States decided to review the cases; two months later, it heard arguments on petitions representing both Hamdi and Padilla. Neither prisoner had been aware until weeks before that the Supreme Court was considering the case. When they were finally allowed to talk with an attorney, the military monitored and then classified all conversations.

Deputy Solicitor General Paul D. Clement underscored his arguments for the Bush administration by using a "trust us" philosophy, telling the justices, "you have to trust the executive to make the kind of quintessential military judgments that are involved."[17]

In response, Frank Dunham, federal public defender representing Hamdi, countered that checks and balances exist in the Constitution because "we didn't trust the executive branch when we founded this government. That's why the government saying, 'trust us' is no excuse for taking away and driving a truck through [the principle] that no man shall be deprived of liberty except upon due process of law."[18]

If the Supreme Court accepted the government's position, "it would mean that for the foreseeable future, any citizen, anywhere, at any time, would be subject to indefinite military detention on the unilateral order of the president," according to the brief presented by the defense.[19]

"Never before in history has this court granted the president a blank check to do whatever he wants to American citizens,"[20] argued defense attorney Jennifer Martinez, on behalf of Padilla. Martinez, professor of law at

Stanford University, also argued that even the broadest interpretation of war powers acts did not allow "executive unlimited power over citizens."[21] In defense of Hamdi, Dunham argued, "We could have people locked up all over the country tomorrow with no opportunity to be heard . . . Congress didn't intend for widespread indefinite detentions."[22] He argued that under the Constitution all prisoners have a right to go to court to challenge their detention.

However, Clement maintained the president's authority is absolute, charging that during war the courts had no rights "micromanaging" how prisoners, including American citizens, were handled. Justice Ruth Bader Ginsburg asked Clement if someone who is detained by the military doesn't have "a right to bring before some tribunal himself" to plead his case. Clement's response that the prisoner could do so during detention, drew Ginsburg's observation, "How about a neutral decision-maker of some kind, perhaps in the military? Is that so extreme?"[23]

Justice Stephen Breyer asked why military detention of civilians was "necessary and appropriate in a country that has its courts open, and that has regular criminal proceedings, that has all the possibility of adjudicating a claim that 'I'm the wrong person' [to have been detained.] . . . Why is it a 'necessary and appropriate' thing to do once you have such a person who is a citizen in this country to proceed by other than a normal court procedure?"[24]

For more than two years, the government refused to release any information on why it held Padilla, and denied him counsel and legal rights. Then, after making its presentation to the Supreme Court, and while that Court was deliberating, the Department of Justice decided to hold a press conference. The pretext for the conference was ostensibly a letter from Sen. Orrin Hatch (R-Utah), chair of the Senate Committee on the Judiciary and a strong supporter of the PATRIOT Act and the Bush administration, who asked both the Departments of Justice and Defense to provide information about American citizens held in custody.

At a nationally televised press conference, Deputy Attorney General James Comey portrayed Padilla as an active recruit of al-Qaeda, although he never became a member of the terrorist organization, who had been trained to attack American targets, specifically American apartment buildings in cities of his choice. "Much of this information has been uncovered because José Padilla has been detained as an enemy combatant and questioned," said Comey.[25] Had the government processed Padilla through the court system, said Comey, "he would very likely have followed his lawyer's advice and said nothing, which would have been his constitutional right. He would likely have ended up a free man."[26]

Padilla never admitted to being an al-Qaeda operative, and claimed only that the use of a "dirty bomb" was nothing more than a ruse to escape from the terrorism in Pakistan and return to the United States.

Andrew Patel, representing Padilla, said Comey's presentation was nothing more than "an opening statement without a trial. We are in the same position we've been in for two years, where the government says bad things about Mr. Padilla and there's no forum for him to defend himself."[27] Comey acknowledged that the information the government says it extracted from Padilla could not be used in a criminal case "because we "questioned him in the absence of counsel."[28] Padilla's attorney, who was monitored every time he talked with his client, was forbidden from making any public statements about what he and Padilla discussed, or even to present a counterargument to the government's public claims.

Comey denied that the press conference was an attempt to influence public opinion or, more specifically, the nine Supreme Court justices. Nevertheless, even conservatives saw the Department of Justice's moves as political not legal. Andrew Napolitano, FOX News judicial analyst, told conservative talk-show host Bill O'Reilly that the Justice Department tactics were "shameful."[29] Scott Turow, a federal prosecutor and defense attorney before he became a best-selling novelist, also questioned the Department of Justice's attempts to manipulate public opinion. "Comey's performance constituted one more legally and ethically dubious maneuver by our government in a case that I already regarded as one of the most troubling in memory," said Turow.[30]

Even if everything Comey claimed Padilla said was accurate, the case brought to the Supreme Court was one not of judging guilt or innocence but of the government's decision to use extralegal and unconstitutional methods. In an observation during oral arguments that would guide the Court's opinion, Justice Breyer suggested, "It seems rather contrary to an idea of a Constitution with three branches that the executive would be free to do whatever they want . . . without a check."[31]

Two months after oral arguments, the Supreme Court dealt the Bush administration a major defeat. In a 6–3 opinion, in the *Rasul* and *al-Odah* cases, it declared the executive branch could not hold foreign-born prisoners at Guantánamo Bay indefinitely without access to the American judicial system and the rights of due process. In an 8–1 decision on the *Hamdi* case, it vacated the opinion of the Court of Appeals for the Fourth Circuit, which accepted the government's arguments that it could deny legal rights to American citizen it declares to be an "enemy combatant." The opinion sidestepped the question of what is an "enemy combatant" and whether tribunals are legal.

In writing the thirty-three page opinion of the Court, Justice Sandra Day O'Connor, while deferential to the president, and seemingly trying to please both sides, nevertheless firmly stated:

Striking the proper constitutional balance here is of great importance to the Nation during this period of ongoing combat. But it is equally vital that our calculus not give short shrift to the values that this country holds dear or to the privilege that is American citizenship. It is during our most challenging and uncertain moments that our Nation's commitment to due process is most severely tested; and it is in those times that we must preserve our commitment at home to the principles for which we fight abroad. . . . (The imperative necessity for safeguarding these rights to procedural due process under the gravest of emergencies has existed throughout our constitutional history, for it is then, under the pressing exigencies of crisis, that there is the greatest temptation to dispense with guarantees which, it is feared, will inhibit government action.) . . . (It would indeed be ironic if, in the name of national defense, we would sanction the subversion of one of those liberties, which makes the defense of the Nation worthwhile.). . .

While the full protections that accompany challenges to detentions in other settings may prove unworkable and inappropriate in the enemy-combatant setting, the threats to military operations posed by a basic system of independent review are not so weighty as to trump a citizen's core rights to challenge meaningfully the Government's case and to be heard by an impartial adjudicator.

In so holding, we necessarily reject the Government's assertion that separation of powers principles mandate a heavily circumscribed role for the courts in such circumstances. Indeed, the position that the courts must forgo any examination of the individual case and focus exclusively on the legality of the broader detention scheme cannot be mandated by any reasonable view of separation of powers, as this approach serves only to *condense* power into a single branch of government. We have long since made clear that a state of war is not a blank check for the president when it comes to the rights of the Nation's citizens. . . .

Whatever power the United States Constitution envisions for the Executive in its exchanges with other nations or with enemy organizations in times of conflict, it most assuredly envisions a role for all three branches when individual liberties are at stake. . . .([I]t was "the central judgment of the Framers of the Constitution that, within our political scheme, the separation of governmental powers into three coordinate Branches is essential to the preservation of liberty") . . . (The war power is a power to wage war successfully, and thus it permits the harnessing of the entire energies of the people in a supreme cooperative effort to preserve the nation. But even the war power does not remove constitutional limitations safeguarding essential liberties.) Likewise, we have made clear that, unless Congress acts to suspend it, the Great Writ of habeas corpus allows the Judicial branch to play a necessary role in maintaining this delicate balance of governance, serving as an important judicial check on the Executive's discretion in the realm of detentions. . . (At its historical core, the writ of habeas corpus has served as a means of reviewing the legality of Executive detention, and it is in that context that its protections have been strongest.) Thus, while we do not question that our due process assessment must pay keen attention to the particular burdens faced by the Executive in the context of military action, it would turn our system of checks and balances on its head to suggest that a citizen could not make his way to court with a challenge to the factual basis for his detention by his government, simply because the Executive opposes making available such a challenge. Absent suspension of the writ by Congress, a citizen detained as an enemy combatant is entitled to this process.

Because we conclude that due process demands some system for a citizen detainee to refute his classification, the proposed "some evidence" standard is inadequate. Any process in which the Executive's factual assertions go wholly unchallenged or are simply presumed correct without any opportunity for the alleged combatant to demonstrate otherwise falls constitutionally short. As the Government itself has recognized, we have utilized the same evidence standard in the past as a standard of review, not as a standard of proof. . . . That is, it primarily has been employed by courts in examining an administrative record developed after an adversarial proceeding, one with process at least of the sort that we today hold is constitutionally mandated in the citizen enemy-combatant setting. . . . This standard therefore is ill suited to the situation in which a habeas petitioner has received no prior proceedings before any tribunal and had no prior opportunity to rebut the Executive's factual assertions before a neutral decisionmaker.

Today we are faced only with such a case. Aside from unspecified "screening" processes . . . and military interrogations in which the Government suggests Hamdi could have contested his classification, . . . Hamdi has received no process. An interrogation by one's captor, however effective an intelligence-gathering tool, hardly constitutes a constitutionally adequate fact finding before a neutral decision maker. ([O]ne is entitled as a matter of due process of law to an adjudicator who is not in a situation which would offer a possible temptation to the average man as a judge . . . which might lead him not to hold the balance nice, clear and true. . . . That even purportedly fair adjudicators are disqualified by their interest in the controversy to be decided is, of course, the general rule. . . . Plainly, "the process" Hamdi has received is not that to which he is entitled under the Due Process Clause. There remains the possibility that the standards we have articulated could be met by an appropriately authorized and properly constituted military tribunal. Indeed, it is notable that military regulations already provide for such process in related instances, dictating that tribunals be made available to determine the status of enemy detainees who assert prisoner-of-war status under the Geneva Convention. . . .

We have no reason to doubt that courts faced with these sensitive matters will pay proper heed both to the matters of national security that might arise in an individual case and to the constitutional limitations safeguarding essential liberties that remain vibrant even in times of security concerns. . . .[32]

Justice O'Connor was joined in her opinion by Chief Justice William H. Rehnquist, and Justices Anthony M. Kennedy and Stephen Breyer. Essentially, the opinion continued to put a burden on Hamdi to present evidence that the government is not wrong in its assertions to his guilt, an essential difference from the "presumed innocent" framework of American jurisprudence. Justices Antonin Scalia, a conservative, and John Paul Stevens, a liberal, also concurred, but argued that the Court's opinion did not go far enough to protect civil rights. "If civil rights are to be curtailed during wartime, it must be done openly and democratically, as the Constitution requires, rather than by silent erosion through an opinion of this court," wrote Scalia. Justices Ruth Bader Ginsburg and David H. Souter also concurred, but further argued that Hamdi's detention itself was improper. Only Justice Clarence Thomas dissented, and agreed with all of the government's contentions about reasons why Padilla, and others, had no rights of constitutional due process. A separate 5–4 decision by the Court declared that Hamdi's detention was lawful; the four dissenting justices had wanted Hamdi to be released from custody.

In a contentious 5–4 ruling the same day as the *Hamdi* decision, the Court sidestepped the constitutional issues to the *Padilla* case and on a technicality declared that the case was filed in the wrong jurisdiction and against the wrong defendant. The *Padilla* case had raised stronger constitutional questions since the defendant, an American citizen, was arrested on American soil and not on a battlefield.

Padilla's attorneys had originally filed a *writ of habeas corpus* in the Southern District of New York, since that was where he was held as a "material witness," and where the court appointed his attorney. But the Supreme Court said the suit should have been filed in the U.S. District Court for the District of South Carolina, where Padilla was imprisoned in the Naval brig. Although Donald Rumsfeld, as secretary of defense, was the brig's superior and had been the one to classify Padilla as an "enemy combatant," the defendant, said the court, should have been the warden of the Naval Brig at Charleston. The Supreme Court reversed the decision of the federal district court in New York and the U.S. Court of Appeals for the Second Circuit, which had ruled the federal government did not have the authority to hold Padilla in a military court and that it had denied him constitutional due process. The Supreme Court allowed Padilla's attorneys to refile in the federal district court in South Carolina, with any appeals to go to the U.S. Court of Appeals for the Fourth Circuit. Although the *Hamdi* decision would strengthen Padilla's petition, he would still be subjected to even longer delays in being brought to trial or released for lack of evidence.

The four dissenters on the Supreme Court (Justices Breyer, Ginsburg, Souter, and Stevens) argued that the Court should have heard the argument because the case presented extraordinary circumstances. In an impassioned dissent, Justice Stevens wrote:

> At stake in this case is nothing less than the essence of a free society. Even more important than the method of selecting the people's rulers and their successors is the character of the constraints imposed on the Executive by the rule of law. Unconstrained Executive detention for the purpose of investigating and preventing subversive activity is the hallmark of the Star Chamber. . . . Access to counsel for the purpose of protecting the citizen from official mistakes and mistreatment is the hallmark of due process. Executive detention of subversive citizens, like detention of enemy soldiers to keep them off the battlefield, may sometimes be justified to prevent persons from launching or becoming missiles of destruction. It may not, however, be justified by the naked interest in using unlawful procedures to extract information. Incommunicado detention for months on end is such a procedure. Whether the information so procured is more or less reliable than that acquired by more extreme forms of torture is of no consequence. The Non-Detention Act . . . prohibits, and the Authorization for Use of Military Force Joint Resolution. . . does not authorize the protracted, incommunicado detention of American citizens arrested in the United States. . . .
>   [I]f this Nation is to remain true to the ideals symbolized by its flag, it must not wield the tools of tyrants even to resist an assault by the forces of tyranny.[33]

About a week following the Supreme Court decisions, an Army JAG attorney announced she will "challenge the lawful makeup" of military tribunals. The Court decisions, said Lt. Col. Sharon Shaffer, "changed in a big way" the few options her client had. Ibrahin Ahmed al-Qosi, a Sudanese man captured in Pakistan, was a prisoner at Guantánamo Bay. Shaffer says the Court decisions "opened the door to challenge the entire legitimacy of the military tribunals."

The Supreme Court decisions on the *Rasul/al-Odah*, *Hamdi*, and *Padilla* cases dealt the Bush administration major blows in its belief that the executive branch wielded unlimited power to bypass constitutional rights and liberties. The cases may have been the most important due process cases in more than two decades.

However, even with the Supreme Court decisions, the federal government was unwilling to yield its authority. The Department of Justice refused to allow any of the detainees at Guantánamo Bay who wished to file a *writ of habeas corpus* to challenge their detention to have access to lawyers. The Department maintained the prisoners were foreigners not in U.S. jurisdiction, and had no constitutional rights.

In the second major response to the Supreme Court decisions, the Pentagon announced it would begin special hearings for the prisoners at Guantánamo Bay. The military allowed seventy reporters to be accredited to cover the hearings; only eight at a time, drawn by lottery, would be allowed within the hearing room each day. Citing national security concerns, the Department of Defense required all reporters and their bureau chiefs were required to sign a contract to allow the government to censor any stories they planned to file, and to get specific permission if they wished to identify any member of the commission, prosecutor, defense attorney, or witnesses.[34]

By the end of the year, the military planned to bring all prisoners, except those personally opposed, before these special hearings. After more than two years without knowing what they were accused of, without being allowed to have legal representation, to bring witnesses, or the right to challenge the evidence, the prisoners, still denied legal representation and facing a tribunal that was devoid of the due process required by the Supreme Court, could try to prove they were wrongfully detained. The process would allow them to face what the military called an impartial board of three officers, none of whom were lawyers or military judges. The impartiality of the officers, even ones of the highest moral character, and who honestly believed they could render a fair and objective decision, was suspect; as with employees of every company, military officers are socialized to understand the wishes and direction of their superiors. Lt. Col. Sharon Shaffer charged the Department of Defense did not allow her adequate resources or personnel to properly represent her client.[35] "The system will not guarantee a fair trial," said Lt. Cdr. Charles Swift, defiantly pointing out, "What you seek is an independent and impartial hearing—and this ain't it."[36] The hearings were nothing less than a last-ditch attempt to subvert the Court's decisions by making the Judiciary believe the military hearings met the Court's requirement, and to keep the prisoners out of the federal judicial system where there would be far more rights. "The government is treating a historic loss in the Supreme Court as though it were a suggestion slip," said Eric M. Freedman, professor of law at Hofstra University, and counsel to some of the detainees.[37] "The entire process is a sham," said Joseph Margulies, principal litigator for the Center for Constitutional Rights, which had brought the primary suits against the federal government.[38] The CCR, representing more than 50 of the detainees, planned to file *habeas corpus* petitions within the federal judiciary. Dozens of other attorneys from several organizations also increased their efforts to represent the detainees and keep the entire process within the federal courts rather than to allow the military to continue to have jurisdiction.

In September 2004, the federal government finally released Yaser Esam Hamdi after more than two years in what Hamdi's attorney called "inhumane" confinement. However, the release, following extensive negotiations with Hamdi's federal public defender, required Hamdi to return to Saudi Arabia, to renounce his U.S. citizenship, and to accept certain travel restrictions.

CHAPTER 6

'Rounded Up Secretly, Jailed Secretly, Deported Secretly'

Less than a month after 9/11, five high-level U.S. intelligence specialists circulated a four-page memo advising law enforcement that spending time on racial, religious, or ethnic profiling was counterproductive to finding terrorists. One of the authors, who requested anonymity, told investigative journalist Bill Dedman why the officials circulated the memo: "Why are we in the situation we're in? We were paying attention to a set of characteristics, instead of a set of behaviors that launch an attack."[1] According to Dedman, the memo warned that profiling "adds no security, and in fact can compromise it" by drawing law enforcement attention to the innocent and away from the guilty.[2] Another of the agents explained:

> It's only human to say these people are different, and the likelihood that an Arkansan will say this country is terrible and blow it up is less than a Jordanian. But fundamentally, believing that you can achieve safety by looking at characteristics instead of behaviors is silly. If your goal is preventing attacks . . . you want your eyes and ears looking for pre-attack behaviors, not characteristics.[3]

The senior agents told Dedman that the nineteen terrorists identified on the four planes did not match the profiles of suicide terrorists in the Middle East.[4]

Profiling, says Margaret Stock, professor of national security law at the U.S. Military Academy, "hurt[s] our security by wasting law enforcement resources on innocent people, isolating the Muslim community, [and] creates distrust, alienating people who might have been able to provide useful information about terrorists."[5]

Anthony Romero says the ACLU is worried "that there is a growing momentum focusing on a specific community, regarding them as suspicious merely because of where they are from. The government should focus on what they have done, not where they were born. . . . That just fuels the fires of xenophobia against Middle Eastern, Arab and Muslim communities."[6]

Nevertheless, under President Bush's directive to "make sure this can't happen again," the Department of Justice vigorously, and many say far too zealously, pursued those who were Muslims or citizens of Arab countries. Within four months of 9/11, the federal government had begun a systematic program of racial and ethnic profiling of American residents.

Under John Ashcroft, the Department of Justice had determined that a person's religious beliefs are subject to scrutiny. The FBI ordered each of its fifty-six regional field offices to survey the number of mosques in regions, and to use demographic data of Muslim communities to base their terrorist investigations,[7] "an action carrying the message for many Muslims that people were being singled out purely because of their religion," according to a report by the California Senate Office of Research.[8] In addition to the surveys, FBI agents have entered several mosques, and monitored dozens of antiwar protests to "observe."[9]

Americans "have every reason to believe . . . they will be subjected to new abuses of power under the PATRIOT Act—and what's worse, under this radical law they may never learn that the government has violated their rights," said the ACLU's Ann Beesen.[10] According to the ACLU, because of the PATRIOT Act and its enforcement:

> Attendance at prayer services, educational forums, and social events has substantially dropped [in the Muslim community]. . . . [B]ecause their members know that the FBI can now demand personal records even if they have done nothing wrong, some plaintiffs have suffered a decline in attendance at their mosques and a dramatic decrease in charitable donations required by religious faith. . . . [T]o lessen the chances that the FBI will demand their records, plaintiffs' members have ceased speaking about controversial political issues and stopped visiting websites that address such issues.[11]

Because of the government's actions, some of the nation's largest contributors to Islamic charities reduced or suspended their annual contributions. "I have children to raise. I have a business to run, and I don't want to take any chances [because I fear] if the F.B.I comes to me and accuses me of something," one Muslim said on why he suddenly reduced his giving from $20,000 to $2,000. Shortly after the invasion of Iraq, the *New York Times* reported, "At the very moment when American Muslims are most eager to send humanitarian aid to Iraq, many say they fear contributing to Islamic charities."[12]

"On the slightest hint of a connection to a foreign church or government," wrote Kate Martin of the Center for National Security Studies, "the FBI is required to share that information with the CIA, which is free to include it in any secret databases."[13] Presumably, that order could apply to members of the Russian Orthodox and Roman Catholic churches, as well as those who are Anglicans, Buddhists, or religions which have membership and offices in countries other than the United States.

The Clinton administration had forbidden the FBI from going on "fishing expeditions." The ACLU reports:

> Ashcroft's guidelines give the FBI a green light to send undercover agents or informants to spy on worship services, political demonstrations and other public gatherings and in the Internet chat rooms without even the slightest evidence that wrongdoing is afoot. . . . The FBI is now very much empowered to conduct

investigative 'fishing expeditions' on First Amendment protected activities even though there is no indication of criminal activity.[14]

Under the Bush administration, there have also been significantly increased levels of arrests and deportations, mostly Muslims from Arab countries. None had any connection to 9/11. Many of those deported, or held for several months and then released, had American spouses or children born in the United States. Some of the government's actions were the result of a stretch of a PATRIOT Act extension of the Immigration and Nationality Act;[15] some of the actions were not authorized within the specifics of the PATRIOT Act, but were initiated under administrative procedures. They show the underlying philosophy that helped identify a nation at fear and at risk.

After 9/11 the federal government detained several thousand individuals, almost all of them from Arab countries, without charging them with any crime, held them in secret locations, didn't release their names, forbade them from having access to legal counsel, or from talking with their families. The restrictions were the same as if they had been captured in Afghanistan and sent to Guantánamo Bay. The Department of Justice later acknowledged only that it detained, in secret and without access to legal representation, fifty people it claimed were "material witnesses," but filed no charges against any of them.[16] About half were held for more than thirty days, according to the Department of Justice.

In contrast, the federal government permitted six chartered aircraft to fly 142 persons, many of them members of the bin Laden family and their friends from the United States to Saudi Arabia about three days after 9/11. The FBI claims it interviewed the group, including twenty-two of the twenty-six members of the bin Laden family, before they left the country. Several watchdog groups claim that the federal government permitted the bin Laden family to leave with minimal interrogation because of long-established financial and political ties between the Bush and bin Laden families. The bin Laden family had previously disassociated with Osama bin Laden. Nevertheless, although probably not part of the 9/11 plot, the family, their friends, employees, and staff may have had information that could have helped authorities identify and pursue those who did. Thousands from Arab countries who had absolutely no knowledge of the plot were arrested and detained, usually without benefit of legal counsel, for several months.

The profiling of Arabs and Muslims, excluding the large bin Laden family, was in stark contrast to the exacting due process and constitutional protection given to the terrorists who destroyed a federal building and killed 168 persons in Oklahoma City in 1997. Certainly, there was no effort to target Southerners, Catholics, or the Scottish community just because one of the terrorists was from the South, was a Catholic, and had ancestors who had come from Scotland.

The Justice Department's inspector general in 2003 reported that the detention of individuals in the United States was "indiscriminate and haphazard," and that there were "significant instances" of "a pattern of physical and verbal abuse," including significant violations of religious practices, repeated and unnecessary body-cavity searches, and beatings of illegal immigrants, most of them Muslim or Arab, almost all imprisoned for minor offenses, by various employees and officials of the Department of Justice. Included were employees of the FBI, Bureau of Prisons, Drug Enforcement Administration, and Immigration and Naturalization Service.[17]

Rep. John Conyers Jr. stated that the inspector general's report "shows that we have only begun to scratch the surface with respect to the Justice Department's disregard to constitutional rights and civil liberties."[18]

John Ashcroft had told the International Association of Chiefs of Police that his department is "committed to treating every crime seriously, every criminal justly."[19] However, his department failed to implement nineteen of the twenty-one recommendations of the inspector general to curtail civil liberties abuses.[20] In December 2001, Ashcroft told the Senate Committee on the Judiciary, "All persons being detained have the right to contact their lawyers and the families."[21] He was correct—the prisoners did have that right. But what Ashcroft didn't say is that the government often didn't extend that right to those it detained.

Khurram Altaf, a thirty-four-year-old man with no criminal record, was detained for two months without counsel, and then deported to Pakistan in 2002 without reasonable due process. Altaf, a United States resident for eighteen years and the father of three American-born children, was general manager of a large New Jersey trucking company. The federal government had no evidence that Altaf, who paid U.S. taxes during his residency, had any ties to terrorist organizations. A year later, Altaf's wife and two of his children joined him in Pakistan; the third child, born deaf and in need of constant medical attention, stayed in the United States.

Mazen al-Najjar was also the target of a Department of Justice investigation. According to David Cole, legal affairs correspondent of *The Nation* and professor of law at Georgetown University:

While the September 11 terrorists were training for and coordinating their conspiracy in Florida, the FBI was spending vast resources investigating Mazen al-Najjar, a Palestinian professor from Tampa who spent three and a half years in detention on secret evidence and charges of political association. Al Najjar was released last December when an immigration judge found no evidence that he posed a threat to national security. And while the terrorists were conspiring in New Jersey, the FBI focused its efforts on Hany Kiareldeen, a Palestinian in Newark detained for a year and a half on secret evidence for associating with terrorists. He was freed after immigration judges flatly rejected the government's charges as unfounded; the FBI's principal source was apparently Kiareldeen's ex-wife, with whom he was in a bitter custody dispute and who had filed several false reports about him.[22]

The federal government detained for five months in secret and without access to legal counsel Mohamed Kamel Bellahouel, an Algerian veterinarian married to an American. Bellahouel had no connection to the 9/11 hijackers other than having been their waiter in a public restaurant. His lawsuit after detention was sealed first by a federal district court, and then by an appeals court. The only way the public knew of these actions was through clerical errors by the court, coupled with aggressive reporting by Dan Christensen, a reporter for the *Miami Daily Business Review*. According to Christensen, the case appeared briefly in March 2003 on the website of the U.S. Court of Appeals for the Eleventh Circuit. The case, *Mohammed Kamel Bellahouel v. Monica S. Wetzel*,[23] although sealed, didn't even appear on the court docket. A government's motion to seal the case was itself sealed. Even if all details are sealed from public view, case citations by law must appear on the public docket.

"I cannot talk about it. I am not allowed," Bellahouel told Christensen, who indicated that the case may have involved a petition for a *writ of habeas corpus* and was filed only after the government released Bellahouel from custody.[24] The government, having denied Bellahouel legal representation and subjecting him to severe interrogation, apparently determined that although he had no connection to any terrorist, his work visa had expired. Christensen's subsequent articles revealed the extent to which the Department of Justice went to keep public records secret while claiming it was in the interest of national security.

For more three years, the federal government detained four Iranian brothers who were once real estate agents in southern California. Each had been in the country at least eight years; one had come to the United States in 1978. Three weeks after 9/11, the INS picked up Mohammed, Mostafa, Mohsen, and Mojtaba Mirmehdi. John Ashcroft claimed the brothers were "security risks." However, they were housed together in a "low-security" area of the detention facility. The government acknowledges they aren't terrorists, but says they supported the Mujahedin-e-Khalq (MEK), an organization the State Department claims is a terrorist organization dedicated to overthrowing the current regime in Iran. It is an organization that John Ashcroft supported while a U.S. senator from Missouri. According to the *Los Angeles Times*, Ashcroft continued to support the MEK even after the Department of State placed it on a terrorist watch list.[25]

The brothers admitted to attending protests against the Iranian government, but denied being members of the MEK. According to the *Times*, the only witness against them at their detention hearing in October "was an FBI agent who testified by telephone that informants told him the Mirmehdis were supporters of MEK."[26] Because of immigration violations—they had lied on applications to come to America by stating they had sought political asylum—the government ordered them deported. But the courts have ruled they can't be deported to Iran where they would face imprisonment and possible death, so they were placed in a detention facility in San Pedro, California. Their arrests were because of "post 9/11 hysteria," charged their attorney, Marc Van Der Hout.[27]

Mohsen Mirmehdi told the *Los Angeles Times* he found it ironic that "the U.S. protested loudly when the Iranian government attacked and arrested students for protesting in the streets in Tehran [but] my brothers protested peacefully and legally [and] the U.S. says that only proves we are terrorists."[28] In July 2004, following a sixteen-month investigation, the Department of State, the FBI, and the Army determined that the MEK had not committed any terrorist acts against the United States during the previous twenty-five years, and that the 3,800 members of that organization who were being held at Camp Ashraf in Iraq had not violated any American laws. However, the Department of State maintained that the MEK was still a terrorist organization, even if individuals did not commit any terrorist acts.[29]

Colleen Rowley, the FBI agent who had sent sharp letters to FBI Director Robert Mueller before 9/11 about intelligence failures, and who was later named *TIME* magazine "person of the year," put many of the detentions and arrests into perspective. In a letter to Mueller, written in February 2003, Rowley pointed out:

> The vast majority of the . . . persons "detained" in the wake of 9-11 did not turn out to be terrorists. . . . [A]fter 9-11, Headquarters encouraged more and more detentions for what seem to be essentially PR purposes. Field offices were required to report daily the number of detentions in order to supply grist for statements on our progress in fighting terrorism. . . . [F]rom what I have observed, particular vigilance may be required to head off undue pressure (including subtle encouragement) to detain or "round up" suspects, particularly those of Arabic origin.[30]

The Center for National Security Studies (CNSS) and several civil rights and media organizations sued the Department of Justice to release the names of more than twelve hundred persons the government detained, often for more than ninety days without counsel, following 9/11.[31] None were charged with any act of terrorism; many were confined solely because they might be potential witnesses. The CNSS charged that failure to release the names violated both the First Amendment and the federal Freedom of Information Act (FOIA). It also charged that the federal government had held innocent Muslims and Arabs, refused to release their names, and then deported them to avoid acknowledging its own errors. In a forty-seven page opinion, Judge Gladys Kessler declared:

Secret arrests are a concept odious to a democratic society and profoundly antithetical to the bedrock values that characterize a free and open society such as ours. . . . The public's interest in learning the identities of those arrested and detained is essential to verifying whether the government is operating within the bounds of the law.[32]

Kessler also ordered the federal government to release the names of defense attorneys. The Department of Justice, in a piece of fiction worthy of any TV show, claimed that by withholding the names of defense attorneys, even if they wanted their names released to the media and the public, it was really protecting them against the embarrassment of representing terrorists.

A 2–1 split by the U.S. Court of Appeals for the District of Columbia Circuit reversed Judge Kessler's ruling.[33] An exemption to the Freedom of Information Act allows federal agencies to withhold "records of information compiled for law enforcement purposes, but only to the extent that the production of such law enforcement records of information . . . could reasonably be expected to interfere with enforcement [proceedings]."[34] The majority opinion accepted the government's claims of national security issues and that release of names "could" interfere with its prosecution. In his dissent, Judge David S. Tatel argued:

While the government's reasons for withholding *some* of the information may well be legitimate, the court's uncritical deference to the government's vague, poorly explained arguments for withholding broad categories of information about the detainees, as well as its willingness . . . to fill in the factual and logical gaps in the government's case, eviscerates both FOIA itself and the principles of openness in government that [the] FOIA embodies.[35]

The Supreme Court, without comment, refused to hear an appeal.[36]

The Immigration and Naturalization Service (INS), under the Department of Justice at that time,[37] deported more than six thousand people. The INS refused to release names or the number it detained. "They were rounded up secretly, jailed secretly, deported secretly," charged Lucy Dalglish, executive director of the Reporters Committee for Freedom of the Press.[38]

An INS decision affirmed the administration's fear and its continued pattern of surrounding itself in secrecy. Ten days after 9/11, Chief Immigration Judge Michael J. Creppy ordered all immigration hearings to be closed. Upon direction of the attorney general, the hearings were to be conducted in secret with "no visitors, no family and no press."[39] Even the docket was to be secret. Four Michigan newspapers challenged that decision.

In Cincinnati, a three-judge panel of the U.S. Court of Appeals for the Sixth Circuit (Michigan, Ohio, Kentucky, and Tennessee) unanimously ruled that holding hundreds of deportation hearings in secret, with absolutely no evidence that any individual posed a security threat, was illegal. In one of the strongest attacks upon the Bush administration's policies, Senior Judge

Damon J. Keith wrote:

> Today, the Executive Branch seeks . . . the power to secretly deport a class if it unilaterally calls them "special interest" cases. The Executive Branch seeks to uproot people's lives, outside the public eye, and behind a closed door. Democracies die behind closed doors. The First Amendment, through a free press, protects the people's right to know that their government acts fairly, lawfully, and accurately in deportation proceedings. When government begins closing doors, it selectively controls information rightfully belonging to the people. Selective information is mis-information. The Framers of the First Amendment "did not trust any government to separate the true from the false for us." They protected the people against secret government.[40]

However, three months after that decision, in a separate case, the Court of Appeals for the Third Circuit (Pennsylvania, New Jersey, Delaware), agreed with the Creppy Directive,[41] reversing a decision by the U.S. District Court for New Jersey.[42] Thus, there were now conflicting interpretations in two of the appeals courts. In May 2003, the Supreme Court refused to hear an appeal from the plaintiffs in the Third Circuit. The Department of Justice did not appeal the unfavorable ruling in the Sixth Circuit.

"The [government's] secrecy gives rise to obvious concerns about what the INS is doing and whether people's rights are being respected and whether the problems [of civil rights and profiling] that arose in the aftermath of 9/11 are being repeated now," Lucas Guttentag of the ACLU told the *Los Angeles Times*.[43]

"Until some other court says otherwise," said Steven Shapiro of the ACLU, "the government can continue the policy of secret arrests that seems fundamentally inconsistent with basic American values, and that we know in this case led to a series of abuses."[44] The policy and practices of the Department of Justice, said Sen. Patrick Leahy during one of the hearings of the Committee on the Judiciary, "seem to be built on secret detentions and overblown press releases."[45]

There was no secrecy to the National Security Entry-Exit Registration System. Following 9/11, the INS required all men over the age of sixteen who are citizens of eighteen countries, most of them in the Arab world, to register and to report any change of address, employment, or job. Even if there were no changes, they had to report to the INS at least once a year. They were also required to provide the federal government with the names of all persons, including American citizens, who they knew. These names were then entered into a database, even if the American citizens had no criminal history.[46] Of the 93,741 individuals who voluntarily registered, the INS deported 13,799, most for minor infractions. The government charged only 143 for criminal activity, none for terrorism-related activities.[47] In December

2002, the federal government detained another one thousand men and boys from the Middle East. The largest sweep was in southern California, but the INS also detained persons in Cleveland, Dallas, and the Minneapolis area.

Although most had stayed in the country longer than their work or student visas permitted, a large number, including dozens of Iranian Jews, had already applied for permanent residence, but the INS had not yet acted upon their requests. Lawyers and organizations claimed the Department of Justice deliberately delayed or refused to process Green Card applications submitted by individuals from certain Middle Eastern countries.[48] Almost no one had a criminal history; many were married to U.S. citizens or had relatives who were citizens.[49] Each of the detainees was allowed to post bail after about a week, but hearings would be several months later. It's doubtful that terrorists would register; it's probable that innocent immigrants would.

Adding to the problems is a decision by John Ashcroft that essentially reduced any due process that immigrants may have believed they had. According to a report prepared jointly by the Center for Democracy & Technology, Center for American Progress, and the Center for National Security Studies:

> In February 2002, Attorney General John Ashcroft ordered the Board of Immigration Appeals, often the last hope for those seeking asylum from a homeland that would subject them to death, torture or other inhumane treatment, to clear its 56,000 case backlog in a little over a year. The Attorney General also announced that, after the backlog was cleared, he would reduce the size of the board from 23 to 11—deciding which members to retain, in part, based on the number of cases each board member had cleared. Immediately, the board members abandoned their traditional three-judge panels in favor of making decisions individually, often taking just minutes to decide. Between March and September 2002, the Board of Immigration Appeals issued over 16,000 decisions without explanation, an exponential growth in such rulings over the previous year, with virtually all upholding the immigration judge's decision.[50]

A year after he weakened immigrant rights, John Ashcroft notified local and state law enforcement agencies, most of which have no training in immigration law, that they had authority to enforce federal immigration laws. Most agencies rejected the attorney general's call. A letter from the president of the California Police Chiefs Association explained why there wouldn't be the "cooperation" the attorney general wanted:

> [I]t is the strong opinion of the California Police Chiefs Association leadership that in order for local and state law enforcement organizations to continue to be effective partners in their communities, it is imperative that they not be placed in the role of detaining and arresting individuals based solely on a change in their immigration status.[51]

Ashcroft later claimed that because of the PATRIOT Act, the United States was able to deport several hundred persons who had specific ties to

9/11. "Actually, the only tie they had to the investigation was that they were taken into custody during the probe," observed Toni Locy in *USA Today*.[52] Of more than five thousand foreign nationals the federal government detained, often illegally, after 9/11, only three were charged; two were acquitted.

"The Arab American Institute found that these interviews created fear and suspicion in the community, especially among recent immigrants, and damaged our efforts to build bridges between the community and law enforcement," said Dr. James Zogby, president of the Arab American Institute.[53] The forced registration of persons from Arab countries, said Zogby, "accomplished nothing of any worth. . . . It is a PR stunt that had a negative impact."[54] Anthony Romero, executive director of the ACLU, said the ACLU had "no problem [with] deporting those who have broken immigration laws, but [the government] should enforce them fairly and uniformly and in a nondiscriminatory way [and not] based exclusively on nationality and ethnicity."[55]

Representing thirteen individuals, the ACLU filed a fifty-page official complaint with the United Nations Working Group on Arbitrary Detention, the first it ever filed, charging the federal government with arrests and deportations that were "arbitrary . . . indiscriminate and haphazard and disproportionately affected Muslims from South Asian and Middle Eastern countries." The ACLU announced it was filing the complaint "to ensure that U.S. policies and practices reflect not just domestic constitutional standards, but accepted international human rights principles regarding liberty and its deprivations." According to Anthony Romero, the ACLU was "sending a strong message of solidarity to advocates in other countries who have decried the impact of U.S. policies on the human rights of their citizens."[56]

Adding to innumerable due process violations, the Department of Justice three months after 9/11 added to the National Crime Information Center (NCIC) the names of several hundred thousand male Muslim immigrants although almost none had a criminal record. In 2003, the Department of Justice exempted the NCIC from the stringent accuracy requirements of its own Privacy Act. The reason, according to the Department, was that "in the collection of information for law enforcement purposes it is impossible to determine in advance what information is accurate, relevant, timely and complete."[57]

Ibrahim Hooper, of the Council on American-Islamic Relations, correctly pointed out that the government's actions "creates the impression that there is a two-tiered justice system: one for Muslims and Arab Americans and another for the rest of society."[58] The interviews, registrations, and detention of Muslims and Arabs is "the most massive case of ethnic profiling since the internment of Japanese Americans during the Second World War," says David Cole.[59]

The racial/religious profiling by federal agencies may have led to an increase in hate crimes directed against persons from Arab countries or who are Muslims. In 2000, only 28 incidents against Muslims were reported to the FBI. The next year, the number rose to 481, most post-9/11, but dropped to 155 in 2002.[60] However, Dahlia Hashad of the ACLU believes the number reported to local law enforcement agencies which then report to the FBI "may be significantly less" than what occurred. "People are reporting these crimes to other agencies than the government," says Hashad, noting, "there is a growing distrust of the government and law enforcement" by the victims in the Arab communities.

More than one thousand incidents of harassment, discriminatory treatment, and violence against Muslims were reported to the Council on American-Islamic Relations in 2003. According to Mohamed Nimer, director of research for the Council on American-Islamic Relations (CAIR):

> Along with an increase in the number of bias-related incidents and experiences, we have also witnessed the negative results produced by government policies that target ordinary Americans based on religion, ethnicity or national origin. It is this guilt by association that has created a sense of siege in the American Muslim community.[61]

The federal government's profiling, harassment, and selective enforcement of immigration law to target persons from the Middle East has caused thousands to leave the United States, according to a special report by the *Sacramento Bee.* "A string of new policies designed to thwart terrorists instead has entangled thousands of immigrants of all nationalities, many of them here legally," wrote Sam Stanton and Emily Bazar in the *Bee.*[62]

Dr. Muhammad Fuad Jan, a second-year medical resident at the Hahnemann University hospital in Philadelphia, is one of those who faced American fears that he might be a terrorist. In 2004, he returned to India for a two-week leave, and then was denied permission to return to the United States; the U.S. embassy said his name was similar to one on a list of criminals and suspected terrorists, according to the *Philadelphia Inquirer.*[63] For four months, he was forced to stay in India; his wife and daughter remained in Philadelphia. Because of immigration rules, his wife, Dr. Hina Mehboob, was forbidden to practice medicine. No one ever explained why a day after *Inquirer* reporter Gaiutra Bahadur began asking tough questions the U.S. government allowed Jan to return to his medical residency.

Jan's problems weren't unique. Because of federal agencies' "cautions," or perhaps because it is so bogged down with checking virtually every immigrant with dark skin, more than one-third of all international physicians who were scheduled to begin training July 1, 2003, arrived late, according to the Educational Commission of Foreign Medical Graduates. The ECFMG also reported that three-fourths of all Pakistani physicians, mostly because of these "cautions," did not arrive at their hospitals on schedule. "Many of these physicians man rural and inner-city hospitals where we can't find American graduates," Omar Attiq, president of the Association of Pakistani Physicians in North America, told the *Inquirer*.[64]

International students, faced with intense delays in processing their applications to study in the United States, of the possibilities that even a quick trip to their home for vacations or to attend to personal matters may jeopardize their studies, and because of pervasive monitoring, are now bypassing opportunities to study in the United States, and are going to Canada, Australia, and dozens of other countries, according to the *Wall Street Journal*.[65] Fewer international students in the United States also means less cultural diversity within higher education, fewer possibilities that these students, often the brightest in their home countries, may remain in the United States to contribute to the arts, health care, business, or technology— and, especially, that they, the future leaders in their own countries might have not just more knowledge and skills because of their training in American universities, but also might have stronger identity with and more favorable beliefs about the United States. Terrorists, of course, have proven they have the means and resources to remain undetected in this country or to live in other countries, moving into the United States when they need to do so.

Before the National Press Club, Anthony Romero told journalists, "history suggests what we do to foreign nationals and immigrants today usually paves the way for what will be done to American citizens tomorrow."[66] However, "tomorrow" was "now."

On a Delta Airlines flight between Atlanta and Philadelphia at the end of August 2002, two federal air marshals detained an American citizen who may have been checking fellow passengers' baggage. One of the marshals pulled the passenger into the first class section, pushed him into a seat, sat on him, and began twisting the handcuffs the more the passenger groaned, according to Bob Rajcoomar, one of the 188 passengers.[67] The other air marshal, his gun drawn, "took control as if he was a terrorist himself," said Rajcoomar. The air marshal, said Rajacoomar, told the passengers, "Nobody move, nobody look down the aisle, nobody take pictures or you will go to jail, nobody do anything."[68] The marshals kept their guns at the passengers for the remaining thirty minutes of the trip, shouting at them to keep their hands and heads out of the aisle, not even to look into the aisle. "It was like a nightmare," said Rajcoomar, who says "the marshals were completely out of control. If they had pulled the trigger, we'd all be dead." His observation was confirmed by Judge James Linberger of Philadelphia, another passenger, who said, "I couldn't believe they would do such a thing."[69] About thirty passengers formally complained to the TSA.

When the plane landed in Philadelphia, one of the air marshals came to

Rajcoomar, yelled at him to put his head down and hands over his head, forcibly took him off the plane, and detained him in a filthy holding cell in the airport for more than three hours. His wife, who had been on the plane, but about thirty rows back since they couldn't get seats together, didn't know what was happening; when she couldn't find him in the terminal, she began frantically calling him, according to the *Inquirer*. He didn't hear her, nor could he answer his cell phone, nor would the police try to find her. Rajcoomar asked why he was being held, and was told by one of the marshals, "We didn't like the way you looked," and "We didn't like the way you looked at us." Rajcoomar, a physician and retired Army lieutenant colonel, is an American citizen, originally from India. Both he and the other passenger who had been detained by the air marshals were released without any charges being filed.

Almost a year after the incident, the Transportation Security Administration acknowledged that its marshals detained Rajcoomar primarily because he was dark-skinned; under threat of a federal civil rights suit, the TSA agreed to make a $50,000 settlement for false arrest, false imprisonment, and emotional distress.[70] The agency, as part of the settlement, also issued a written apology and initiated changes in the hiring and training of air marshals.

At a news conference, Rajcoomar said, "I hope that other people won't have to go through this horror." Unfortunately, his wish would not become reality.

CHAPTER 7

A Need to Raid Nudie Bars

Based upon Department of Justice statements, initially unchallenged by most of the establishment media, Americans felt secure that although noncitizens had no rights and, thus, the government could do what it wanted to them, that American citizens Yaser Esam Hamdi and José Padilla were "enemy com- batants" and constitutional rules didn't apply to them, and that racial and ethnic profiling may be necessary, even if directed against dark-skinned Americans, at least all other American citizens were safe from intrusion by the government.

"U.S. citizens cannot be investigated under this act," Mark Corallo, spokesman for the Department of Justice, said a year after the PATRIOT Act was signed.[1] A few months later, Corallo said that civil libertarians were "completely wrong" in their accusations that the Act could be used against American citizens.[2] "The public has . . . been misled. [The Act] is not directed at U.S. Persons," added Viet Dinh, assistant attorney general for legal policy between 2001 and 2003 and primary writer of the PATRIOT Act.[3] In April 2003, a month after Dinh's statement, the U.S. attorney for Alaska, parroting official Department of Justice statements, emphasized that the PATRIOT Act "can't be [used against] U.S. citizens."[4] They were wrong.

"Nowhere does this statute [FISA] indicate that United States citizens cannot be targeted," the ACLU points out. "[T]he statute," states the ACLU, makes it clear that an 'investigation of a United States person' *can* be conducted, so long as it is not based solely on activity protected by the First Amendment. . . . The statute defines 'United States persons' to include both citizens and permanent residents."[5]

Before the Senate Committee on the Judiciary in December 2001, John Ashcroft had stated, "Each action taken by the Department of Justice, as well as the war crimes commissions considered by the president and the Depart- ment of Defense, is carefully drawn to target a narrow class of individuals— terrorists. Our legal powers are targeted at terrorists. Our investigation is focused on terrorists. Our prevention strategy targets the terrorist threat."[6] John Ashcroft was deliberately wrong on that statement as well. Most of the mainstream media never challenged him. The federal government's implementations of the Act's provisions go well beyond intercepting and obstructing terrorism.

The use of the PATRIOT Act to target individuals and organizations with no terrorist connections dates almost to the beginning of the Act.

"Within six months of passing the PATRIOT Act," said Dan Dodson, official spokesman for the National Association of Criminal Defense Attorneys, "the Justice Department was conducting seminars on how to stretch the new wiretapping provisions to extend them beyond terror cases."[7]

In May 2002, the Foreign Intelligence Surveillance Court, which had granted every government request for two decades, had enough of John Ashcroft's attempts to circumvent the Constitution, and unanimously denied a Department of Justice request to use the authority under the PATRIOT Act to investigate criminal activity. The court ruled the federal government must not "direct or control the use of FISA procedures to enhance criminal prosecutions" not directly related to terrorist threats.[8]

The FISA Court of Appeals, which had never met, overturned the lower court's decision five months later, affirming the government's belief that the USA PATRIOT Act allows investigation into criminal activity if obtaining foreign intelligence is of "significant purpose" as opposed to the more rigorous "primary purpose" originally required by FISA.[9]

The American Bar Association (ABA) was so concerned about possible misuse of the PATRIOT Act that its Section on Individual Rights and Responsibilities issued a report in February 2003 that specifically addressed the federal government's intent and its possible constitutional violations:

> There is now a significant danger that if the government can show a "measurable" foreign intelligence purpose in a given situation, it will elect to use FISA procedures rather than the more exacting standards of Title III [of the Omnibus Crime Control and Safe Streets Act of 1968], even in a case where the overriding purpose is to bring a criminal prosecution. This situation puts at risk core guarantees of our Constitution, including the Fourth Amendment's protections from unreasonable searches, associational rights protected under the First Amendment, and the Fifth Amendment privilege against self-incrimination.[10]

Based upon the preliminary report, the ABA House of Delegates, in a strongly worded resolution, urged Congress to consider an amendment to the PATRIOT Act that would "ensure that FISA is used only for bona fide foreign intelligence-gathering purposes, as contemplated by the Act, and not to circumvent the Fourth Amendment requirements applicable to domestic law enforcement investigations." It further asked Congress "to conduct regular and timely oversight . . . to ensure that government investigations undertaken pursuant to [FISA] comply with the First, Fourth, and Fifth Amendments to the Constitution."[11]

In May 2003, the Department of Justice finally admitted it used the Act to pursue non-terrorist activities.[12] Mark Corallo, trying to justify the Act's use, claimed that "certain provisions could be used in regular criminal investigations."[13] John Ashcroft argued there was no distinction between using the tools provided by the PATRIOT Act to conduct criminal investigations or to pursue terrorist threats. Contradicting Ashcroft, Sen. Patrick Leahy (D-Vt.), former chair of the Senate Committee on the Judiciary, stated that upon approving the PATRIOT Act, "We sought to amend FISA to make it a better foreign intelligence tool. But it was not the intent . . . to fundamentally change FISA from a foreign intelligence tool into a criminal law enforcement tool."[14] Bob Barr, who had been a representative from Georgia at the time of 9/11, said he voted for the PATRIOT Act "with the understanding the Justice Department would use it as a limited, if extraordinary power, needed to meet a specific, extraordinary threat. Little did I, or many of my colleagues, know it would shortly be used in contexts other than terrorism, and in conjunction with a wide array of other, privacy-invasive programs and activities."[15]

Nevertheless, the Department of Justice circumvented the intent of the PATRIOT Act and cited Section 314 as its justification to launch "Operation G-Sting," an investigation and subsequent arrest of the owner of a Las Vegas strip club who may have given bribes to local officials and been involved in moneylaundering. The PATRIOT Act permits investigations into about two hundred crimes related to money-laundering. The use of the PATRIOT Act in the surveillance and subsequent arrest of the strip club owner "has absolutely nothing to do with terrorism, which is why it's so troubling," said Gary Peck, executive director of the ACLU of Nevada.[16]

The FBI said the PATRIOT Act "was used appropriately and was clearly within the legal parameters of the statute."[17] "If that's true," argued the *Las Vegas Review-Journal*, which has been out front in coverage of PATRIOT Act issues, "then major portions of this law need to be promptly repealed, unless the [Supreme Court] can get at them and overrule them first."[18]

"The Attorney General didn't tell Congress he needed the PATRIOT Act to raid nudie bars," said Laura W. Murphy of the ACLU in November 2003.[19] "The law was intended for activities related to terrorism and not to naked women," added Sen. Harry Reid (D-Nev.).[20] Rep. Shelley Berkley (D-Nev.), who had voted for the PATRIOT Act, said, "It was never my intention that the PATRIOT Act be used for garden-variety crimes and investigations."[21] It certainly wasn't Congress's intent it be used against American citizens. Whatever the intent, the Department of Justice was using the PATRIOT Act against American citizens not suspected of terrorism.

In July 2004, at the end of the Democratic National Convention—in what some saw as a suspicious coincidence to detract from the Democrats' message, and to bulk its reasons why the PATRIOT Act needed to be continued—the Department of Justice announced it had used the PATRIOT Act to charge fifteen persons, American and Canadian citizens, none of whom could be remotely considered to be terrorists, with smuggling marijuana. The fifteen were charged with bulk-cash smuggling for having moved at least $10,000 out of the country without reporting it.

Between the time when the federal government was using the PATRIOT Act to check into the habits of a strip club owner and when it arrested marijuana smugglers, it was also looking into the life of a woman with no criminal past. In 2003, Becky Foster, a resident of a Las Vegas suburb, found out the government had her in its website. Foster, a court clerk, was president of a homeowners association. When she tried to change banks, the new bank sent notices to all officers that the PATRIOT Act "requires banks to check all signers on all accounts to determine if there are any terrorist links."[22] The Community Association Banc informed the officers it was required to obtain names, social security numbers, driver's license information, and date of birth. Foster told the *Sacramento Bee*:

> When they sent us the letter, we just all kind of looked at each other. We didn't take a vote on it, we just said we're not going to do it. This is another example of how far the tentacles reach into private people's lives. I had no idea it was going to affect us on a level like this, at a homeowners association. It's silly, I think.[23]

These cases, said Gary Peck, "are exactly why the PATRIOT Act is a threat to liberties and must be corrected."[24] Peck pointed out, "It's just as the ACLU said from the start. The PATRIOT Act, which was originally passed off as dealing solely with terrorism, in fact expands government power in areas that have nothing to do with terrorism."[25]

A year after he said the PATRIOT Act was to be used only against terrorists and couldn't be used against American citizens, Mark Corolla now claimed, "I think any reasonable person would agree that we have an obligation to do everything we can to protect the lives and liberties of Americans from attack, whether it's from terrorists or garden-variety criminals."[26]

An investigation by Michael Isikoff in *Newsweek* revealed that the Department of Justice wasn't the only agency to use the PATRIOT Act to justify investigations not only of persons never suspected of any criminal act, like Becky Foster, but also investigations of non-terrorist crimes. The Treasury Department reported that in 2003, based upon requests from several federal agencies, under authority of the PATRIOT Act it had directed all financial institutions to search their records for information against 962 suspects; it then issued subpoenas against more than six thousand banks to release all financial data about the suspects. More than two-thirds of the "hits" were "in money-laundering cases with no apparent terror connection," according to Isikoff.[27] Dozens of other "hits" were the result of nothing less than fishing expeditions in the belief that someone "may" have been associated with someone who "may" have committed a crime, or "may" have known someone who "may" have committed a crime. Other federal departments and agencies that used the PATRIOT Act against non-terrorist crimes were the Internal Revenue Service, U.S. Postal Service, the Secret Service, and even the Department of Agriculture.[28]

In 2003, for the first time, requests for authorization to use wiretaps were more for terrorism and espionage cases than for criminal cases. Federal and state courts authorized 1,442 wiretaps, an increase of 6 percent from 2002, for criminal cases, according to the Administrative Office of the U.S. Courts; the courts denied no requests.[29] The FBI reported that the Foreign Intelligence Surveillance Court authorized more than 1,700. Each of the warrants led to monitoring hundreds or thousands of conversations, not just who were targeted but also those of innocent persons who didn't expect their calls to be recorded, their every word subject to being used in other investigations.

The increase of authorizations for terrorism wiretaps could have been because either the Department of Justice had placed a higher priority upon terrorism cases, or because federal law enforcement was using the less stringent FISA requirements to get more warrants against criminal cases. "The fact that it is now a secret court that is overseeing the majority of surveillance activity, in cases that do not require probable cause, does raise significant privacy and constitutional issues," said David Sobel, general counsel of the Electronic Privacy Information Center.[30]

The Department of Justice "continues to play the 'trust us, we're the government' game with the American people," said ACLU Legislative Counsel Charlie Mitchell, "even though its aggressive use of the PATRIOT Act in contexts unrelated to terrorism and a series of internal reports that show a culture of disdain for civil liberties suggest a growing credibility gap."[31]

CHAPTER 8

'It's Not the Government's Job'

Between a diner and a pet shop in a small strip mall in Bloomsburg, Pennsylvania, is Friends-in-Mind, a small independent bookstore.

On the first floor are more than ten thousand books on shelves that create aisles only about three feet wide. On top of the shelves are stacks of ten, fifteen, even twenty or more books. On the floor are hundreds more, stacked spine out three or four feet high. There are books in metal racks, drawers, and on counters. It's hard to walk through the aisles without bumping into a pile in the store that's about the size of a medium one-bedroom apartment. In the basement are at least two thousand more books.

"Sometimes I order four or five copies of a title, but often I order only one copy, but I want to have whatever my customers want," says owner Arline Johnson, who founded the store in 1976 after working almost two decades as a clinical psychologist and teacher. Unlike the chain stores with magazine and newspaper racks, wide aisles, track lighting, and a coffee shop, Friends-in-Mind has only books and some greeting cards. Also unlike the chain stores with large budgets for space and promotion to attract hundreds of customers a day, Johnson says she sees "on a real good day" maybe twenty-five or thirty people; often she sees fewer than a dozen.

In September 1984, she saw someone she didn't want to see. A week after the Naval Institute Press shipped three copies of Tom Clancy's Cold War thriller, *The Hunt for Red October*, the FBI showed up. The FBI, which apparently got the information from the publisher, "wanted to know where the books were and who purchased them," says Johnson. She says she told the two men that she couldn't remember to whom she sold two copies, but acknowledged she sent one copy to her cousin, who had served aboard a nuclear submarine "and had all kinds of clearances." Johnson says she wasn't pleased about the interrogation—"and my cousin definitely wasn't happy about anyone checking on what he was reading." The FBI visit to Johnson's bookstore was an extension of its "Library Awareness Program" during the 1970s and 1980s that had agents ask librarians to identify who was using specific magazines, articles, and books. The FBI never returned to Friends-in-Mind, but occasionally residents in this rural conservative community complain about what's in the store. She's been challenged for selling books about Karl Marx, gay rights, and even dinosaurs. Johnson says she tells the "book police" that "it's important that people learn and read about everything, whether they believe it or not." She also stocks copies of the Constitution and the Federalist Papers. Leftwing. Rightwing. Business. Labor. Anti-establishment. Everything's available in her store. "It's not the government's job to tell me or anyone what they can read or write," she says. But, over the years, the government has made it "its job."

In 1798, Congress, influenced by the Federalist administration of John Adams, passed the Alien and Sedition Acts, a series of four acts written at a time when the government believed extensive subversive activities by foreigners threatened the security and freedom of the decade-old country. However, Adams' vice president, Thomas Jefferson, argued that the laws were unconstitutional and meant primarily to silence opposition. Jefferson and James Madison campaigned for the presidency on the promise to defeat the laws. In 1801, upon the inauguration of Jefferson as president and Madison as vice president, the Alien and Sedition laws expired without being tested in court.

During the antebellum era, the federal government under Andrew Jackson made it a crime to ship abolitionist newspapers to the South. In 1873, the federal government established a rigorous antiobscenity statute that allowed the Post Office to declare almost anything, including contrary views, to be declared obscene. The penalty, still on the books, of mailing any such publication (or even personal letter) is a fine of $5,000 and imprisonment for a maximum of five years.

Near the end of World War I, under the administration of Democrat Woodrow Wilson, Congress passed the Espionage Act of 1917, which forbade any interference with the recruiting of troops, and the Sedition Act of 1918, which made it a felony to publish "any disloyal, profane, scurrilous or abusive language about the form of government of the United States or the Constitution, military or Naval forces, flag, or the uniform." The federal government used both acts to prosecute more than two thousand persons who exercised their free speech rights to criticize the government. Most were sentenced to terms up to twenty years imprisonment.

Between 1918 and 1921, Wilson's attorney general, A. Mitchell Palmer, encouraged by a vast majority of the American people, viciously attacked the free speech rights of resident aliens as well as American citizens. Using a rabid hatred for the reemerging Communist philosophy, Palmer's Department of Justice, without warrants, raided the homes and offices of those he believed opposed the administration, raised critical and significant social issues that may have questioned the philosophical base of the traditional Democrat-Republican party structure. Under Palmer's direction, more than 16,000 persons, were arrested, many of them beaten and forced to sign phony confessions. None were ever convicted of attempting to overthrow the federal government by force. Before the House of Representatives, Palmer declared the "foreign filth" his Department detained had "sly and crafty eyes, lopsided faces, sloping brows and misshapen features," and that their minds were "tainted by cupidity, cruelty, and crime."[1] That same year, in a memoir, Palmer declared, "tongues of revolutionary heat were licking the alters of the churches, leaping into the belfry of the school bell, crawling into the sacred corners of American homes, seeking to replace marriage vows with libertine laws, burning up the foundations of society."[2]

Four landmark Supreme Court cases within seven years affirmed the government's power to deny certain constitutional protections.[3] Strong dissents by Justices Louis Brandeis and Oliver Wendell Holmes Jr., however, would help reestablish later cases for constitutional freedoms in times of crisis.

During World War II, out of fear, the American government arrested, seized their property, and confined to detention camps more than 100,000 Japanese–Americans, most of them American citizens. The Supreme Court, in a decision that disregarded constitutional protections and is now regarded as a major blemish upon that Court, agreed with the government.[4] The "chilling effect" assured there would be fewer voices of dissent by any ethnic group—or by Americans opposing a wide-scale destruction of civil liberties.

Shortly after World War II, America entered its second "Red Scare" era, this one under the direction of FBI director J. Edgar Hoover, who had been a special assistant to A. Mitchell Palmer three decades earlier, and by Sen. Joseph McCarthy who was vicious and merciless in his attacks upon those he believed were Communists. The attacks focused upon the entertainment industry, then spread to other groups. And, as had occurred three decades earlier, almost none of the accused had ever advocated the undermining and overthrow of the United States. Once again, America suppressed dissent in the belief it was supporting freedom.

In 1950, a congressional committee had ordered Edward A. Rumely, secretary of the Committee for Constitutional Government, to turn over lists of the names and addresses of all customers who contributed any amount exceeding $1,000, including bulk purchase of books, pamphlets, and other literature. Congress also required the organization to identify specific dates and purposes of each transaction. The stated purpose was to determine direct influence by lobbyists upon Congress. Most organizations went along with congressional demands. When Rumely refused to identify the customers, he was indicted for contempt of Congress. The U.S. Court of Appeals for the District of Columbia Circuit reversed that indictment, but it was appealed. In March 1953, the Supreme Court determined the congressional committee had no authority to require individuals or organizations to produce such records if there was no direct contact with Congress. It didn't look at the broader issue of whether providing any records of direct contacts with Congress was constitutional.[5]

During the 1960s and 1970s, the FBI destroyed antiestablishment news-papers and spread disinformation about the nature and purpose of the alternative press. Among thousands who the FBI decided needed to have "files," usually because they were social activists challenging conventional authority, was the Rev. Dr. Martin Luther King Jr. Civil rights issues, peaceful protest, and dissent of the government's will, by the FBI's reasoning, apparently were un-American.

The most recent series of intrusions upon First Amendment rights began in 1998 when special prosecutor Kenneth Starr demanded two Washington-area bookstores to release records of what presidential playmate Monica Lewinsky had purchased. It was a sweeping allegation that had no reasonable basis of establishing any groundwork in Starr's attacks upon President Bill Clinton. Since then, there have been several cases in which police, operating with warrants issued in state courts, have demanded a bookstore's records.[6]

The PATRIOT Act, claims the Department of Justice, "specifically protects Americans' First Amendment rights" while protecting the nation's security.[7] Throughout the country, librarians, booksellers, writers, publishers, and numerous religious and civil liberties organizations disagree. Their primary concern is Section 215, which allows federal agents to seize "any tangible things (including books, records, papers, documents, and other items)." The Act's "gag orders" effectively block all parties from even acknowledging if an inquiry was made.

In one of its strongest resolutions, the 64,000-member American Library Association (ALA) declared it "opposes any use of governmental power to suppress the free and open exchange of knowledge and information or to intimidate individuals exercising free inquiry. . . . ALA considers that sections of the USA PATRIOT ACT are a present danger to the constitutional rights and privacy of library users."[8] The South Carolina Library Association, one of dozens throughout the country, condemned the PATRIOT Act as "a present danger to the constitutional rights and privacy rights of library users," and called for Congress to take an "active oversight" of the Act and to call for hearings "to determine the extent of the surveillance on library users and their communities."[9]

The Santa Cruz, California, City-County Library System was the first in the country to post signs warning its patrons that under the PATRIOT Act, "records of the books and other materials you borrow from this library may be obtained by federal agents." It also warned patrons that "federal law prohibits library workers from informing you if federal agents have obtained records about you." The signs followed a resolution by the Santa Cruz Library Joint Powers Authority Board that not only directed the main library and its nine branches to post the signs, but also directed its librarians to strengthen protection of reader confidentiality, and to require the library director to notify the media "to draw public attention to the issues raised by the USA PATRIOT Act."[10]

The signs "did what we wanted them to do—create a public stir," says

Anne Turner, library director, who says "probably 99 percent of the county's residents oppose the PATRIOT Act." Because she would be forbidden under the PATRIOT Act to even mention to anyone, including her staff and supervisor if the FBI demanded any patron's records, she now tells her library board every month she has not been contacted by the FBI. "The month I don't say it, the board will know I have been contacted," says Turner.[11]

In June 2003, three months after the signs first appeared, a half-dozen students from the University of California at Santa Cruz staged a protest at the main library, and got even more media attention by pulling dozens of books from the shelves—"anything that the government thought might be subversive," says Turner, "and began reading them in the library."

Hundreds of libraries now display signs warning patrons about possible loss of privacy; dozens of libraries now have lists of what to do if the FBI produces a search warrant.[12] And most librarians agree with Alice Bernstein of the Sun City, Arizona, Public Library. "This [Act] is a disgrace to the United States," she says.[13]

Hundreds of libraries have begun destroying certain records identifying which books patrons borrowed, and have also destroyed logs of who used which computer. Their actions are legal, as long as the shredding is done before any government-issued subpoena. All fifty states have laws or court cases which assure protection of the privacy of library records. However, federal law overrides state laws.

Neal Coonerty, owner of Bookshop Santa Cruz and president of the American Booksellers Association in 2000–2002, has been outspoken about the PATRIOT Act. "We don't believe that reading a murder mystery at the beach here means you're plotting a murder," Coonerty wrote in his customer newsletter.[14] Bookstores are especially susceptible to government intrusion upon customer records. Like all businesses, the Internal Revenue Service requires them to keep financial records for three years.

Linda Ramsdell, president of the New England Booksellers Association, and Trina Magi, president of the Vermont Library Association, initiated a letter-writing campaign in Fall 2002 to rally support against many provisions of the PATRIOT Act. Among those responding were Michael Katzenberg and Linda Prescott, owners of Bear Pond Books in Montpelier, Vermont, who deleted all titles from the records of their store's 3,000 Readers' Club accounts. "A citizen's right to free speech explicitly covers the right to read any book," says Katzenberg, "and implicit in that is the right to privacy in which a reader's choice of books is protected from government scrutiny." A story in *Seven Days,* a weekly newspaper in Burlington, Vermont, led to an Associated Press story, and reaction from throughout the country. In the first weeks, the owners of the 3,200-square-foot independent bookstore received several "very negative" e-mails. However, Katzenberg recalls "about 95 per-cent of more than several hundred letters have been very positive." Many of the letters, says Katzenberg, came from readers who switched their online purchasing from megastores and chains, which have numerous reasons to track customers' purchases, to smaller independent bookstores because of a fear of the invasion of privacy not by the stores but by government officials.

Amazon.com, the largest online bookstore, has a database of forty-one million customers, with every transaction recorded. So comprehensive and efficient is that database that the company can notify customers when new books are published in areas they have purchased similar books—or even if they "visited" the site's online description of a book but didn't buy it. Hundreds of larger independent bookstores and small chains also have online purchase capabilities. At numerous bookstores and the larger chains, customers can take advantage of discount cards. Even if the customer pays for a book with cash, the transaction is recorded in a database if the customer uses that card. There is no evidence the federal government has tried to access bookstore databases; however, the PATRIOT Act permits law enforcement to get that information, and all parties are bound by gag orders against disclosure that any attempt was even made. Even if the companies refuse to provide that information, and are willing to risk a long and costly court fight, the nature of computerized databases is such that, even with extensive firewalls established, they are susceptible to being hacked, their data scrutinized.

Arline Johnson at Friends-in-Mind, like many independent booksellers, says she doesn't keep computer records, accept credit cards, or even have a store newsletter, all of which can be seized, compromising the constitutional protections of her customers.

The shredding of customer records by bookstores and libraries to avoid governmental interference into Americans' privacy is one thing; official governmental intrusion into their sources of information is another, and one that has a shaky legal authority. "In the topsy-turvy world after September 11, guardians of information have been transformed into destroyers of data," Dan Malow reported in the *Fort Worth Weekly*.[15] Some of the destruction is because a fearful government has forced librarians to destroy information it thought terrorists might be able to use. "We used a razor blade to make it unreadable," Brenda Barnes of Texas Christian University told the *Weekly* about the government's demand to destroy CDs of the public water supply. Other libraries reported similar incidents involving other kinds of public records. Of course, the only ones denied the information were American citizens who have every right to know about their local government; terrorists would have little difficulty getting that same information elsewhere.

The *Los Angeles Times*, in a sharply worded editorial sixteen months after the passage of the PATRIOT Act, stated: "Allowing G-Men to, in essence, play their hunches about who might be a terrorist or supporter based on the books or movies he or she reads or watches was a perilous idea to begin with and could choke free debate on unpopular ideas."[16]

The effect of the USA PATRIOT Act upon businesses that loan, rent, or sell books, videos, magazines, and music CDs is not to find and incarcerate terrorists—there are better ways to investigate threats to the nation than to check on a terrorist's reading and listening habits—but to chill constitutional freedoms.

The ACLU, representing six organizations, filed suit in July 2003, charging that Section 215 violates several First, Fourth, and Fifth Amendment protections of the rights of free speech, privacy, and due process.[17] Four months after the ACLU filed its suit, three separate coalitions of bookseller, library, and writer organizations filed *amicus curiae* ("friend-of-the-court") briefs to support the ACLU suit.[18] "The PATRIOT Act authorizes the FBI to engage in fishing expeditions in bookstore and library records and then bars booksellers and librarians from protesting even after the fact. Such an unprecedented extension of prosecutorial power demands immediate court review," said Chris Finan, executive director of the American Booksellers Foundation for Free Expression (ABFFE), upon the filing of the brief to oppose the government's request to dismiss the suit.[19]

A coalition of ten organizations, led by the ABFFE, in filing an *amicus curiae* brief in U.S. District Court November 2003, charged:

> Section 215 of the PATRIOT Act provides the government with an unchecked and unprecedented power to obtain materials protected by the First Amendment whenever the government wants. [It] requires no showing of relevance or need to obtain the requested material and provides no means of challenging an order once issued. . . .
> [It] authorizes the production of First Amendment materials without any governmental showing that the information would actually further a terrorism investigation . . . [Its] automatic gag rule violates the First Amendment because it unjustifiably imposes a blanket ban of secrecy upon recipients or orders in the absence of any showing of need by the government for such secrecy. . . .
> [It] threatens the core constitutional rights of amici and their patrons . . . [T]he government's ability to obtain confidential private information about a bookstore or library patron's reading practices likely will have a dangerously broad chilling effect on the exercise of basic First Amendment liberties. Patrons will curtail their expressive activity if they fear that their reading habits might be scrutinized by the government and possibly . . . form the basis of a criminal investigation.[20]

Early in 2004, the American Booksellers Association, the American Library Association, and PEN American Center began a petition drive to secure signatures of persons who oppose Section 215. The petitions were placed in bookstores, libraries, and were available on a website. "This isn't about stripping law enforcement of the power to investigate terrorism [but] about restoring confidence that our reading choices aren't being monitored by the government," said Larry Siems, director of PEN's Freedom to Write Campaign.[21] The petitions were supported by forty organizations representing almost every major writer, bookseller, and library organization, as well as more than eighty companies, including the nation's largest book publishers and bookstore chains.

Many booksellers, especially those in rural communities, were leery of placing the petitions into their stores, fearing that a controversial issue might alienate some customers, thus reducing sales. But the fears were unfounded, according to the American Booksellers Association. "I haven't heard a single bookseller complain of fallout from this campaign," says Oren Teicher, American Booksellers Association chief operating officer.[22] "We just put [the petition] on the counter and people just sign it," said Nancy Beattie of Bookstore Plus (Lake Placid, New York), who says she "may be more conservative than most booksellers." Other booksellers also report they had little difficulty getting customer signatures.[23] More than 120,000 persons in about four hundred stores signed the petitions in the four months leading up to the annual BookExpo, the largest convention for those in the bookselling and book publishing industries. Following the June 2004 convention, which included special sessions about the effects of the PATRIOT Act and the petition drive, more bookstore owners placed petitions near their checkout counters.

"Terrorism investigators have no interest in the library habits of ordinary Americans," according to an official statement from the Department of Justice.[24] Elaborating upon the statement, Mark Corallo said not only doesn't the Department of Justice "have any interest in looking at the book preferences of Americans, [it doesn't] care, and it would be an incredible waste of time."[25] However, the Department of Justice also stated that "historically, terrorists and spies have used libraries to carry out activities that threaten our national security. If terrorists or spies use libraries, we should not allow them to become safe havens for their terrorist or clandestine activities."[26] Historically, spies and terrorists also used bookstores, schools, sports arenas, and bedrooms of unsuspecting homeowners. If the government's contention about the use of libraries is to be accepted as a reason for governmental intrusion, then by extension the government would have authority to monitor, with minimal or no judicial oversight, every place where people congregate online.

Nevertheless, Assistant Attorney General Viet Dinh told the House of Representatives Judiciary Committee in May 2003 that FBI agents contacted fewer than fifty libraries, and most of them had first contacted the FBI to report suspicious activity.[27] However, about half of the 906 library directors responding to a survey by the Library Research Center of the University of Illinois, October 2002–January 2003, reported federal or local law enforcement personnel visited their libraries and requested them to turn over data about their patrons; 219 of them voluntarily turned over data, 225 did not.[28] The Department of Justice tried spinning the facts. It claimed that what Dinh really stated was that FBI agents contacted the fifty libraries in the course of "criminal" investigations, and that the number of investigations under the guise of terrorism was classified.[29]

About eighteen months after that survey, the American Library Association announced plans to conduct its own more intensive survey, promoting the spokesman for the Department of Justice to say he'd "be happy for them to do it [because] the idea that agents are running around libraries is absurd."[30] Barbara Comstock, John Ashcroft's director of public affairs and a former official in the campaign to elect George W. Bush, argued, "We've had so much erroneous hysteria out there about our counter-terrorism authority and how it's used."[31] Ashcroft himself was caustic. In a speech in Memphis, Ashcroft claimed, "The charges of the hysterics are revealed for what they are: castles in the air, built on misrepresentation, supported by unfounded fear, held aloft by hysterics."[32] The Department of Justice claims statements opposing Section 215 from the American Library Association and other opponents are little more than "baseless hysteria."[33] Mark Corallo, speaking on behalf of the Department of Justice, was forced to modify that statement by saying that what the attorney general really meant was that the nation's librarians were "duped by those who are ideologically opposed to the PATRIOT Act."[34] Corallo said Ashcroft's comments were not meant to attack librarians but the ACLU and other civil rights organizations.

The Department of Justice innumerable times claimed the PATRIOT Act, especially the controversial Section 215, could not be used to obtain information from persons not suspected of being terrorists or spies. But, an internal memo, distributed October 29, 2003, and which the Department of Justice reluctantly released under a federal court order in June 2004, revealed that federal agents could invoke the provisions of the PATRIOT Act against persons who were innocent of any crime.[35]

The Department of Justice also claims that Section 215 is "essential" to law enforcement, that its provisions could not be narrowed or modified without compromising national security. But, when it appeared that opposition was increasing against Section 215 and its potential to chill First Amendment freedoms, John Ashcroft declassified the Department's own records to claim that in the two years following the terror of 9/11, it never used the power of Section 215.[36] Less than a month after Ashcroft made that announcement, the FBI prepared a request to the FISA court to invoke a Section 215 warrant.[37] Acting on a Freedom of Information suit filed in December 2003, a federal court in May 2004 ordered the Department of Justice and FBI to release copies of memos, as well as statistical data, about the use of Section 215. That suit had been filed by the American Booksellers Foundation for Free Expression, Freedom to Read Foundation, ACLU, and

Electronic Privacy Information Center.[38] The government had attempted to block the release and postpone delivery of information until June 2005, a request the court denied. Judge Ellen Segal Huvelle ordered the Department of Justice to produce all documents. Citing national security issues, the Department of Justice provided no statistics or proof that it did or did not invoke Section 215; because of the mandated gag order against all parties in a Section 215 warrant, it is impossible to know the extent of the Department's surveillance on private citizens.

CHAPTER 9

'The Most Dangerous of All Subversions'

To an audience at Tsinghua University, President George W. Bush said that "life in America shows that liberty paired with law is not to be feared. In a free society, diversity is not disorder, debate is not strife, and dissent is not revolution."[1] That assertion is accurate, but the president didn't tell the Chinese students about the formal suppression of dissent during the administrations of John Adams and Woodrow Wilson, nor about how his own administration dealt with debate and dissent. Nor did he tell the students about his own political–religious beliefs. In a statement made to *Free Inquiry Magazine* in Fall 1988, and which seemed to reveal how the future president felt about opinions not in line with his own, George Bush had stated, "I'm not sure that atheists should be considered citizens, nor should they be considered patriots."

The Department of Justice's official statement is that "Peaceful political discourse and dissent is one of America's most cherished freedoms, and is not subject to investigation as domestic terrorism."[2] However, the truth is not in the public relations statements put out by the Department. John Ashcroft and Dick Cheney have labeled dissent, even by leaders of both major political parties, to be unpatriotic. The vice president had called those who questioned the president "irresponsible."[3]

Three months after 9/11, John Ashcroft told the Senate Committee on the Judiciary what he thought of those who opposed the PATRIOT Act:

> [T]o those who scare peace-loving people with phantoms of lost liberty, my message is this: Your tactics only aid terrorists—for they erode our national unity and diminish our resolve. They give ammunition to America's enemies, and pause to America's friends.[4]

Agreeing with Ashcroft, and slurring those who oppose the PATRIOT Act as aiding the enemy, was Kris W. Kobach, his counsel from 2001 to 2003. In an Op-Ed rant in the *New York Post*, Kobach charged:

> Foreign terrorists have an unwitting ally in the American Left. Several liberal protest groups are waging a campaign to unilaterally disarm our government. If they succeed, it could hobble the United States in the War on terrorism and eventually exact a toll in American lives.
> The liberals' campaign is mainly a propaganda war—a massive and pervasive disinformation effort meant to convince the nation that the PATRIOT Act infringes

upon the civil liberties of ordinary Americans. . . .

The ultimate danger is not that the Left will defeat the PATRIOT Act in court. The danger is that it will succeed in pressuring Congress to let provisions of the Act expire in 2005 and succeed in tying the hands of police departments across the country. If this happens, terrorists will have cause to celebrate and American lives will be put in jeopardy.[5]

"Where I fault [the Department of] Justice and the attorney general is in the disingenuous way they defended the Patriot Act and then tried to imply that anyone who faults the act is either in league with terrorism or not sensitive to terrorism," David A. Keene, chairman of the American Conservative Union, told *Vanity Fair* contributing editor Judy Bachrach.[6]

Jack P. Calareso, president of Ohio Dominican University, called the nations' universities to be more open to public debate:

Ashcroft should be taken to task for implying that one who questions the Bush Administration's policies as they relate to civil liberties is unpatriotic and a threat to our nation. Does dissent equate to turncoat? Hardly. Open debate is a cornerstone of our democracy, and individuals must be able to express themselves openly, whether they support an administration or disagree with its policies. Those who dissent don't love their country any less than those who support the president.[7]

During World War I, reiterating statements he had made for several years, former president Theodore Roosevelt wrote, "To announce that there must be no criticism of the president, or that we are to stand by the president, right or wrong, is not only unpatriotic and servile, but is morally treasonable to the American public."[8]

Few outside the Bush administration would call Gen. Wesley Clark, supreme commander of NATO before his retirement, unpatriotic; but even his loyalty has been challenged by vigorous supporters of the president and of the PATRIOT Act. "I don't believe in the PATRIOT Act [because] I don't think you can win the war on terrorism by giving up the very freedoms that we're trying to defend," said Gen. Clark.[9]

The *Dayton* (Ohio) *Daily News*, observed: "Ashcroft's scowling, swaggering, dyspeptic antipathy for anyone who questions his methods and authority is transforming him and his office into mere caricature."[10]

As Texas governor, George W. Bush had ordered peaceful protestors away from the governor's mansion. As president, he directed there be "free-speech zones," areas often as much as a half-mile from any presidential cavalcade or speech, for anyone protesting his policies. It makes no difference if the protestor is a Quaker or anyone else opposed to violence, the rules are all the same—all protestors must not be anywhere near the president. For those who refuse, even peacefully, to enter into these remote and generally obscure "free-speech zones," local police arrest them for disorderly conduct, and then detain them until the president or vice president is out of the area, and the media leave. Anyone not carrying a protest sign or carrying a pro-administration sign is allowed to be in the visual range of the president and vice president. Obviously, anyone wishing to harm the president needs only to carry a sign praising the president, or not to carry one at all.

By creating a protest zone hundreds of yards away, the Bush administration's actions are designed not so much to protect the president as to give the political illusion of the president's "popularity." The media, especially the television media, focus upon the president and crowds that are carefully selected and deftly manipulated to show enthusiastic support of Bush and his policies. Because they believe the "story" is with the president, they usually ignore dissenters, especially if they're away from the president. It gives a false picture of the president and of the country, yet is politically clever.

On June 4, 2001, the Tampa, Florida, police arrested grandmothers Sonja Haught and Janis Lentz, and thirty-seven-year-old gay rights activist Mauricio Rosas on a variety of charges, including disorderly conduct and trespassing after warnings. Their offense? They were peacefully holding protest signs while attending a political rally for President Bush and Florida Gov. "Jeb" Bush at Legends Field, a publicly owned baseball stadium. One of the 8-1/2-inch by 11-inch paper signs challenged the election of President Bush, another stated that "June is Gay Pride Month." About 150 others carried protest signs, but they were placed into a "First Amendment Zone" a half-mile away. Among those cordoned off were members of the Sierra Club, the National Organization for Women, and several gay and lesbian alliances.[11] Others admitted to that rally also carried signs, but theirs supported the president, the governor, or certain conservative values; they were allowed to be close to the speakers. Apparently, some of the pro-Bush crowd thought it was proper to block the voice of any dissenter, and began to jostle them, kick dirt at them, or try to take away their signs.[12]

Soon, a member of the Republican event staff came to the protesters and shouted, "I've called the police!" He had claimed the event was "private," although the field is considered to be a public place; the three protestors, like everyone else on the field, had tickets. Shortly after that, Tampa police did arrive and told the three that unless they took down their signs they would be arrested. "Lose the sign and you can stay," a police officer told one of the protesters. They asked why others were allowed to carry signs, and were told, "Don't push the issue." The Republican staffer then placed persons with larger signs praising the president and governor in position to obscure the protest signs from the media.

According to a suit filed in federal court, three police officers handcuffed the protesters and "through excessive use of force," which caused each of them bruises and lacerations, took the three from the field, dragging Rosas, who has a physical disability, "across the field and down a flight of stairs." When the protesters asked if they could then go to the "First Amendment Zone," the police declared they were "through protesting for the day."[13]

A police spokesman told the *St. Petersburg Times*, "They [the Secret Service] said that you can't be within eyeshot of the president with those signs because it's a security issue. Most of this is bigger than us. We work within their parameters."[14] However, a Secret Service spokesman later stated, "hecklers and people with signs we don't consider a security risk, so we don't remove them." He told the *Tampa Tribune* the local police removed the protestors at the request of the Republican party.[15] "Since when did the Tampa Police Department become the bouncers for a political party?" asked *Tampa Tribune* columnist Daniel Ruth.[16]

The Hillsborough County State Attorney's Office declined to prosecute. The three took their case to federal court, alleging violations of the First and Fourteenth amendments. Among the charges in the suit were that the police actions constituted "a prior restraint upon free expression [creating] an impermissible 'chilling effect' on constitutionally protected speech and expression."[17] The suit, said Rosas, was "to show that the freedoms established by the Constitution are more important than those established by a mob."[18]

However, the federal court disagreed, and dismissed the complaint under the belief that the violations by the police did not show a pattern of unconstitutional action. Judge James D. Whittemore ruled that the plaintiffs did not show "that the City maintained a widespread practice or 'custom' of enforcing a 'First Amendment Zone. . . . [and that] Plaintiffs fail to present evidence demonstrating that a 'First Amendment Zone' was designated at the rally or that they were evicted from the rally for violating a 'First Amendment Zone' policy."[19] "Essentially, the court determined Haught, Lentz, and Rosas were arrested for trespassing, not for dissenting. The plaintiffs later abandoned an appeal to the U.S. Court of Appeals for the Eleventh Circuit (Alabama, Florida, and Georgia) for reasons that did not deal with the merits of the case, according to attorney Luke Lirot.

In August 2003, Lirot filed another challenge to the "free-speech zones." Adam Elend, Jeff Marks, and Joe Redner had attended a political rally, November 1, 2002, for Gov. "Jeb" Bush, attended by President Bush. Elend and Marks, social issues documentary film producers, and Redner, a nightclub owner, were at that rally specifically to protest the "free-speech zones." They raised protest signs—and handed out literature with information about free speech issues decided by federal courts. The three men were about 150 feet outside the entrances to the stadium where the president would speak; all three were peaceful.

University of South Florida (USF) police and Hillsborough County sheriff's deputies, who claimed to be under Secret Service orders, directed the three men to move more than a quarter-mile away. When the men refused, they were charged with obstructing without violence, disorderly conduct, and violation of "trespass after warning."[20] A Hillsborough County, Florida, judge later dismissed the charge, but with the reason that USF had not given the Republican party contractual rights over the property.[21] The Republicans had claimed the president's visit was a "private event" at a public university.

In a related incident, six persons, each with a ticket to the event, each wearing a campaign button for Gov. Bush's opponent in the forthcoming election, were refused admittance. The individuals said they hadn't planned any protest, were at a public university, and just wanted to hear the president.[22]

In a subsequent federal suit on behalf of Elend, Marks, and Redner, Luke Lirot charged, "The arrests of the plaintiffs ... in reliance upon a constitutionally impermissible plan to regulate speech, acted as a complete and total prior restraint of [Plaintiffs'] ability to communicate their political messages in the manner deemed appropriate, a right that is guaranteed by the First Amendment." The complaint further charged that the protest zones "have been widely utilized as a reflection of [Secret Service] custom and practice of implementing constitutionally impermissible restrictions on protected political speech at virtually every domestic presidential appearance." The complaint charged that the police actions violated the First, Fifth, and Fourteenth amendments.[23]

In Columbia, South Carolina, local police, again claiming they were acting under Secret Service orders, arrested a fifty-four-year-old man for violating a protective bubble around the president. Brett Bursey was one of thousands at the Columbia Metropolitan Airport to see the president during a political campaign rally six weeks after 9/11. Bursey's offense was that he was peacefully carrying a sign, "No More War for Oil," and refused to go to a "free-speech zone" about a half-mile away. When the local authorities declined to prosecute, the Department of Justice took up the charge, prosecuting under a federal law that gives the Secret Service authority to restrict access to anyone in areas in which a president visits. The fine could be as much as $5,000; imprisonment could be as long as six months. Eleven members of Congress, including members of the House Committee on the Judiciary and the Committee on Homeland Security, wrote John Ashcroft asking that the federal prosecution be dropped, calling the prosecution of the criminal charges "a threat to the freedom of expression we should all be defending." Ashcroft refused their request. In a narrow ruling more than a year after the arrest, a federal magistrate sidestepped any constitutional issues and fined Bursey $500 for not obeying a Secret Service directive.[24]

In Stockton, California, in August 2002, several hundred protestors who had a city permit to hold a demonstration were ordered by police, again claiming they were acting on Secret Service orders, to go to a "free-speech zone." This zone was established behind several buses and big rig tractor-trailers that were placed in position to keep the protestors away from the media and the president's supporters who were allowed much closer access. The president was in Stockton for a political fund-raiser. Among the protestors were those opposed to the probable war in Iraq, as well as dozens who opposed the president's environmental and antilabor policies, and about twenty severely disabled persons who protested California's budget impasse.[25]

The Kalamazoo, Michigan, police arrested Antoine Jennings, a Western Michigan University student, for refusing to go to a "free-speech zone" about two hundred yards from the president's supporters, and behind a building. The reason Jennings apparently presented such a security risk was that he was carrying a sign, "Welcome to Western, Governor Bush," a reference to the disputed 2000 election. In a subsequent trial, he was fined $100 for trespassing.[26]

In Evansville, Indiana, at a political rally attended by Dick Cheney, police arrested John Blair, who had won a Pulitzer Prize for news photography, for holding a 30-inch by 40-inch sign declaring, "Cheney—19th Century Energy Man." Blair had begun walking to the "free-speech zone" when he asked an accompanying officer, "Could I go down to that parking lot where the people are?" That's when he was arrested and charged with disorderly conduct and resisting arrest. The police eventually dropped charges, but only after hand-cuffing him, keeping him in custody for several hours, and well after the president left the area.[27]

A few miles south of Pittsburgh, a sixty-five-year-old retired steelworker was arrested when he refused to go to the "free-speech zone." According to Bill Neel:

> I had gone to [the] protests . . . on Labor Day of 2002. And they had taken my sign. I was standing on the street in front of the so-called free speech zone. And they told me that I had to go inside the cage [a six-foot high chain link fence] which . . . was surrounded by police officers, which to me seemed to be incarcerating me for being a protester. And I refused to go in there. And I was off the street and out of everyone's way. At the same time, people with pro-Bush signs were walking up and down the street and carrying signs and exhibiting them without being forced into this so-called free speech zone.
>
> I told the officer that there was no such thing as a free speech zone, the whole country was a free speech zone, and he eventually arrested me [handcuffed me] and took me into custody.[28]

A district justice found no cause for the arrest, and ruled the police "went a little too far" in their zealous attempt to curb protest.[29]

In 1999, George and Laura Bush bought a ranch near Crawford, Texas, a rural community of seven hundred residents in the central eastern part of the state. Within weeks of Bush's election as president a year later, the city council passed an ordinance that would essentially shut down any protest. That ordinance required any individual or group that wished to hold a "procession, parade or demonstration" to pay a $25 fee, tell all the details of their plans and obtain permission from the county sheriff at least fifteen days before the event. The ordinance also required any protest to be held only on the high school football field.

On May 3, 2003, about a hundred persons decided they wished to protest the war in Iraq on a day the president was scheduled to be at his ranch. According to news reports, some of the protestors were driving through town, but didn't plan to protest until they were outside the town limits. Patricia Major told the Associated Press one of the reasons she went to Crawford from Dallas was to show her teenage daughter, "dissent is an important part of democracy and that people can dissent in a peaceful manner and have their voices heard and that bad things won't happen to them in this country."[30] When Major and four others got out of their cars at a police barricade to talk with the officers, the police arrested and handcuffed them, and then held them overnight in jail.

In a subsequent trial in municipal court, the police chief said that even persons who were standing around, not protesting anything, but were wearing a "peace" button could be arrested.[31] Each of the five was fined $200–$500. Major told the Associated Press a reality of the justice system in some parts of the country:

> I think that we had a jury of people who live in a small town, so they're going to have to face their neighbors and their public officials and their law enforcement personnel every day. We're not the most popular people in this town, and it would take an enormous amount of courage to bring back an innocent verdict.[32]

About five months later, Judge Tom Ragland of the McLennan County Court dismissed all charges, ruling the ordinance under which the five were convicted was "overly broad on its face and in the manner in which it was implemented and enforced by the City of Crawford and therefore contravenes the First Amendment."[33]

A decision in the U.S. District Court for the Eastern District of Pennsylvania restricted the exclusionary practices of the "free-speech zones." The ACLU had filed suit to challenge the "free-speech zones" as a violation of the First Amendment.[34]

The complaint began when ACORN (the Association of Community Organizations for Reform Now, a group of 150,000 low- and moderate-income families) was denied the right to protest near President Bush on July 24, 2003. The president was scheduled to speak at the Treasury Financial

Facility in Philadelphia, which was issuing about twenty-five million Child Tax Credit checks. ACORN planned the protest to point out that the president and the Republican leadership had not done anything to relieve the tax burden of what they called "the working poor." The Philadelphia police and Secret Service both determined that no group or individual, no matter what their beliefs, would have access to the sidewalk across the street from the facility. Their reason was to protect the president's safety, although it also restricted any protestor from being able to see the president—or from him seeing their concerns.

On the morning of the president's visit, several persons were in the "no-protest" zone, actively supporting the president. No law enforcement officer or government official removed them. Senior Judge John P. Fullam granted an ACLU complaint requesting immediate preliminary and permanent injunctive relief. That order, the day of the president's visit, required police officials "to permit plaintiffs to demonstrate peacefully . . . no farther away from the Treasury Financial Facility Building than other demonstrators."

In an amended complaint filed in September, the ACLU added three other organizations and broadened the scope to challenge the Secret Service's "policy and/or practice of discriminating against peaceful political protesters," and to include all law enforcement agencies. The effect of that suit led to less restrictive policies against protestors. In May 2004, Judge Fullam dismissed the ACLU claim, citing the Secret Service's elaborate written regulations which specifically provide for nondiscrimination on the basis of the views sought to be expressed by protesters. He noted that both plaintiff and defendant agree "that demonstrators opposed to the administration have the legal right to be treated no worse than pro-government demonstrators." However, in denying the plaintiffs' suit, Judge Fullam also established a precedent that would dictate that not only the Secret Service but all law enforcement agencies during presidential visits had a responsibility to follow the Secret Service's own rules to assure there was not discriminatory treatment between protestors, supporters, or those who expressed no views.[35]

In addition to the exclusionary "free-speech zones," the Bush administration has a long history of smothering opposition in other ways. All persons wishing to attend any event in which the president or vice president appear are prescreened. They are asked to provide their names, addresses, birth dates, and social security numbers. This information often goes into a computerized database. In some places, the Republican party officials make notes on the "guest list"—among those notes are "judge's son" and "carpenter's wife." When persons ask why they must give personal information, they are often told the Secret Service requires it. "We don't require that information," says Tom Mazur, official spokesperson for the Secret Service. The information, says Mazur, is solely a "staff issue." The Republicans exclude those it finds may not support the president; the Democrats don't set any rules on political beliefs. The Secret Service will screen all persons at the time they enter an event, but it's only to see that no weapons are brought into the venue.

In addition to prescreening the audience, the Republican functionaries give the audience campaign buttons and signs, and often "warm up" the audience to create an illusion for the TV cameras that the president or vice president are immensely popular. Anything not on the unofficial "approved" list is contraband. In January 2003, four months before the invasion of Iraq, and long before the president declared his intention to run for reelection, staffers at a rally for George W. Bush in Scranton, Pennsylvania, ordered a woman to remove a small gold peace sign. "I was told it was an unauthorized symbol," said Jean Golomb, president of the Northeast Pennsylvania Association of Hospital Auxiliaries, who bought it at a Hallmark store.

In Saginaw, Michigan, the Republican campaign confiscated a rolled-up T-shirt from a family of three who had tickets to a rally for the president. The T-shirt had a pro-choice message, "It's your choice . . . not theirs." Barbara Miller, a fifty-year-old chemist and undecided voter, said she was told, "We don't accept any pro-choice non-Republican paraphernalia at this event."[36] An hour later, the campaign ordered the family, which had been seated and unobtrusive, ripped up their tickets, and ordered them to leave. At the time, Miller says she was threatened by staffers who said if she didn't comply, they would bring in the Secret Service. Another staffer, said Miller, shouted out, "She's trying to smuggle in anti-Bush T-Shirts!"[37]

In Albuquerque, persons who were unknown to the Republicans were required not only to provide detailed personal information—name, address, phone number, e-mail address, driver's license number—but also to sign loyalty oaths to the Bush administration. Persons not signing the loyalty oath were denied admission. Michael Ortiz y Pino, a Vietnam combat veteran, told the Associated Press he was asked by the Republican organizers to identify if he was with any groups that were associated with veterans, pro-life/pro-choice, gun rights, or teachers. The Republican response was that the Secret Service demanded the information; the Secret Service did not suggest a check upon a person's affiliations nor that they sign loyalty oaths.

State Rep. Dan Foley, representing the Republican party, claimed "a known Democrat operative group" had planned to protest. Americans Coming Together, a pro-Kerry organization, denied any effort to infiltrate and disrupt the event. There were no interruptions or protests at the speech; in addition to screening all possible protestors, the Republican organizers created a protest zone about a half-mile from the speech. Heather Layman, spokesperson for the Republican National Committee, said requiring "loyalty oaths" is not RNC policy, but "when we see there are Democrats who try to come to Republican events and disrupt them," the RNC might ask for the oaths. "We just want to assure a positive experience for those attending," said Layman.

A month earlier, pro-Bush protestors attended a Kerry–Edwards rally in Albuquerque; none were asked to reveal personal information to get a ticket, to protest, or to sign a loyalty oath. The Kerry campaign had actually urged their supporters to be tolerant to the protestors.[38]

The president's exclusionary politics continue to show the world that dissent was not acceptable. But, Bush–Cheney '04 and Victory '04, the two major umbrella campaign organizations for the Republicans, were able to claim that political rallies were "private." The media reported; they didn't investigate. And then the president spoke in Charleston, West Virginia. It was July 4, 2004, the 228th birthday of a revolution founded in dissent and the libertarian belief that all views had a right to be heard in the "marketplace of ideas."

The president's speech on the steps of the state capitol was billed as a presidential address, not a campaign rally. Because it wasn't a political rally, the Republicans didn't have to pay the $53,000 cost the budget-strapped state had to cover for local security,[39] nor any federal costs associated with transportation, security, staffing, and promotion. Even if the Republican organization believed the First Amendment didn't apply to "private" political rallies, there was absolutely no way an official appearance on public land could even be considered to fall outside constitutional protections. But that's exactly what happened that Independence Day.

Persons who wished to attend the speech had to apply for tickets. A two-page list of instructions informed them they couldn't bring food, beverages, umbrellas, signs, and banners. They also couldn't bring video-recording equipment, perhaps because the Republican party believed that, like banners, camcorders could be used as weapons, rather than as a tool permitted under the First Amendment to record a public event. Not included on the list of forbidden objects were T-shirts and buttons with political messages.

Apparently, either in ignorance of, or in defiance of, the federal court order in Philadelphia the previous September, the local political committee decided that a "free-speech zone" across the street from where the president was to speak was necessary. Trouble began when some people decided the Constitution trumped political realities.

Fourteen-year-old Katharine Nyden, who had a ticket to the speech, was one of those threatened with arrest. She and her eleven-year-old brother were wearing T-shirts that offended the Republican organizers and the police. On the front of the T-shirt was a silk-screen picture of Edward Munch's painting, "Scream," with the words "Bush Again?" On the back was a cowboy hat with a slash through it. According to Nyden, whose experiences were typical of thousands not allowed to attend rallies or who were thrown out of rallies although they had tickets:

I was soon stopped by a young man who told me that I would have to take off the pins and turn my shirt inside out. . . . I simply walked on without changing anything. As I looked around, I saw many people staring at us with utter disgust. I simply looked them straight in the eye and smiled. We were stopped by a woman who told us that we had to remove our pins and get rid of the shirts because she said that it wasn't a political campaign trip.

I looked at her for a second and then asked, "Well what about the people wearing Bush T-shirts? And how is your hat not political?" She claimed that she hadn't seen anyone wearing Bush shirts. I found that a bit hard to believe considering the fact that I had only been there for about five minutes and had seen many.

She then said, "Ma'am if you don't remove the pins and fix the shirt, I will have to ask you to leave. It's the law." I laughed and said, "Well what law would that be?" She simply gave me an annoyed look and said, "Young lady it is not my job to understand the law!" I glanced at her hat again and said, "You work for a congresswoman and it's not your job to understand the law?" She was really getting annoyed and she soon grabbed the friend of my parents by the arm and told us that we needed to leave. After much discussion, she finally gave up and left.

We picked up some American flags from a box to declare our patriotism. We were all growing very hot and we soon saw the young man who had originally told us to take off our pins and fix our shirts. He was carrying a large box filled with cups of water. My mother told me to get some. But as I approached him, he backed off. "Oh so now you want some water? I don't think so!" he said as he veered away from my brother and me. In the process of running away, he spilled all of the water all down the front of his pants. My whole family thought it was hilarious and we began to laugh.

As he came back around with his drenched pants I smiled at him and said "Nice one, buddy!" He looked completely outraged. He then spent a few minutes talking with some state troopers. Pretty soon, a few of the troopers were headed our way. They approached us and asked us to leave. My mother then asked why. "One of our event coordinators told us that you were causing problems and we'd like you to leave," the trooper said. "Why should we have to leave because he embarrassed himself by dumping water all over his pants?" I asked as the trooper asked us to leave again. "This is an invitation only event. We can make you leave whenever we want," he said. My mother then whipped out the tickets and said, "But we have invitations."

The trooper then told us that we needed to leave or we would get arrested. "What is this like a police state?" my mother asked. We refused to leave and so the trooper came back and told us that he was going to arrest us. "Can you show me the law that permits you to just arrest us for no reason?" I asked. "Ma'am, I don't have to show you anything. I'm not a man that lies. I don't have to tell you why I'm arresting you!" he said impatiently. I couldn't believe what I was hearing. I asked him again to see the law but he only raised his voice and said he didn't have to show me anything.

By this time, he was getting very angry and turning red. I found it a bit ironic that as the trooper was telling us to leave, Bush was talking about freedom of speech. My mother held her flag in the air and waved it as Bush said this. As she did, a row of elderly people gave her a shocked look. My father and his friend moved back because they thought that they might get arrested.

Apparently, someone called the White House and someone there told the state troopers that they didn't think it was a very good idea to arrest us. Soon there were at least ten to fifteen state troopers behind us. I could almost feel them breathing on our necks because they were so close. After a while, they backed off, but there were still a number of people staring at us.

Katharine Nyden was threatened, but she wasn't arrested. Nicole and Jeffery Rank were.

Nicole Rank, an environmental scientist working as a reservist with the Federal Emergency Management Agency (FEMA), had come to Charleston a little more than a month earlier following heavy flooding; her husband was an oceanographer who had accompanied her, but wasn't working with FEMA.

On their own time, they decided to attend the rally. They had tickets, and were quietly standing with the rest of the crowd of about 6,500. On their T-shirts were the words, "Love America, Hate Bush." When the Ranks refused to turn their T-shirts inside out or to move to the "free-speech zone" as directed, they were handcuffed, taken from the rally, arrested, fingerprinted, and had mug shots taken. A White House official told the *Charleston Gazette* that persons are discouraged from bringing any campaign items, no matter what their message, to official presidential visits, and that the White House did not have any role in asking for or ordering the arrests.[40]

Charleston Mayor Danny Jones told the *Gazette* that his city police were acting under direct orders of the Secret Service when they arrested the Ranks. "We work with the local law enforcement, but they do not work under the direction of the Secret Service," says Tom Mazur, spokesperson for the Secret Service. Then, in an incredible twist of logic, Jones claimed, "The officers, quite frankly, feared for the safety of the Ranks." The Democratic candidate for sheriff told the police, "You can't arrest them for this." A state police officer bluntly replied, "I don't have to tell you." FEMA terminated Nicole Rank's assignment and cut off her pay, although her supervisor had given her a mark of "excellent" for her work in Charleston.

Rather than returning home to Corpus Christi, Texas, the Ranks stayed in Charleston, living in a motel, to fight the charges. "It was difficult for us financially," Jeff Rank told the *Gazette*.[41] Two weeks later, the Ranks, represented by the ACLU, went to court. In minutes, it was over. Municipal Court Judge Carole Bloom quickly dismissed all charges, stating that because the event occurred on state property, the city's trespassing ordinance didn't apply.[42] "If we had to do it again," said Police Chief Jerry Pauley, "we would file in state court."[43] Mayor Jones refused to apologize to the Ranks. "They were there to get arrested. They succeeded," he told the Associated Press. "We're going to get on with our lives and go back to Texas and get jobs," Jeff Rank said, noting he and his wife "will continue to exercise our right to free expression when we see fit [but] we're not professional protesters."[44]

A day after the court dismissed the case, Sen. John Kerry came to Charleston for a political rally. "The only reason you would be asked to leave," said Amy Shuler Goodwin, Kerry's spokesman for West Virginia, "is if you were disrupting the event or causing harm to someone."[45] In contrast, Reed Dickens, a Bush campaign official, told the *Gazette* that persons "interested in supporting the president's message" are welcome at Republican campaign events, and erroneously claimed that even on public land, "campaign events are private events, and therefore, by their nature, it's up to the discretion of each campaign who comes in."[46]

One week after the Republican National Convention, the Secret Service, which claims it is unconcerned about hecklers, supervised the arrests of seven AIDS activists from Act Up at a Bush campaign rally in suburban Philadelphia. According to the *Washington Post*, one of only a handful of media that even reported on the arrests, the seven persons "were shoved and pulled from the room—some by their hair, one by her bra straps—and then arrested for disorderly conduct and detained for an hour."[47] The *Post* reported that police, apparently upon advice of the Secret Service, told reporters if they approached the protestors or tried to talk with them, they would not be allowed to continue covering Bush's speech. The president's personal aide apparently personally kept one reporter from approaching the protestors.

The administration's mistrust of the people and refusal to accept dissent as a part of the American political process, its swaggering and arrogant display of self-righteous power disguised within a blanket of "national security," extended to the media, which had often been compliant during the first years of the administrations. In Tucson, it changed. Bush–Cheney '04 required the news media to identify the race of some of the journalists reporting on the speech of the vice president. "It was such an outrageous request, I was personally insulted,"[48] said Teri Hayt, *Arizona Daily Star* managing editor. The campaign had requested to know the race of photojournalist Mamta Popat, but not of other staff reporters and photographers. In requesting the information, a Republican organizer told the *Daily Star* the request was made to identify the race of the photojournalist in order to distinguish her from someone else who might have the same name. "It was a very lame excuse," said Hayt who refused to provide the information.[49] The campaign officials later allowed Popat to cover the speech.

News media willingly provide the names, dates of birth, and social security numbers of journalists covering the president or vice president; racial identification is not one of the criteria the Secret Service requires. Although the *Daily Star* refused to accede to what appeared to be a request that could have been racial profiling, a clerk at the *Tucson Citizen* provided the campaign with the race of one of its staffers—a senior editor said had the request come to her, she "would have been hesitant" to identify the staff photographer by race. Assistant news directors at local television stations KVOA and KOLD did provide the racial information that the Bush–Cheney '04 campaign had sought on one person from each of the stations.[50]

A campaign spokesperson claimed the Republicans made the request for information at the request of the Secret Service; he didn't explain why the

Secret Service and not the reelection campaign organization hadn't requested the information directly. The Secret Service, which didn't respond to reporter C. J. Karamargin's initial request for information, three days after the event stated that racial identification is a "personal identifier" needed for background checks.[51] If it was a policy, it was randomly or selectively enforced; reporters needed only to provide their names, organizations, titles, and addresses.

In Bloomsburg, Pennsylvania, a week before the Republican National Convention, the Bush–Cheney '04 campaign organization escalated its distrust of the people and denied admission not only to persons who weren't in complete agreement with the Bush–Cheney message—at least three long-time community leaders were denied tickets—but to reporters as well. Dick Cheney was scheduled to speak at Bloomsburg University, a public state university. The university did not require the campaign to pay rent for the field house/basketball court venue. It did provide dozens of staff "volunteers," most of whom wore Bush–Cheney stickers, to assist on the day of the speech. About ninety minutes before the speech, Republican staffers ordered two reporters to leave the area. The reporters had an authorized press credential issued by Bush–Cheney '04 and tickets to the speech. Three Republican staffers who refused to identify themselves—"we don't have to tell you anything"— did say that a "spot check" of the names revealed these two reporters weren't "welcome" at the speech. They were told where the "protest zone" was—it was about a mile from the speech.[52] When the reporters, who had previously been at the "protest site" to cover that event, said they weren't at either the isolated protest or the speech to protest but to report, one of the staffers arrogantly said, "You're protesting now." When the reporters, who were on public land outside the field house again clearly stated they were members of the media, they were told they had two choices—leave the premises or be escorted off the grounds. The university's director of police told them if they didn't leave the area voluntarily, he would arrest and incarcerate them; in response to a question, he refused to indicate what the charges would be.[53] The university later claimed it was acting under authority of the Secret Service. The Secret Service denied the university's claim. Ironically, the university, which allowed the campaign committee to decide who was allowed to be at the rally, and which didn't challenge the campaign workers who demanded the two reporters not be allowed on the premises, had trumpeted in a news release two days before the vice president's visit:

> As a university, it is our duty to provide a forum for the exchange of ideas. . . . We are pleased to welcome Vice President Cheney to our university and to have this opportunity to participate in the American Democratic process.[54]

Exclusionary zones for all groups, protestor and supporter, are not new with the Bush administration. The Secret Service with all presidents, vice presidents, and major political candidates creates security zones to keep the public, protestor or supporter, away from posing threats. When candidates choose to "walk the rope line," shaking hands with the public, the Secret Service understandably becomes more concerned.

Both major political parties had used exclusionary zones before, most often at national conventions. The Department of Justice and the City of Boston planned to establish a "protest zone" far enough away from the July 2004 convention of the Democratic convention as to be unseen by the delegates as they walked into the convention hall. The site, after negotiations, was moved closer to the convention hall, but still established a confined atmosphere for protest. That site, beneath an abandoned elevated train line, was bound by chain-link fences covered by mesh, nets, and razor wire. "One cannot conceive of what other elements you would put in place to make a space more of an affront to the idea of free expression than the designated demonstration zone," stated Judge Douglas P. Woodlock. However, because of arguments from law enforcement and the Department of Justice, represented by three assistant United States attorneys, apparently unchallenged by the Democratic National Committee, he ruled that the protest zone was constitutional in order to protect the safety of the spectators and delegates.[55] In opposition to the Department of Justice and the City of Boston, he did permit a protest parade during a two-hour block on Sunday before the convention. All of the protests, even illegal ones outside the zone, were peaceful. Police made only a half-dozen arrests.

For the first time since its founding in 1856, the Republicans decided to hold their convention in New York City, then pushed back the quadrennial convention from its traditional July or early August dates to August 30–September 2. The Republican response to charges of continuing to politicize the September 11 tragedy was that there was no coincidence. Few believed the reasons for selection of the most Democratic and liberal major city in America or the September date was because "New York is the capital of the world, and what better place to highlight the president's vision of America than New York," as RNC press secretary Leonardo Alcivar tried to spin.[56]

But a day before the convention, Dick Cheney held a press conference on Ellis Island, with the skyline of lower Manhattan behind him, and praised President Bush for his role after 9/11. Throughout the four-day convention, the Republicans repeatedly invoked the memory of 9/11.

But, by placing the convention in New York, the Republicans had to deal with the largest protests in several decades. A federal judge had to intervene to keep the City of New York and the Republican National Committee from creating an even more restrictive set of conditions than what existed at the Democratic National Convention. U.S. District Court Judge Robert Sweet ruled that the city could not create interlocking metal "pens" for protestors without assuring that citizens had the right to enter and leave at their choosing, that police needed to have a reasonable suspicion and probable cause to do general searches of all bags of protestors, and that the city, which planned to close several streets near Madison Square Garden, site of the convention, had to inform the public about other ways to get to planned protest sites. In a seventy-eight page ruling, Judge Sweet pointed out:

> Difficult issues of standing and constitutional law complicate the achievement of the delicate balance between these powerful concepts. That balance is of particular importance to citizens and their government in times of heightened political tension and threatened challenges to public safety.[57]

The city granted permits for about twenty rallies in Manhattan parks, but several times rejected petitions by United for Peace and Justice (UPJ), a coalition of about a hundred organizations, to hold a rally for 250,000 in Central Park the day before the convention. Mayor Michael R. Bloomberg told UPJ, "You'll ruin the lawn." When challenged that the city had no problem with allowing more than 500,000 in Central Park in 1982 for a peaceful "Nuclear Freeze" protest, 600,000 to attend a Paul Simon concert in 1991, 250,000 to attend a Garth Brooks concert in 1997, and 75,000 to attend a Dave Matthews concert in 2003, as well as several other free concerts in the park, the mayor replied that the city's grass was newly sod, and the people would ruin it.

In response to concerns about restricting First Amendment rights, Deputy Police Commissioner Paul J. Browne said the city "devoted a lot of resources and worked very hard to allow unfettered free speech despite the fear of terrorism." About two weeks before the convention, Mayor Bloomberg, a Republican, warned possible protestors, "if we start to abuse our privileges, then we lose them."[58] The mayor may have believed that the First Amendment was a "privilege." What the city was offering, however, was "peaceful political activists" buttons. Those buttons would allow persons to get discounts at dozens of restaurants, museums, and stores. The city had no way to determine if someone who got a button would peacefully protest or was a terrorist. And most protestors said they refused to be compromised by what appeared to be a publicity stunt.

The city assigned more than ten thousand police in the area around the convention site; it was about the number of American troops chasing terrorists in Afghanistan. The protests began on the Friday before the convention when five thousand persons on bicycles rode through midtown Manhattan; police arrested 264 of them on a variety of minor charges, and held each of them for up to twelve hours while slowly processing them through the booking procedures. A day later, about twenty-five thousand pro-choice activists peacefully marched across the Brooklyn Bridge and to the mayor's office.

The day before the convention, about 200,000–250,000 people, representing a wide range of social issues, as well as almost universal views against the war in Iraq, organized by the UPJ, crowded together on a two-mile route and marched past Madison Square Garden, the convention site. Innumerable "street guerilla theatre" presentations dotted the city during the convention, including Paul Revere impersonators who rode down Lexington Avenue protesting, "The Republicans are coming!" Because of the intense media coverage, police, government officials, and the Republican leaders did the "politically correct" thing—they looked into the TV cameras and emphasized they believed in freedom of speech. Protests, mostly peaceful, continued the next four days, as individuals and small groups confronted delegates.

During the convention, several persons seemed to easily outwit the extensive security system and protested on the floor of the convention before being arrested. One person was arrested when she held an antiwar banner inside the convention center. Eleven persons from Act Up, all of whom had legitimately issued official floor passes, were arrested when they stood on chairs during a speech by Andrew Card, President Bush's chief of staff, revealed T-shirts that proclaimed, "Bush: Stop AIDS," and shouted "Bush Kills, Bush Lies." It was a protest against the lack of funding for AIDS research.[59] In contrast to the nonviolent protest by Act Up, several Young Republicans attacked the protestors, with one of them beating a young woman while she was dragged to the floor. The protestors were arrested by police and the Secret Service because "they were not who the convention committee wanted to be there," according to Ann Roman, Secret Service spokesperson.[60]

In contrast to the professional restraint of law enforcement before and during the first day of the convention, preemptive arrests and incarceration in filthy conditions for innumerable minor offenses plagued the city the last three days of the convention. On the second day of the convention, police cordoned off a city block, and with absolutely no warning to disperse arrested the first two hundred of about one thousand persons who had just begun a peaceful march from Ground Zero. The War Resisters League had earlier negotiated a limited approval for the march from the police who reneged on the deal without notice. Wildly swinging their batons or charging on motor scooters into crowds, police arrested more than twelve hundred persons that day.

In less than a week, police arrested more than eighteen hundred persons, most of them nonviolent, all of them believing they had the First Amendment rights of free speech, assembly, and to address the administration for a redress of grievances. Those who were arrested were handcuffed, often tightly causing bleeding and swelling, left for as many as three hours on the streets, and charged with disorderly conduct or parading without a permit, violations in the same legal category of unpaid parking fines.

They were taken to Pier 57 where police had established a holding area of chain-link cages with razor wire on top within a three-story garage that once housed city buses. Signs on the garage walls declared there were hazardous materials inside; the concrete floor was oily from years of diesel fuel and antifreeze spillage, washed over by massive amounts of Clorox. Many of those detained later complained of rashes from contact with whatever it was on the floor. There were few benches inside the cages, each of which held thirty to a hundred individuals, forcing most of those arrested to take turns sitting on the benches and to sit or sleep on the floor; blankets were not provided. Food was usually corn flakes, warm and sour milk, rotting apples, and near-stale cheese or bologna sandwiches; persons had to share them with each other and, sometimes, the roaches in their cells. There were no trash bins, and portable restroom facilities were filthy.

Mayor Bloomberg and Police Commissioner Raymond Kelly claimed most of the protestors were held only ninety minutes, and that all of those arrested were booked and released within eight hours. Most of the compliant media—at least the few not busy covering the infomercial proceedings at Madison Square Garden or taking advantage of the Republicans' large supply of free food and complimentary massages and manicures solely for the media—didn't challenge the city's statements. The truth was that most of the protestors were forced to remain as "missing persons" in the system for up to sixty hours. Persons not involved in the protests who were arrested on misdemeanors were incarcerated, booked, and released within a day. There was a general feeling that police intended to keep the protestors confined until after the convention closed, a tactic used by Philadelphia police four years earlier at the Republican National Convention there.

Only after New York State Supreme Court Judge John Cataldo ordered the city to immediately release almost six hundred persons or face a $1,000 fine for each person for every day that person was not arraigned and released within twenty-four hours of arrest, as required by law, did the city reluctantly—and slowly—release the protesters and bystanders who had been caught in an elaborate web created by the police and city administration. The judge initially ordered a fine of about $600,000 for contempt of court. However, the city lawyers in a subsequent hearing complained that the massive number of arrests caused the system to bog down, although the Manhattan district attorney, who agreed to prosecute almost all of those arrested, had previously stated the city could easily handle one thousand cases a day. The city's attorneys then argued the judge had not given the city enough time to comply with the judicial orders. The city, said Judge Cataldo, was "well aware of these orders [and they] were repeatedly not complied with." The city's delays in complying with the judicial orders, said Judge

Cataldo, was "willful and intentional."[61]

It may be shocking, even frightening, that the federal, state, and local governments, often in direct violation of the Constitution, have attempted to shut down the rights of dissent. However, large segments of the American public also oppose those whom they falsely believe aren't "patriotic" or who refuse to support the Bush administration. Whether it's a protest about a domestic program or the war in Iraq, Americans seem to be less tolerant than the Founding Fathers had wished. In letters to the editor, newspaper "call-in" columns, and on radio talk shows, they often argue that protestors deserve to be restrained, even arrested. A photography professor at Kent State sent an anonymous e-mail to one of two student reporters who were arrested and incarcerated for almost two days while covering the Republican convention, stating he "didn't care" about their arrest, what happened to them or anyone else, nor did anyone else care. Following a lengthy interview, published in the *Bloomsburg* (Pennsylvania) *Press Enterprise*, of a woman who was arrested and incarcerated at Pier 57, several anonymous readers complained—not at the treatment, but at the woman. Among their comments were that she was a "childish simpleton" and "anti-american"[*sic*]; some implied she was a radical or a Communist. One, reflecting the views of many, argued that "protesting [President Bush] is just like spitting on our troops." Some attacked the newspaper for giving her a "forum to spout an ideological diatribe."[62]

No reporters were arrested during the Democratic National Convention. Police and the Secret Service detained or arrested dozens during the Republican convention. At least ten reporters contacted the Reporters Committee for Freedom of the Press, which had established a twenty-four hour legal assistance hotline for the convention.[63] Several more who didn't contact the Reporters Committee were detained or arrested. Among them was a sixteen-year-old student at Malverne (New York) High School. Benjamin Traslavina, editor of the *Malverne Mule*, and a credentialed reporter to the convention, was arrested when he tried to photograph a protest on the floor of the convention. The Secret Service detained him, turned him over to the New York police, who then handcuffed him, confiscated his credentials, destroyed his film, and charged him with inciting to riot, assault, and disorderly conduct. He was finally released, with charges still against him, after about thirty hours, most of them spent at the Pier 57 cells.[64] Dozens more were subjected to intense scrutiny of their credentials, threatened with revocation of their credentials for filming protests, or even thrown out of the convention site.

One of those thrown out was Irene Dische, a novelist/journalist whose works appeared in the *New Yorker*, the *Nation*, and dozens of major European newspapers. Dische, who had floor passes, attended the convention the first three days. The fourth day, she went into the convention site in the evening, was handed a small flag to wave, but politely declined to do so.

"Immediately, I felt a hand on my shoulders, and was taken away," she says, by two persons—"thugs" she called them—and one person she believed was from the Secret Service. The two "thugs" were soon identified as New York City detectives. They took her documents and held her for an hour. Using her cell phone, she called her daughter. "You don't speak in a language we can't [*sic*] understand here," she was told. In a nearly all-White convention in the nation's most multicultural city, apparently no one knew she was speaking German to her daughter. They confiscated her cell phone. Soon, two Immigration agents came to interview her. She says she doesn't know who called them—police or the Secret Service—possibly because she spoke with an accent, possibly because she spoke German. Dische, an Austrian–American Jew, is an American citizen. But, since they couldn't throw her out for failing to wave a flag on cue or for speaking a foreign language, the people "protecting" the delegates had to find another reason. They "kept telling me I wasn't a real journalist," she says, "that I was deceptive." She asked the "good cop," possibly the Secret Service agent, to "Google me up." The two city detectives and the agent escorted her to the street, "trying to make nice on the way."

The federal government, the Bush administration, or various political committees don't even have to be directly involved in invoking prohibitions against public speech. Prior to the Masters Tournament in 2003, the National Council of Women's Organizations announced plans to picket the Augusta National Golf Course, the all-male club that was host of the national professional golf tournament. Possibly taking a cue from the president's political advisors, the city of Augusta, Georgia, soon after passed an ordinance restricting protest to at least a half-mile away. In a 2–1 decision, the U.S. Court of Appeals for the Eleventh Circuit ruled against the city.

In 1972, Lewis F. Powell, less than a year after being appointed to the Supreme Court by Richard Nixon, during a time of war and when the Nixon administration initiated countless civil rights violations in security versus freedom issues, articulated why those who created the foundation of the United States were concerned that all citizens have the rights of free speech:

> History abundantly documents the tendency of Government—however benevolent and benign its motives—to view with suspicion those who most fervently dispute its policies. [constitutional] protections become more necessary when the targets of official surveillance may be those suspected of unorthodoxy in their political beliefs. The danger to political dissent is acute where the government attempts to act under so vague a concept as the power to protect "domestic security". Given the difficulty of defining the domestic security interest, the danger of abuse in acting to protect that interest becomes apparent.[65]

There is an even greater shadow in the new millennium than during the 1960s and 1970s when the FBI, under J. Edgar Hoover, raided dozens of bookstores, alternative newspapers, and the offices of organizations that opposed the Vietnam War, the Nixon administration, or Hoover himself. Because of constitutional abuses under COINTELPRO, the government's counterintelligence program, restrictions were placed against FBI investigations of political activities.[66] John Ashcroft, citing "national security," loosened those restrictions. Under the PATRIOT Act, the federal government may again search newsrooms and reporters' records "without proof of probable cause—or even reasonable grounds to believe—that the person whose records it seeks is engaged in criminal activity," according to Lucy Dalglish of the Reporters Committee for Freedom of the Press.[67] The effect of Section 215 also reaches to supersede state shield law protections that give reporters the ethical authority to protect their sources. Once the veil is removed by law enforcement, "whistle-blowers," informants, and sources such as Watergate's "Deep Throat" would be rendered meaningless to the pursuit of truth. "Sadly, our government has an ugly history of using its investigative powers to squelch dissent," says ACLU associate legal director Ann Beesen.[68]

The newest paranoia of fear has trapped thousands of Americans who have done nothing more than say what they believe. In Santa Fe, New Mexico, a former assistant public defender was detained by local police, handcuffed, questioned by the Secret Service for five hours, and held overnight in jail either because of comments he may have made in a computer chat room, which he denied, or because of a comment he made in a college library, in which he said he thought the president was "out of control."[69] In San Francisco, an FBI agent questioned a retired phone company employee after someone in his gym reported an argument he and six others had about the president's policies. At no time did he threaten the safety of the president.[70]

The FBI and law enforcement agencies are increasing their use of undercover agents to infiltrate political organizations opposed to the Bush administration,[71] and are monitoring antiwar demonstrations and collecting information about dissidents, especially those opposed to the war in Iraq.[72] Police departments, working with the FBI, have skirted the constitutional issues and figured out better ways to collect data, even if the evidence was flimsy or just plain wrong.

Antiwar activists and other opponents of the Bush policies are routinely scrutinized at airport check-ins, according to a report by Paul Harris in London's *Observer*.[73] In Wisconsin, twenty antiwar activists about to board a plane for a Washington, D.C., rally were denied boarding privileges. In San Francisco, Jan Adams and Rebecca Gordon, peace activists and executives of *War Times*, an antiwar newspaper, were detained before they boarded a flight to visit Gordon's father in Boston. Adams and Gordon were told they were on the federal government's "no-fly" list as possible terrorists. Following several checks, they were each given a boarding pass with a large red "S."[74] They were never told what the "S" meant. A subsequent ACLU suit under the Freedom of Information Act revealed the previously secret "no-fly" list, but no information about how people are included on it and, more important, how they could be removed from that list. Gordon told CBS News she believed the list had a primary purpose "to frighten people and to make people realize there will be consequences to exercising free speech."[75] The Transportation Security Administration, which receives names from several federal agencies, denied that political activity had anything to do with who was placed on the list.

Sometime after 1999, the Denver, Colorado, police began gathering massive intelligence data about individuals and organizations. In March 2002, the ACLU of Colorado revealed this formerly secret practice by the police to monitor and record peaceful protests fully protected by the First Amendment. According to documents uncovered by the ACLU, the police had recorded license plate numbers, home addresses, and personal descriptions of individuals who attended rallies, and then created files marked "permanent." The files also included information from intercepted e-mails, apparently none of which hinted at or suggested the use of any violence.

The Denver police further labeled certain organizations as "criminal extremist." Among those organizations were the American Friends Service Committee, a nonviolent Quaker organization; Amnesty International; and End the Politics of Cruelty, a Denver organization that monitored police activity.[76] Persons who attended a peaceful protest rally against Columbus Day were also monitored, their personal data included in the "permanent" file. Apparently not having learned about rights of privacy and the First Amendment, the police one month after the first disclosures were still recording data from participants in peaceful protests. Ironically, it was a rally to protest the illegal surveillance that led police to record license plate numbers of protestors.

Two peace groups, Citizens for Peace and the Pikes Peak Justice and Peace Commission, obtained documents that revealed that the "Spy Files," as they became known, were apparently shared with other cities and the FBI Joint Terrorism Task Force (JTTF), created after 9/11, which also had been conducting surveillance against peaceful protestors throughout the country.[77] A city police detective and a county sheriff's detective were assigned full time to work with the Denver-area JTTF.

"The police have no legitimate reason to keep files on the peaceful expression of political views and opinions," said Mark Silverstein, ACLU's legal director, who charged that such actions serve only to create a chilling effect upon free speech. Mayor Wellington E. Webb—who, along with elected officials, labor leaders, and civil rights advocates had been subject of a similar FBI spy operation in the 1970s[78]—had not known about the Denver police's current practice. Soon after the ACLU brought the case to public attention, Webb ordered a preliminary investigation. He concluded there was an "overly broad interpretation" of established policies for intelligence gathering, and had reported on "organizations that do not pose a threat."[79] He revealed that the police held 3,200 files on residents and 208 files on organizations, almost all created within a three-year period. He called for an investigation of the city's policies, an independent third-person investigator to review each file, and a regular audit by the city attorney's office of any intelligence file to determine if there was a legitimate reason to create that file. Within a week, the Denver City Council, which had planned to pass a resolution opposing civil rights violations in the USA PATRIOT Act, amended that resolution to reaffirm the city's existing policy to protect citizen rights on intelligence gathering by the police.[80]

Six months after the first announcement, and three months after the mayor accepted almost all of the recommendations of an independent panel, the police decided to release the files, but only if citizens personally came to the police department; the department refused to identify which citizens were targets, prompting thousands to want to see if they were subjects.[81] Those who did see their files were outraged that some of the information had been blacked out by the police.[82]

The controversy continued several more months, with the police maintaining it had no written policy and could, therefore, collect intelligence data, a direct contradiction to statements made by the mayor and a former police chief.[83] Subsequent information revealed that the police had intelligence files, some from the 1990s, in their homes, and that other police departments provided information to Denver.[84]

Finally, in May 2003, about a year after the first disclosures, the ACLU and the City of Denver settled a class action suit. Among the provisions, the city/county would give persons a chance to learn what was in their files, and to purge/destroy the files.[85] A federal judge later ordered the city to pay almost $470,000 in legal fees to the plaintiffs.[86]

On October 6, 2002, Carol Gilbert, Jackie Hudson, and Ardeth Platte, three nuns with a long history of antiwar activism, cut a chain-link fence at an Air Force base near Greeley, Colorado, went to the lid of a Minuteman III missile silo, hit the silo with a ball-peen hammer, and then using their own blood painted crosses on the lid, and held a prayer vigil. They were arrested, handcuffed, left on the ground for three hours, and then jailed for seven months before trial.

The nuns claimed they were using symbolic free speech to protest America's potential use of weapons of mass destruction and the impending war against Iraq. The Department of Justice knew it couldn't charge the nuns with exercising their First Amendment rights, but may have wanted to send a chilling message to other antiwar protestors. Charged with sabotage and with obstruction to national defense under PATRIOT Act provisions, the nuns—ages fifty-five, sixty-six, and sixty-eight—faced up to thirty years imprisonment. Senior Air Force officers testified that the nuns' actions did not threaten national security, and that the monetary damage was minimal. The government said it wanted each of the protestors sentenced to at least six years imprisonment, the minimum under the PATRIOT Act.

They were tried and found guilty in April 2003, during the peak of the war against Iraq; it was a time, the defense claimed, when patriot fervor was at its highest. Judge Robert Blackburn, calling the nuns "dangerously irresponsible," fined them $3,080.04, the cost the government claimed was needed to fix the fence, and sentenced each to thirty to forty-one months imprisonment.[87] It was the only conviction of sabotage since President Bush signed the PATRIOT Act.

On September 27, 2002, Washington, D.C.'s Metropolitan Police Department arrested in Pershing Park about four hundred persons following a relatively peaceful protest in front of the World Bank and International Monetary Fund. Those arrested were handcuffed, wrist to opposite ankle, with a loose chain in between; the protestors could neither stand nor lie prone, and were detained up to eighteen hours. The district attorney refused to prosecute any of those arrested, which included spectators who had been in the park at the time and not part of the protest.

The United States Park Police, although on site, did not arrest anyone. An internal investigation by the Metropolitan Police Department revealed that the Park Police had told Metropolitan Police that the protestors' actions, based upon Park Police standards, did not rise to the level for mass arrests.[88] That same internal police department investigation indicated the arrests were improper.[89] In several suits, the protestors charged the government violated their First, Fourth, and Fourteenth Amendment rights.[90]

In Phoenix, Eleanor Eisenberg, executive director of the Arizona ACLU, was arrested when she took pictures of mounted police moving into a crowd of about four hundred peaceful protestors. She was charged with disorderly conduct; the charges were later dismissed.[91]

In April 2003, the New York Police Department arrested and detained for up to twelve hours, seventy individuals following a peaceful antiwar protest outside the offices of the Carlyle Group, an investment firm that has ties to both the Bush and bin Laden families. All charges were dismissed.

"It was frightening to learn how easy it is to be arrested without warning and hauled away for peacefully exercising your free speech rights," Sarah Kunstler, one of those arrested, told the Center for Constitutional Rights (CCR).[92] In February 2004, the CCR, which defines its mission as "advancing the rights guaranteed by the U.S. Constitution and the Universal

Declaration of Human Rights," filed suit in the U.S. District Court for the Southern District of New York on behalf of fifty-two of those arrested and against the New York Police Department. The CCR charged:

> By itself, defendants' arrest and prosecution of plaintiffs without any basis what-
> soever, much less the probable cause required by law, is unacceptable. When paired,
> however, with defendants' obvious distaste for plaintiffs' political message, their
> attempt to squelch plaintiffs' speech and discourage future dissent is reprehensible. .
> . .
>
> Instead of treating plaintiffs with the respect due all citizens exercising their core
> First Amendment rights, defendants chose to punish plaintiffs for having the
> temerity to question and criticize our government.[93]

Two incidents in February 2004, more than two years after the enactment of the PATRIOT Act, showed how far the government had gone in its belief that dissent and First Amendment rights are secondary to a political agenda. At the University of Texas at Austin, two Army intelligence agents, a week after a public conference on the role of Islam in the lives of women, tried to get a videotape of that conference and the names of those who attended.

In attendance were Army officers who attended the conference and claimed they were approached by "suspicious" persons from the Middle East. Among those interviewed was Jessica Biddle, a third-year law student and coeditor of the *Texas Journal of Women and the Law*, which had donated funds for the conference at the university's law school. "I thought it was outrageous. He was intimidating and was using the element of surprise to try to get information out of us," Biddle told the *Houston Chronicle*.[94] Sahar Aziz, a student who organized the conference, and had been told by other students that the agent wanted to interview her, said she was "flustered, and suffered a lot of anxiety that they would come to my house that night." She said she "kept wracking my brain, 'Did anything happen at the con-ference?'"[95] James Harrington, director of the Texas Civil Rights Project, said that the agent's door-to-door tactics to gain information were meant "to intimidate and scare people from using their First Amendment rights."[96]

In the second episode, a Polk County Sheriff's deputy, identifying him-self as a member of the FBI Joint Terrorism Task Force, delivered a sub-poena to Drake University (Des Moines, Iowa) on February 3, 2004, and demanded the university surrender a list of the names of persons who had attended an antiwar forum on November 15, 2003, sponsored by the student chapter of the National Lawyers Guild. The forum, which included workshops and nonviolence training sessions, had occurred the day before a peaceful protest against the war in Iraq at the Iowa National Guard headquarters.[97]

U.S. District Judge Ronald Longstaff issued the subpoena at the request of U.S. Attorney Stephen Patrick O'Meara. Included in the broad sweep of the subpoena was a demand to turn over all information the university had about the National Lawyers Guild, including names of its officers, minutes of its meetings, and the annual report for the previous year. He replaced his original subpoena three days later with one less broad, but which demanded all university records relating to the forum three months earlier. The U.S. attorney's office also issued subpoenas against four individuals—the president of the Catholic Peace Ministry, a staff member of the Catholic Workers House, a former coordinator of the Iowa Peace Network, and an antiwar activist who had visited Iraq, all of them forty-two to fifty-two years old—to appear before a grand jury. O'Meara later said the FBI's sweeping investigation was meant solely to produce the name of one individual.[98]

Under authority of the PATRIOT Act, the federal government may demand entire databases without identifying to a court the name of the individual it is targeting or even if those individuals in the database have any connection to terrorism. Because of the sealed gag order issued by Judge Longstaff, who was following PATRIOT Act legislation, the university was forbidden to tell anyone, including the students or the media, that subpoenas were even issued or that it intended to turn over the records.

The federal government's actions, said Heidi Boghosian, executive director of the National Lawyers Guild, was not only "a clear First Amendment violation," but also "a clear attempt to intimidate lawful expression."[99] She said she believed the government's action was a "political maneuver . . . to intimidate the American people to keep them from dissenting from President Bush and his administration."[100]

Equally strong opposition came from the American Association of University Professors. In a written statement a week after the first subpoenas were issued, the AAUP charged that "such sweeping demands are suspect in any context [and] intrudes deeply and dangerously into the affairs of a group of students and encroaches upon freedom of expression and association."[101] Apparently from "leaks" by the National Lawyers Guild and those individuals who were subpoenaed, the *Des Moines Register* began printing stories about the subpoenas and the gag order within three days of the issuance of the first subpoena.

"They want to kill speech. They want to put fear into the antiwar movement in Iowa," Sally Frank, professor of law and the advisor to the Drake chapter of the National Lawyers Guild, told the *Times-Delphic*, Drake's weekly student newspaper, which published the story a day before its normal publication date.[102] Journalism professor Herbert Strentz said the government's action was "an unwarranted exertion of government power."[103] Kathleen Richardson, the *Times-Delphic* advisor and one of the more outspoken critics of the government's actions, says most Drake students "didn't know what was going on" or some of the critical issues of free expression and association until the *Times-Delphic* printed the story.

"Our country has experienced dark episodes in which the government has curtailed citizens' civil liberties in the name of fighting enemies," Sen. Tom Harkin (D-Iowa) wrote to John Ashcroft, and called for the attorney general "to help ensure that we do not see another such episode in Iowa or anywhere in America."[104] Under the glare of the media's lights, extensive opposition by innumerable national organizations, and possibly because of Harkin's vigorous protest, O'Meara withdrew all subpoenas. Judge Longstaff then removed the gag order. "Whatever one's views of the political positions articulated at that meeting, the University cherishes and protects the right to express those views without fear of reprisal or recrimination," said Drake president David Maxwell.[105]

Three months later, during a week when John Ashcroft claimed al-Qaeda was plotting another attack upon the United States, heavily armed FBI, Immigration, and IRS agents searched the Philadelphia home and adjacent mosque of Muslim cleric Mohamed Ghorab. The iman, a conservative Muslim leader, had previously condemned the 9/11 attacks, terrorism, and those who wanted to enter Afghanistan to become part of the jihad movement.[106] However, he was vigorous in his opposition to the war in Iraq and many of President Bush's domestic policies. He had been interrogated by the FBI the previous year and cleared of any terrorist connections. The raid was conducted ostensibly as part of a federal tax investigation. However, there was "no connection" between the raid and Ashcroft's announcement of impending terrorism, according to the U.S. Attorney's office for the Eastern District of Pennsylvania. Rich Manieri said the timing was "unfortunate but coincidental."[107] Most in the Muslim community believed otherwise. "It's because of what he was saying, and the way it was reported to them," Ayman Ahmed of the mosque al-Hedaya told the *Philadelphia Inquirer*.[108]

In Spring 2004, the FBI began a systematic plan to interview "potential" protestors or those who may have had information about protests at the Democratic and Republican national conventions. Many of the protests were to be against the war in Iraq; several would focus on President Bush's domestic policies; others, at the Democratic National Convention, would demonstrate against pro-choice and other liberal agenda items.

In Missouri, the FBI kept three young activists under twenty-four hour surveillance for about a week, then interviewed them and their families, asking questions about their political activities. "We believe they were targeted because of their outspoken political activities," said Denise Liberman, legal director of the ACLU of Eastern Missouri. Among the political issues the three men—ages twenty, twenty-two, and twenty-four—spoke out about were the environment, globalization, and the war in Iraq. None of the three had any history of violence or threats against individuals;

the only arrests any of the three had, said Lieberman, were for mis-demeanors—jaywalking and hosting a loud party.

They had planned to attend the Democratic National Convention to protest the failure of the two-party system. However, the Grand Jury issued a subpoena for them to testify the day they had planned to be in Boston for the protest. "We tried to get the U.S. attorney to delay the hearing for two days so they could have adequate counsel," said Lieberman, "but it was denied." The testimony lasted less than five minutes for each of the three. None of the three were charged with anything; none were held in custody.

The surveillance, questioning, and subsequent Grand Jury investigation, said Lieberman, was nothing less than "a tactic of intimidation." The three men, "shaken and frightened by all this," said Liberman, not only didn't go to the Democratic National Convention, two chose not to go to the Republican convention. After the three men, who had asked the ACLU to protect their identities "out of fear of retaliation," were declared "targets" of an investigation, ten others who had planned to attend the Democratic con-vention also cancelled their plans. The FBI interrogations, said Lieberman, created nothing less than "a chilling effect upon free speech."[109]

In Colorado, the FBI visited several antiwar activists in three different groups. "It's an abuse of power, designed to intimidate these kids from exercising their constitutional right to protest government policies and asso-ciate with others who want to protest government policies," Mark Silverstein, legal director of the ACLU of Colorado, told the *Rocky Mountain News*.[110]

The FBI response was that it was "not monitoring groups, or interviewing individuals, unless we receive intelligence that such individuals or groups may be planning violent and disruptive criminal activity or have knowledge of such activity."[111]

One of those individuals the FBI may have believed was "planning violent and disruptive criminal activity" was Sarah Bardwell, an intern with the nonviolent antiwar American Friends Service Committee, a part of the Society of Friends (Quakers), which received the Nobel Peace Prize in 1947. Four FBI agents and two Denver Police officers went to Bardwell's home to interview her and her four housemates. Bardwell told the *Rocky Mountain News*, "[I]t was an intimidation tactic and it was designed to threaten people who are analyzing our current government and its policies and the system in the United States—an intimidation tactic that is used to crush any form of resistance or dissent or public expression of disapproval.[112]

The FBI claimed individuals "were free to talk to us or close the door in our faces."[113] Few Americans faced by a half dozen FBI agents and police officers know they have the legal rights not to say anything, especially when one of the questions the FBI agents asked was if the subjects knew it was a federal offense to withhold any information about possible criminal activity.

"The kinds of questions asked of these activists . . . are not the kind of questions being asked in good faith to elicit information on criminal activity," Silverstein said.[114]

The *Denver Post* charged the FBI and the Joint Terrorism Task Force with having "gone about their mission aggressively, with little regard for basic human rights and without evidence that the people they are trying to dissuade are actually intending any criminal activity."[115]

The *New York Times* strongly argued against the government's overt efforts to chill free expression:

> The knock on the door from government investigators asking about political activities is the stuff of totalitarian regimes. . . .
>
> The F.B.I.'s questioning of protesters is part of a larger campaign against political dissent that has increased sharply since the start of the war on terror. . . .
>
> The government must not be allowed to turn a war against foreign enemies into a campaign against critics at home.[116]

The *St. Louis Post-Dispatch* was especially vigorous in its condemnation of the government tactics:

> FBI harassment of nonviolent protest interferes with First Amendment rights.
>
> Two years ago, when Mr. Ashcroft expanded the FBI's power to snoop, he pledged not to repeat J. Edgar Hoover's abuses. Mr. Ashcroft hasn't kept that promise. Surveillance of antiwar protesters was ordered by an FBI intelligence bulletin last October. It asked local police to watch out for protest tactics including Internet use, fund-raising activities, videotaping of events and "peaceful" techniques (that) can create a climate of disorder.
>
> All of those activities are protected by the First Amendment. But the FBI's Office of Legal Counsel upheld the legality of the investigative techniques. The *Times* reported that the legal counsel concluded that "given the limited nature of such public monitoring, any possible 'chilling' effect caused by the bulletins would be quite minimal and substantially outweighed by the public interest in maintaining safety and order during large-scale demonstrations."
>
> By using valuable FBI resources to snoop on antiwar protesters, Mr. Ashcroft's Justice Department displays a troubling lack of balance and perspective that puts American freedom and security at risk.[117]

A month after stories began appearing in Denver, and one day after *The New York Times* published information about the FBI interrogations, Reps. John Conyers Jr. (D-Mich.), Jerrold Nadler (D-N.Y.), and Robert C. Scott (D-Va.), members of the House Committee on the Judiciary, sent a letter to the FBI inspector general to determine why there appeared to be "systematic political harassment and intimidation of legitimate antiwar protesters." They asked for an investigation to examine "the means, techniques and extent of FBI interrogation and investigations of political and antiwar protesters," and to determine if the investigations focused upon actual threats of violence "or merely involved legitimate political and antiwar activity."[118]

Sections 411 and 802 of the PATRIOT Act extended the U.S. Code to create the term "domestic terrorism."[119] The Act specifies that domestic terrorism involves:

(A) [A]cts dangerous to human life that are a violation of the laws of the United States or any State;
(B) appear to be intended—
    (i) to intimidate or coerce a civilian population;
    (ii) to influence the policy of a government by intimidation or coercion; or
    (iii) to affect the conduct of a government by mass destruction, assassination or kidnapping . . .

Sections 411 and 412 permit the secretary of state to designate American groups as "terrorist organizations." A broad and loose definition, especially of Section 802, permits the government to define any organization opposed to governmental policies or which is involved in civil disobedience as being a terrorist threat to the security of the United States, and to deny them the privilege to do advocacy or fund-raising within the United States. Section 802 "has a suppressive, Orwellian effect on speech and political advocacy, especially direct action advocacy, arguably the most effective grassroots technique to influence political change,"[120] according to Bob Barr. Among other organizations which could fall within Section 802 are the National Education Association (NEA) and Greenpeace.

In February 2004, Secretary of Education Rod Paige called the 2.7 million member NEA a "terrorist organization." Facing public outrage and a political embarrassment to the Bush administration, Paige retracted his comments, stating, "I should have chosen my words better," but still accused the NEA's lobbyists as using "obstructionist scare tactics."[121]

In a blistering letter to Paige, Jane Buck, president of the American Association of University Professors (AAUP), charged that his words were "at best, intemperate and, at worst, malicious. The flimsy . . . apology that you gave to the NEA membership, but from which you pointedly excluded the national leadership, is insufficient and fails to repair the damage you have inflicted on educators and their profession."[122]

Although having the potential of chilling political commentary, Paige's comments were only words. The Department of Justice actively sought to possibly declare Greenpeace to be a terroristic organization.

The Department of Justice had to go back to an 1872 law to prosecute Greenpeace. That law, informally known as "sailormongering,"[123] was originally designed to prohibit prostitutes and tavern and boarding-house owners from boarding ships as they approached continental waters, getting sailors drunk, stealing their money and possessions, or luring them to their taverns and boarding houses. It was used only twice, the last time in 1890.

The case against Greenpeace, an international organization opposed to destruction of the environment and also a strong opponent of the Bush administration's environmental policies, began in April 2002. Two Greenpeace members had boarded the *APL Jade*, a 965-foot container vessel, more than five miles from Miami. Their intent was to unfurl a banner, "President Bush: Stop Illegal Logging." They had no intention to interfere with the ship's mission. The *APL Jade* had been carrying about seventy tons of mahogany from Brazil, in violation of Brazil's own laws designed to help protect the rain forests. Most of the world's illegal mahogany is unloaded at American ports. According to Nancy Hwa at Greenpeace, "the activists carried out their protest with full attention to safety and protection of property." Greenpeace policies do not allow anything other than peaceful protests.

The *APL Jade* crew called the Coast Guard. Six activists were arrested, spent a weekend in jail, and then were sentenced only to time served. But, fifteen months after the federal government allowed the Jade to enter the Port of Miami and to unload its illegal cargo, the Department of Justice filed criminal charges against Greenpeace, and charged it under the "sailor-mongering" statute. That prosecution established Greenpeace as the first organization to be prosecuted for nonviolent protest by its members.[124] If the federal court found Greenpeace guilty, it could fine the organization up to $10,000, the IRS could revoke its nonprofit tax-exempt status—and the Department of Justice could declare it a "terrorist organization." The federal government, under Section 106, could seize all assets and property. If the organization received probation, its fund-raising and protest activities would have been restricted for five to eleven years, and the government would have had access to its membership rolls. The purpose of the government's actions, according to the Daytona Beach *News-Journal*, was "repression by intimidation."[125]

The *Miami Herald*, among dozens of metropolitan newspapers and national organizations, also opposed the government's actions:

[T]his indictment is a puzzlement. . . . There seems no point to it beyond the vindictiveness toward a group that riles the administration. Is this the best use of federal law-enforcement resources? Is it selective prosecution? . . . Using the mantra of domestic security to justify an overzealous prosecution doesn't parse. The Greenpeace violators were justly punished at the time. The case should be closed and all resources focused instead on genuine threats to homeland security.[126]

Prior to trial, Judge Adalberto Jordan observed that the indictment "is a rare—and maybe unprecedented—prosecution of an advocacy organization for conduct having to do with the exposition of the organization's message."[127] Judge Jordan also observed, "As late as 1998, a high-level Department of Justice official told Congress that the DOJ does not 'go after [advocacy] groups,' and instead prosecutes people who commit criminal conduct. . . . This case may, therefore, signal a change in DOJ policy" under a new political administration.[128]

Jordan also granted Greenpeace a jury trial; the Department of Justice had opposed trial by jury. But the jury never decided the case. After the Department of Justice presented its case, and before Greenpeace could defend itself, Judge Jordan dismissed the case. He didn't address constitutional issues, but ruled that the government's claim under the "sailor-mongering" statute the ship was about to enter the port was inconsistent with the facts since it was more than five miles offshore at the time it was boarded.

The Bush administration and its allies "seem bent on stifling our tradition of civil protest, a tradition that has made our country stronger throughout our history," said John Passcantando, Greenpeace USA executive director.[129]

Attempting to "spin" the decision, a spokesman for the Department of Justice said, "The U.S. attorney's office remains undeterred in prosecuting those persons who illegally attempt to board ships at the Port of Miami or otherwise threaten port security."[130]

In two different jurisdictions, federal courts have ruled that the procedures for ruling an organization as a "foreign terrorist organization" are unconstitutional. In one case decided in the nation's capital in 2001, the U. S. Court of Appeals for the District of Columbia Circuit ruled:

> [T]the aggrieved party has had no opportunity to either add to or comment on the contents of [the] administrative record; and the record can, and in our experience generally does, encompass "classified information used in making the designation," as to which the alleged terrorist organization never has any access. . . .[131]

Seizing upon that precedent, the U.S. District Court for the District of Central California in June 2002 dismissed a fifty-nine-count indictment against five Iranians and two Iranian–Americans who had allegedly raised money for an organization that the Department of State declared to be a "foreign terrorist organization." Judge Robert M. Takasugi ruled that because the 1996 law, incorporated within the PATRIOT Act, gives organizations "no notice and no opportunity" to challenge their designation, it is "unconstitutional on its face," and that such designation may not be used as a basis for bringing criminal charges against individuals who may support that organization, since defendants are "deprived of their liberty based on an unconstitutional designation they could never challenge." He declared he would not "abdicate my responsibilities as a district judge and turn a blind eye to the constitutional infirmities" of the law.[132]

Nevertheless, the federal government disregarded those two federal court decisions and continued to seize documents and assets of organizations it either identified as terrorist organizations or had ties to such organizations. In such cases, the organization has to burden to prove it is not a terrorist organization—and is hampered by not having access to its own records.

In December 2001, the FBI had seized records, property, and about $5 million from the Holy Land Foundation for Relief and Development (HLF), which provided food and money to Palestinian refugees as well as victims of regional wars in Bosnia and Kosovo, for victims of an earthquake in Turkey, and to food banks in Texas and New Jersey. The organization also claimed to have provided a fund for victims of the 9/11 attacks. The government, with evidence provided by law enforcement agencies, claimed the charity also provided funds for Hamas, a Palestinian terrorist organization. The Foundation denied the accusation and claimed the government provided no evidence of its accusations.[133] In July 2004, the HLF filed a formal complaint with the Department of Justice's inspector general, charging that the FBI "fabricated a case" against it, and that the FBI memorandum leading to the designation as a terrorist organization was in almost every instance materially misleading," and that the translations were "either intentional or in reckless disregard of the truth." The HLF charged that the FBI translators misled the courts on translations from Arabic to English, as well as translations to English from Hebrew, originally accurately transcribed from the Arabic by Israeli intelligence agents.[134] The day after the Foundation filed its complaint, a federal grand jury in Dallas returned a forty-two count indictment charging the HLF and seven of its officers with providing $12.4 million to organizations linked to Hamas between 1995 and December 2002 when the government froze its assets. Among the government's charges was that the HLF contributed money and assistance to the families of Hamas terrorists who had been killed or imprisoned, and for channeling funds to Palestinian hospitals, schools, and orphanages that may have been run by Hamas. One of the hospitals the HLF funded, and which was cited in the indictments, also received funding from the U.S. Agency for International Development.[135]

John Ashcroft claimed the indictments came about because of the use of the PATRIOT Act to obtain evidence from wiretaps. HLF attorney John Boyd said not only was the indictment without merit, but its timing "in the middle of the Democratic National Convention" in July 2004 was suspect. "Every allegation in the indictment," Boyd told the *Fort Worth Star-Telegram* "is something the Department of Justice was fully aware of two-and-a-half years ago."[136]

A week after the raid on the HLF in December 2001, the FBI raided the offices of the Global Relief Foundation (GRF) and the Benevolence International Foundation (BIF), two of the nation's largest Muslim-based charities. The Department of the Treasury froze all assets of the GRF. Both organizations denied funneling money to terrorist organizations, and the federal government did not release any specifics as to which organizations the two charities may have sent money.[137]

In January 2004, the U.S. District Court for the Central District of California struck down as unconstitutional a specific part of the PATRIOT Act. The Humanitarian Law Project, a group of four organizations and one individual, had filed suit charging that sections 302, 303, and 805 of the Act, which prohibited experts from giving advice to what the federal government designated as terrorist organizations, was vague and overbroad. David Cole, one of the plaintiff's attorneys, pointed out that his clients, who had been prohibited by the federal government from continuing a humanitarian mission, "sought only to support lawful and nonviolent activity, yet the PATRIOT Act provision draws no distinction whatsoever between expert advice in human rights, designated to deter violence, and expert advice on how to build a bomb."[138]

In agreeing with the plaintiff, and affirming that First and Fifth Amendment rights were violated, U.S. District Judge Audrey B. Collins said that the law was not "sufficiently clear . . . to allow persons of 'ordinary intelligence a reasonable opportunity to know . . . what is prohibited.'" And that the defendants' "contradictory arguments on the scope of the prohibition underscore the vagueness of the prohibition [and] could be construed to include unequivocally pure speech and advocacy protected by the First Amendment."[139] The Department of Justice appealed; the Court of Appeals for the Ninth Circuit was expected to rule by November 2004.

The government's loss at the district court level in California didn't deter it from filing against a doctoral student in computer science at the University of Idaho. The case would be a major confrontation between the First Amendment, passed under George Washington's administration in 1789, and the PATRIOT Act, passed under George W. Bush's administration in 2001.

In February 2003, about a hundred FBI and law enforcement personnel moved into Moscow, Idaho, interviewed the entire Muslim community, as well as dozens of others, and arrested Sami Omar al-Hussayen. According to the Department of Justice, al-Hussayen forwarded money to support terrorism and, as a volunteer, set up and ran websites used by a terrorist organization. That "terrorist organization" is the Islamic Assembly of North America, a charity that provides copies of the Koran to libraries and to prisoners. The federal government has repeatedly stated that the Islamic Assembly has terrorist ties, although it is not listed as a terrorist organization. Al-Hussayen, a married Saudi citizen with three children and a reputation not only for intellect but also for a respect for Western traditions, had spoken out against the 9/11 terrorism, and had organized a blood drive for its victims.

However, in opening arguments, Assistant U.S. Attorney Kim Lindquist told the court that al-Hussayen had a "dual persona—one face to the public, and a private face of extreme jihad."[140] The government added several charges of fraud and filing false statements; its claims were based upon the premise that al-Hussayen claimed he was entering the United States solely to study but that he was also in the country to help terrorists. At no time did the government adequately explain why al-Hussayen had to be in the United States to create and maintain "terrorist" websites, and couldn't have done his work in his native country. While imprisoned for more than a year awaiting trial, al-Hussayen continued his studies.

The prosecution argued that the websites recruited terrorists. However, the defense's only witness, Frank Anderson, a former CIA expert on terrorism recruitment methods, methodically picked apart the government's claim. The rest of the Defense case consisted of intense cross-examination and emphasis upon the government's constitutional violations.

David Nevin, al-Hussayen's attorney, argued the government had violated his client's First and Fifth amendment protections. He maintained that al-Hussayen had only volunteered to set up and maintain a website of an association that promoted the understanding of Islam, and that he never advocated or believed in violence. But, even if all of the government's charges were true, Nevin told the jury, "This is America, and in America you have a right to express an opinion."[141] He argued, "It's impossible to base criminal punishment on protected speech."[142]

In his instructions to the jury at the end of the seven-week trial, District Court Judge Edward Lodge said that although the First Amendment is not absolute, the Constitution protects free expression "even if those beliefs advocate the use of force or violation of law, unless the speech is directed to inciting or producing imminent lawless action."[143]

While the jury was deliberating, the city council of Moscow, Idaho, home of the University of Idaho and site of the trial, passed a resolution condemning profiling and PATRIOT Act civil liberties violations, and called upon Congress to "continue to actively work for the repeal of any portions that violate the guaranteed civil liberties enumerated in the Bill of Rights."[144]

In the seventh day of deliberation, the jury found al-Hussayen not guilty on three charges of terrorism, specifically those of creating an Internet network to finance and recruit terrorists, one count of making false statements, and two counts of visa fraud. Had he been convicted, al-Hussayen would have faced up to fifteen years imprisonment on each of the terrorism charges, twenty-five years on the visa fraud charge, and five years for each false statement. When the jury became deadlocked on eight lesser counts of visa fraud charges, Judge Lodge declared a mistrial for those counts.

"There was a lack of hard evidence," juror John Steger told Bob Fick of the Associated Press who had been the primary reporter on the arrest and subsequent trial. Fick said the jury believed, "There was no clear-cut evidence that said he was a terrorist so it was all on inference."[145] Steger said the jury didn't think any of the hundreds of pages of documents or the 29,000 intercepted e-mails the government presented showed any evidence of terrorism. "It seemed it was pretty innocent what he was doing," said Steger.[146]

Nevin told reporters the federal government needs "to focus on real terrorism cases. There are plenty of ways to do that without dismantling the Constitution."[147] Tim Gresback, one of the attorneys who assisted other Muslims caught in the initial sweep in Idaho, said after the verdict not only did it show "the government was out of control," but that Americans "cannot contain terrorism by allowing government zealots to act like terrorists."[148] Frank Anderson, the CIA expert, told the media he was "embarrassed and ashamed that our government has kept a decent and innocent man in a jail a very long time."[149] Within a couple of days of the verdict, the government said it would deport al-Hussayen. Because of that decision, he was not released from custody. His wife and children had earlier returned to Saudi Arabia to avoid deportation. Even with the acquittals, the conflicts between the PATRIOT Act and the First Amendment would continue.

About three weeks after the verdict, the Department of Justice dropped charges on the eight lesser offenses, in return for al-Hussayen not fighting a deportation order. Trying to get a "last word" over a case which probably should not have been brought to trial, U.S. Attorney Tom Moss told the media, "It is in the best interests of the people of the United States that Mr. Al-Hussayen leave the country as soon as possible."[150] Moss never explained why he thought it was "in the best interest of the people" as opposed to the "best interest" of the Department of Justice. Even with his acquittal, al-Hussayen remained in jail an additional six weeks. The delay, according to officials of the Department of Justice, was because of certain bureaucratic "delays," some because resources were spent on executing John Ashcroft's order in July for the FBI to interview Muslim, Arab, and students from Mideastern countries; Ashcroft said he believed there was a terrorist plot developing.[151]

At the time he was arrested, al-Hussayen had completed all coursework and was within three months of defending his Ph.D. dissertation, according to Dr. John Dickinson, his academic advisor and one of his strongest supporters. The sixteen months of confinement, subsequent trial, and time spent in jail after acquittal, although he continued to try to stay current, set al-Hussayen back at least six months. However, the University of Idaho, says Dickinson, will allow al-Hussayen to complete his dissertation and then defend it by video conferencing from any location of his choosing.

Al-Hussayen wasn't the only one directly affected by the Department of Justice's prosecution. Three weeks after the FBI arrested al-Hussayen, the federal government arrested, detained, and then restricted the activities of Abdullah al-Kidd, a University of Idaho graduate who the prosecution claimed was a material witness. Al-Kidd, who had converted to Islam, was arrested at Dulles International Airport in the nation's capital prior to boarding a flight to Saudi Arabia where he had a four-year fellowship. According to the Associated Press, federal prosecutors "maintained . . . that Al-Kidd's testimony was crucial to their case . . . and if he was permitted to go to Saudi Arabia it was unlikely he could be forced to return for the trial." Following detention, the government forbade him from traveling outside of Nevada, the residence of his wife, or Idaho, California, and Washington where he had relatives. Al-Kidd, who had been a counselor for homeless teenagers, was never called as a witness.[152]

Because of the vagueness of many of the PATRIOT Act's provisions, "there is an uncertainty that breeds caution among those who might seek to speak, or write, or broadcast freely," says Irwin Gratz, president of the Society of Professional Journalists. Because of this "chilling effect," says Gratz, "we can never know what information we are denied, or what wisdom we won't have because someone, somewhere, was too scared by the PATRIOT Act to speak their mind."

"The FBI is dangerously targeting Americans who are engaged in nothing more than lawful protest and dissent," Anthony Romero, ACLU executive director, told the *New York Times* in November 2003. "The line between terrorism and legitimate disobedience is blurred," he said, "and I have serious concern about whether we're going back to the days of [FBI Director J. Edgar] Hoover."[153]

Almost as troubling as the restrictions upon First Amendment rights and civil liberties is the attitude of most Americans. In 2002, almost half of Americans believed that the First Amendment "goes too far in the rights it guarantees," according to a survey by the First Amendment Center. That same survey revealed that about 42 percent of Americans also believed that the media had "too much freedom," and half believed that the media, which had given the president a wide latitude to enact and conduct the "war on terrorism" following 9/11, nevertheless, "has been too aggressive in asking government officials for information about the war on terrorism."

Among other findings were that about 40 percent of respondents believed neither the press nor professors should be allowed to criticize the U.S. military policy, and that "the government should have greater power to monitor the activities of Muslims living in the United States than it does other religious groups,"[154] a direct violation of First Amendment guarantees.

Two years later, as the terror of 9/11 diminished and the nation began to see the effects of civil rights violations, about two-thirds of Americans said they supported the basic First Amendment freedoms, but one-third still said that the First Amendment went too far in protecting Americans' rights. Unfortunately, says the First Amendment Center, "only one of the five freedoms was identified by more than half of those surveyed."[155] Part of the problem, said the Center, was that only about 28 percent of Americans believed the nation's educational system was doing a "good" or "excellent" job of teaching students about the First Amendment.

During the "Red Scare" and McCarthy era in the 1950s, Supreme Court Justice William O. Douglas told the nation: "Restriction of free thought and free speech is the most dangerous of all subversions. It is the one un-American act that could most easily defeat us."[156] The president's actions leave one to wonder how he could claim to be the leader of a country that values diversity, debate, and dissent. The lack of knowledge by Americans and a blind belief that the Constitution gives Americans too many rights may, as Justice Douglas said, be the most important factor that undermines this nation.

CHAPTER 10

'An Allergy to Any Kind of Legal Restraint'

In his speech at Tsinghua University, President George W. Bush stated, "Our liberty is . . . overseen by a strong and fair legal system. . . . The president, me, I can't tell the courts how to rule. And neither can any other member of the executive or legislative branch of government. Under our law, every one stands equal. No one is above the law and no one is beneath it."[1]

However, in May 2001, four months after taking office, President Bush withdrew the country from being a signatory to protocols of the International Criminal Court. Among that court's requirements is that it would not allow prisoners to be turned over to countries that are in violation of the Geneva Conventions. The U.S. response was that it could be trusted.

Mocking the Bush claims, Harold Hongju Koh, dean of the Yale Law School, said "Trust us, we're Americans and we don't need judicial oversight. [The prisoner abuse in Iraq] absolutely undermines that rationale."[2]

Cloaking itself behind a mantra of "national security," the Department of Justice refused to comply with both congressional requests and federal court orders. "The Justice Department has foiled numerous attempts by lawmakers and civil libertarians to learn how the administration has deployed new tools granted under the Act," according to Nancy Kranich, senior research fellow with the Free Expression Policy Project, a national organization which conducts research and provides analysis on First Amendment and censorship issues.[3]

"Rather than inviting congressional involvement [the Bush administration] discourages it—both out of an ideological attachment to executive power and out of an allergy to any kind of legal restraint on its conduct," the *Washington Post* editorialized slightly more than two years after the president signed the PATRIOT Act.[4]

The *Dayton Daily News* charged that Ashcroft uses "fear-mongering and invective to minimize accountability of federal law enforcement and undermine the authority of the judicial branch of government."[5]

The Justice Department "has largely ignored repeated congressional requests for . . . information, with appropriate safeguards. Constructive oversight by both the Congress and the courts helps ensure that the Justice Department uses its enormous power appropriately, both to protect our national security and to uphold individual rights," Sen. Patrick Leahy, at that time chair of the Senate Committee on the Judiciary, stated in August 2002.[6]

A little more than a year later, Leahy, now the committee's ranking member, again castigated Ashcroft for failing to appear at oversight hearings. "I understand that the attorney general is a busy man," Leahy said, "but he has found time to travel the country to make other appearances" to promote the PATRIOT Act.[7]

In June 2003, frustrated with the Department of Justice's failure to provide adequate information, the House Judiciary Committee sent fifty specific questions to the attorney general. The Department of Justice refused to answer several questions. One month later, following an oversight hearing within the Senate, Sen. Patrick Leahy asked Ashcroft to provide the answers to ninety-three questions; thirty-seven were not answered.[8] Sens. Patrick Leahy, a liberal Democrat; Arlen Specter (R-Pa.), a moderate Republican; and Charles Grassley (R-Iowa), a conservative Republican, stated that such actions by the attorney general were "making exercise of our oversight responsibilities difficult."[9]

A year later, things weren't any better. Speaking to the combined annual convention of the American Society of Newspaper Editors and the Newspaper Association of America, Sen. Leahy bluntly outlined the problem of oversight:

> [W]hen it comes to Congressional oversight, cooperation from this Administration has been sparse and grudging. I have been here with six administrations. I have never seen such a lack of cooperation. Oversight letters sent by both Republicans and Democrats to the Justice Department go unanswered for months, sometimes for years. The Attorney General has been reluctant to appear before the authorizing committees to answer questions, he has testified less frequently than any of his predecessors in modern times, and this during a period when there is so much to be accountable for. . . . Some have even gone so far as to equate their oversight questions to giving aid and comfort to our enemies. One of the main officials of the Administration said that in asking these questions we are giving aid and comfort to the enemy.[10]

Two months later, in opening remarks to a hearing by the Committee on the Judiciary, the first one Ashcroft had attended in fifteen months, Sen. Leahy reaffirmed comments he made before the journalists, and emphasized: "Too often we on this Committee, on both sides of the aisle, get the sense that under your direction and example, the Justice Department and its agencies consider oversight by Congress to be nothing more than a nuisance."[11]

During the first eight months of the Bush–Cheney administration, Dick Cheney met with several individuals to establish a national energy policy. Critics argued that Cheney, a former oil company CEO, had brought together only corporate representatives to establish a policy friendly to the energy industry; no environmentalists were invited to those meetings. The Sierra

Club, an association primarily of liberals, and Judicial Watch, a public oversight organization composed primarily of conservatives, consolidated separate suits to challenge the administration to release the names of the members of the National Energy Policy Development Group to determine if the vice president's actions violated federal law. Under the Federal Advisory Committee Act, the membership and records of all advisory panels are public documents, except when "composed wholly of full-time officers or employees of the federal government."[12] If private individuals participated, the entire committee was required to be balanced, rather than representing one political policy. The Sierra Club and Judicial Watch wanted to know not only if private citizens were invited into meetings and discussed issues but the extent of their participation, even if they had no vote. The vice president, arguing "executive privilege," refused to disclose the names of anyone involved in the discussions.

The U.S. District Court for the District of Columbia granted the right of "discovery" and denied the federal government's motion to dismiss the case, stating that the administration's tactics were to "cloak what is tantamount to an aggrandizement of executive power with the legitimacy of precedent where none exists."[13] The administration appealed. A three-judge panel of the U.S. Court of Appeals for the District of Columbia pointed out it did not have jurisdiction because the case was still in the federal district court.[14] The administration appealed to the full appeals court. By a 5–3 vote, the full court decided not to hear the administration's arguments.[15] However, the Supreme Court of the United States agreed to hear the government's appeal, even though the U.S. District Court had not determined which documents Cheney had to turn over to the plaintiffs. Before the Supreme Court, Solicitor General Theodore B. Olson argued:

> The Constitution explicitly commits to the president's discretion the authority to obtain the opinions of subordinates and to formulate recommendations for legislation. Congress may neither intrude on the president's ability to perform these functions nor authorize private litigants to use the courts to do so.[16]

Olson further claimed that a "constitutional immunity" protects the president and his staff from having to disclose information, except under a criminal investigation. Agreeing was Justice Antonin Scalia:

> I think executive privilege means whenever the president feels that he is threatened, he can simply refuse to comply with a court order. He has the power . . . to say, "No, this intrudes too much upon my powers. I will not do it."[17]

Prior to the oral arguments before the Supreme Court, the Sierra Club had asked Scalia to recuse himself since not only was he was a personal friend of Cheney, but had recently gone on a duck-hunting adventure with

Cheney on land in Louisiana owned by an executive of an oil rig service corporation. Scalia defiantly refused to recuse himself. Some of the toughest questions during oral arguments were directed by Scalia to the plaintiffs.[18]

"At some point, the Bush administration is going to have to realize that the American people want to know what kind of influence energy corporations had over America's energy policies," said David Bookbinder, senior attorney for the Sierra Club.[19] He pointed to current legislative proposals as justification for the request:

> President Bush is today touting a plan to weaken clean air standards for power plants. And he's promoting an energy bill largely inspired by these secret meetings. The public deserves to know who actually wrote these plans.[20]

The Supreme Court, stating the federal district court acted "prematurely" in granting the right of discovery of the names, vacated the lower court's order and remanded it for further consideration. The Court's ruling essentially gave the administration, which had almost three years to protect the list of persons who primarily determined the administration's policies favorable to the energy and oil industries, another two years of legal maneuvering, thus preventing the release of any embarrassing data until after the November 2004 elections. Dissenting, and voting to have the district court order executed for release of information, were Justices Ruth Bader Ginsburg and David H. Souter. Justices Scalia and Clarence Thomas, who usually vote as a block, were harsher upon the petitioners than the other justices, claiming that the district court "clearly exceeded its authority" to order documents under the open government law, and argued the lower court order be reversed.

The administration's refusal to divulge what may be critical public documents extended into the investigation into the 9/11 terrorism. President Bush initially refused to create an independent panel to review events that preceded 9/11. Under public and political pressure, he finally created the National Commission on Terrorist Attacks Upon the United States. Vice President Dick Cheney told the Senate leadership in February 2002 that the Bush administration officials would defy all attempts to question them about what they knew before and after the September 11, 2001, attacks. For more than two years, the Bush administration maintained it would not provide information nor would it allow any member of the executive branch to testify, citing "executive privilege."

Only after Richard Clarke, antiterrorism expert under three presidents, testified in April 2004 about failures in the Bush administration to deal with evidence that might have prevented the 9/11 terrorism, and with the mounting evidence becoming a political embarrassment, did President Bush and Vice President Cheney agree to testify. However, under an agreement to get their version of what happened before, during, and after 9/11, the Commission was forced to agree that the president and vice president would testify together, their testimony would not be under oath, and would not be recorded. Both former President Bill Clinton and former Vice President Al Gore previously testified separately, with electronic records made of their testimonies.[21]

CHAPTER 11

The 'Ambiguous' Administration

The United States, as both a colonial and sovereign nation, has had a long history of the people wanting less secrecy in government—and the government wanting more secrecy. Before the delegates to Virginia's convention to debate and possibly ratify the Constitution of the United States, Patrick Henry argued that exact point. "To cover with the veil of secrecy the common routine of business is an abomination in the eyes of every intelligent man and every friend to this country," he forcefully declared.[1] In making his argument for openness in government, Henry also recognized there were some limitations when it came to national security issues, but that in almost all instances openness of governmental actions is what best serves the people and the Republic.

Almost two centuries later, a controversial Supreme Court decision essentially determined if the government believes something should be kept from public view because of issues of national security, then it should be kept from public view. By a 6–3 decision, the Supreme Court decided in *Reynolds v. U.S.* (1953), that the widows of crewmen killed in a B-29 crash in Georgia in 1948 had no right to look at crash data investigations that could help prove their wrongful death suit and negligence by the Air Force. The Court had not even looked at the data to determine if the government was correct in its assertion of national security. Both a federal district court and an appeals court had agreed with the plaintiffs that the information should be provided. The Supreme Court reversed lower court rulings and sealed the data.[2] Decades later, the unsealed documents revealed no national security issues, only that the Air Force had failed to install heat shield protectors on the plane's engines, and hadn't properly trained the civilians on board in emergency procedures.[3]

In 2003, the Supreme Court agreed with the pleas of the Bush administration's solicitor general not to reopen the case, even with the new evidence. Timothy Lynch, of the Cato Institute, a conservative think tank, argued:

> This petition [to reopen the case] is a vivid reminder that government officials can use the veil of "national security" to shield themselves from criminal prosecution for misconduct, civil legal liability or embarrassing revelations. The only way to minimize those kinds of abuses is to treat legal claims of national security with a healthy dose of skepticism.[4]

Armed with the precedent of the *Reynolds* decision, the Bush administration has used the pretext of national security, whether real or imagined, to cloak its actions, and has applied it in innumerable creative ways. It has cited the case as a justification to withhold all information about its actions in deportation hearings and treatment of prisoners. It has also used "national security" arguments to interfere in a lawsuit filed against United Airlines by the widow of a victim of 9/11;[5] the government ordered the airline not to turn over any information, claiming to do so would violate national security. That widow, Ellen Mariani, later filed a RICO (Racketeer Influenced and Corrupt Organizations Act) suit against the president and several members of his administration.[6] Her attorney, Philip Berg, former Pennsylvania deputy attorney general, told the media that the president "is invoking a long standard operating procedure of invoking national security and executive privilege claims to suppress the basis of this lawsuit that [he and his administration] failed to act and prevent the '911' attacks [and that] for financial and political reasons [they] have obstructed justice" and refused to cooperate with the Congress and independent commission investigating the causes of 9/11.[7]

The Bush administration has also brought out the PATRIOT Act to justify its obsession with secrecy, and has used it to tighten what is available under the Freedom of Information Act. Under the PATRIOT Act, the government has wide latitude to classify documents, including those which were previously public documents. The abuse of classification leads to an abuse of the Freedom of Information Act. President Bush granted classification authority not only to Defense, State, and Justice departments, but to several other departments (including Agriculture and Health and Human Services) and agencies (including the Environmental Protection Agency) as well. The Nixon administration classified documents not to preserve national security but to prevent being embarrassed by their disclosure. The Bush administration seems to have the same policy.

Under the pre-9/11 FOIA, only certain "records" were exempt; under the PATRIOT Act, "information," a much broader category, is exempt. Under the FOIA, "critical infrastructure" of a business was narrowly defined, and generally exempt from public disclosure. Under the Critical Infrastructure Information Act, incorporated within the Homeland Security Act which created the Department of Homeland Security, not only is there a much broader definition of "critical infrastructure," but corporations also can use authority granted under that Act to restrict critical and vital documents from public scrutiny. These documents, if first presented to the Department of Homeland Security, which would declare them to be "trade secrets" and keep them from public disclosure, could include not just financial documents, but also environmental and public health issues.

"This provision created new opportunity for big polluters or other offenders to hide their mistakes from public view just by stamping 'critical infrastructure information' at the top of a page," said Sen. Patrick Leahy.[8] The exemptions could also affect public knowledge about critical health issues. The PATRIOT Act establishes criminal penalties for disclosure of information, both classified and unclassified. In April 2004, the Department of Agriculture approved an Animal Identification System, expected to cost about $500 million over a six-year period, to identify critical health problems including "Mad Cow Disease." However, the National Cattlemen's Beef Association agreed to cooperate only if the information on animals was exempt from all Freedom of Information laws.[9]

In addition to the PATRIOT Act provisions, a number of federal agencies and regulatory commissions, operating under advice of the White House or from presidential executive orders and directives, further restricted release of critical infrastructure information. Beginning August 2004, the Nuclear Regulatory Commission no longer issues public records that reveal security gaps at the nation's 103 nuclear reactors. "We need to blacken some of our processes so that our adversaries won't have that information," said Roy Zimmerman of the NRC.[10] However, innumerable consumer watchdog groups quickly attacked the NRC decision as nothing more than a cover-up of embarrassing problems that could affect the public safety and health. Among problems which had been public, but now would be classified, would be guards and control room personnel falling asleep, inadequate training, and falsification of security logs. According to the Associated Press, the energy industry had contributed about $3.7 million to Democrats and $9.2 million to Republicans during 2004.[11]

Under the National Environmental Policy Act (NEPA) of 1970, all federal agencies must file public Environmental Impact Statements. However, the Department of Homeland Security, under an exemption, now can hide that information. This could include, but not limited to, causes of oil spills or impact that new projects, both federal and private, would have upon the environment.

The National Highway Traffic Safety Administration now forbids public disclosure of data relating to unsafe motor vehicles. Among the classified information are industry tests and consumer complaints. The logic behind the decision, according to the agency, is that if such information is made public it would cause "substantial competitive harm" to manufacturers.

Congress has also been a party to the increased classification of previously public records. A little-noticed provision, submitted by the White House, in the $350 billion transportation bill for 2004–2005 exempts the Transportation Security Administration from complying with the Freedom of Information Act on any document it considers "Sensitive Security Information." In attacking the classification, a wide range of journalistic and consumer advocate organizations pointed out that such classification could hide from public view "a lot of environmental and public health information, from nuclear waste transport routes to toxic spills near shipping facilities."[12] The classification of hazardous materials incidents, for example, would aid not the nation from terrorists but corporations from public accountability; further, a failure to identify hazardous materials spills could significantly endanger the public's health.

"We believe in more transparency to make sure our facilities are safe and the democratic process works," said Rick Blum of OMB Watch.

The Clinton administration had directed federal agencies to provide public documents quickly and efficiently if there was no "foreseeable harm." An executive order in April 1995 opened up documents for public review. However, two months after his inaugural, President Bush issued an executive order that restricted public release of innumerable historical documents, including most of those from his father's administration, and could have easily been interpreted to have included public records of his own administration while governor of Texas.[13] In keeping with its policy of classification and secrecy, the Bush administration about nine months after the inaugural told federal agencies to consider "institutional, commercial, and personal privacy interests" when replying to FOIA requests,[14] a change from the open policies of disclosure established by Janet Reno, his predecessor, and not to comply with FOIA requests if any appeared to be "ambiguous." Most requests, at least to the government, appeared to be "ambiguous."[15] Two years later, a survey by the General Accounting Office in September 2003 revealed that almost one-third of all federal agencies said they revealed less information about public records following the Ashcroft memorandum.[16]

So obdurate had the Department of Justice become three years after the president's inauguration that it was routinely delaying and then denying even the most innocuous FOIA requests. A request for "a copy of each press release issued by the U.S. Attorneys Offices containing a terrorism-related indictment"[17] was denied. The reason, according to the Executive Office of United States Attorneys, which responded about five weeks after the request, was:

> The records you requested would pertain to particular individuals in the context of criminal prosecution. It is the policy of the Executive Office neither to confirm nor deny that such records concerning living third parties exist. Further, any release to you of such records if they do exist, would be in violation of the Privacy Act. . . . [The] disclosure would result in an unwarranted invasion of person privacy.[18]

The Department of Justice never explained how previously released public statements originally meant to "puff" the Department's activities could months or years later even remotely be considered to invade anyone's privacy. Nor did it adequately explain how the indictment of any individual, by law a public record, would compromise anyone's privacy.

Under the Bush administration, "we saw the greatest roll back of FOIA in the history of that wonderful legislation," according to Sen. Patrick Leahy.[19]

The Bush administration, charged former Vice President Al Gore, has used "unprecedented secrecy and deception in order to avoid accountability to the Congress, the courts, the press and the people. . . . Rather than accepting our traditions of openness and accountability, this Administration has opted to rule by secrecy and unquestioned authority."[20] In 2003, the federal government spent about $6.5 billion to classify fourteen million new documents, according to an investigation by OpentheGovernment.org, a coalition of thirty-three national journalism and consumer organizations. It was more almost four times the number classified in 1995 during President Clinton's first term. The report also concluded that for every dollar spent declassifying documents, executive branch agencies spent about $120 to create and keep documents secret. Although there has been a significant increase in public requests under the Freedom of Information Act, "resources devoted to handling public requests for information has held steady," the coalition concluded.[21]

The ACLU and the Electronic Privacy Information Center (EPIC), among dozens of other individuals and organizations, have learned how difficult it is to get public documents from the Department of Justice. The ACLU and EPIC filed an FOIA request in August 2002 to force the Department of Justice to release documents related to its enforcement of the PATRIOT Act, specifically how the federal government was monitoring private communications of citizens not accused or suspected of any crime. Ignoring a ten-day requirement to provide or deny the requested documents, the Department of Justice delayed the request for more than two months. A court order at the end of November directed the Department to provide information by January 15, 2003.[22] That order was ignored. "The release of the records we have asked for would not jeopardize ongoing investigations or undermine the government's ability to respond to new threats," according to EPIC general counsel David Sobel, who emphasized that the request would "allow the public to determine for itself whether the new surveillance powers are necessary and whether the FBI is abusing them."[23] Eventually, the Department of Justice provided 341 pages, with significant and substantial sections blacked out; it refused to provide fifty-three pages.[24] Among what the ACLU and EPIC did find was a massive program of surveillance against American citizens.

EPIC also tried to get records from the Office of Homeland Security (OHS), at that time in the executive branch. The Center had petitioned the OHS under the Freedom of Information Act for "all records relating to efforts to standardize driver's licenses across the country [and] proposals being considered . . . that rely upon biometric technology to identify citizens and visitors to America," as well as a proposal to identify and establish a database for all airline passengers.[25] The OHS denied the request, claiming it wasn't required to provide information since it wasn't bound by FOIA rules.

The OHS, in response to a suit filed by EPIC in U.S. District Court for the District of Columbia, asserted that federal courts hold no jurisdiction. EPIC then tried, under the FOIA, to access papers from OHS to present to the court proof that the federal agency was in fact bound by the FOIA. The OHS refused to provide even those papers, claiming that because it wasn't bound by the courts or by the FOIA, it also didn't have to provide documents proving it fell under FOIA regulations.[26] District Judge Colleen Kollar-Kotelly denied the government's petition to dismiss and ordered it to provide EPIC with the information it needed. Reluctantly, the OHS did provide much, but not all, of the information.[27]

Attempts by the *San Diego Union-Tribune* to learn how many fugitive immigrants had been apprehended by the INS following 9/11 resulted in a memo from the INS headquarters to all its field offices directing them not to assist. The INS claimed it did not receive permission from the Department of Justice to release the information.[28]

Even a routine request for information about lobbyists for foreign governments has led the Department of Justice to provide a creative way to avoid releasing that information. All foreign governments, companies, and foundations that conduct any form of lobbying are required to file extensive reports. Included are the names of individual Americans, as well as law firms, and advertising, and PR agencies that work for foreign governments, and the fees they have been paid. In Spring 2004, the Department of Justice told the Center for Public Integrity, which had filed a Freedom of Information request, that it couldn't provide an electronic copy of the data, something almost every government agency can do, because the computer system was "too fragile"; even making the electronic copy, said the Department of Justice, "could result in a major loss of data, which would be devastating."[29] The department says it meets the requirements for disclosure because individuals can still get the information, just not from a computer system that is old, fragile, and subject to constant malfunction. No one would explain how the system was allowed to deteriorate, especially since there has been extensive budget upgrades since 9/11. The hard copy is available for fifty cents per page; the CPI says that individuals must know precisely which pages they want, and that there are often hundreds of pages per item. In July 2004, the Center filed suit against the Department of Justice for failure to provide information required under the Freedom of Information Act.[30]

Rick Blum, director of OpentheGovernment.org, asks, "How can we make decisions if we don't know what they're doing? We believe in more transparency to make sure the democratic process works."

The Department of Justice "has simply become a black hole, a room without windows [and] nothing gets out," says Charles N. Davis, executive director of the Freedom of Information Center at the University of Missouri. What the Department does release, says Davis, "is tightly managed for maximum propagandistic effect."

Often, reasons to deny public records is because the government claims such release would hinder the conduct of the president's "war on terrorism." The Department of Defense, understandably with more secrets than the Department of Justice, has routinely denied FOIA requests, especially when the documentation could be politically embarrassing. A request by five national organizations[31] in October 2003, seven months before the scandal broke in the major American media, for information about prisoner abuse in Iraq, was shuffled into a bureaucratic limbo. In denying the request for expedited processing, the Department of Defense claimed such action wasn't warranted because there was neither "breaking news" value nor a "compelling need" as provided by law. Providing immediate release of information was unnecessary, claimed the Department of Defense, because the refusal to grant expedited processing would not "endanger the life or safety of any individual." In June 2004, the five organizations filed suit against the Department of Defense and other government agencies for illegally withholding public records. The suit demanded release of records of abuse or torture of prisoners, investigation reports about the deaths of prisoners, policies governing inter-rogation of prisoners, policies of sending prisoners to countries which use torture, and all records regarding the government's response to Red Cross concerns about safety of prisoners.[32] Two months later, U.S. District Judge Alvin K. Hellerstein ordered the Department to comply with the request.[33]

About four thousand government officials have authority to classify documents, according to Rep. Christopher Shays (R-Conn.), chair of the Government Reform Committee's national security panel. The system, he told a committee hearing, "often does not distinguish between the critically important and the comically irrelevant,"[34] Among the comically irrelevant that were classified, said Shays, was a satiric plot against Santa Claus and what cocktails former Chilean dictator Augusto Pinochet preferred. The Bush administration," said Shays, "believes the less known the better."[35]

A *Washington Post* analysis revealed that Americans are learning more about the president's activities from news releases and websites of foreign governments than from the White House. Both routine presidential and political visits are often released by others well before any White House confirmation, according to the *Post*. A trip by the Palestinian Authority's prime minister in July 2003 to meet with President Bush was first announced by the prime minister and reported in the *Jerusalem Post*, but never revealed by the White House. The White House even refused to disclose the visit of a Little League team in 2002.[36]

"Patriotism means . . . not trying to hide from accountability through excessive secrecy and privacy," said Gen. Wesley Clark, former Supreme commander of NATO, and a frequent critic of the Bush administration.[37]

The "zeal for secrecy adds up to a victory for the terrorists," said Bill

Moyers, former press secretary to Lyndon Johnson, publisher of *Newsday*, and winner of more than thirty Emmys for television news and documentaries. "Never has there been an administration like the one in power today, so disciplined in secrecy, so precisely in lock-step in keeping the information from the people at large and in defiance of the Constitution from their representatives in Congress," said Moyers in a keynote speech to the annual convention of Society of Professional Journalists in September 2004.[38]

"Looking back at the past three years reveals a pattern of secrecy and dishonesty in the service of secrecy," wrote Walter Cronkite in April 2004.[39] Cronkite, a combat correspondent during World War II, and former CBS-TV anchor who has covered eleven presidential administrations beginning with that of Harry Truman after World War II, was emphatic in his condemnation of the Bush administration:

> One sometimes gets the impression that this administration believes that how it runs the government is its business and no one else's. It is certainly not the business of Congress. And if it's not the business of the people's representatives, it's certainly no business of yours or mine.
>
> But this is a dangerous condition for any representative democracy to find itself in. The tight control of information, as well as the dissemination of misleading information and outright falsehoods, conjures up a disturbing image of a very different kind of society. Democracies are not well-run nor long-preserved with secrecy and lies.[40]

According to Sen. Patrick Leahy:

> [W]hat I see from a perspective of 29 years in the Senate is government secrecy being ratcheted up—sometimes conspicuously, sometimes imperceptibly. Even before the war on terrorism began, we saw an Executive Order limiting the release of presidential records that sharply curtailed the ability of journalists and researchers to look at these historical documents.[41]

Even John Dean, White House legal counsel for Richard Nixon, whose penchant for secrecy was a defining part of his administration, finds the Bush–Cheney secrecy to be excessive. In *Worse Than Watergate* (2004), Dean writes:

> George W. Bush and Richard B. Cheney have created the most secretive presidency in my lifetime. . . .
>
> Not only does this secrecy far exceed anything at the Nixon White House, but much of the Bush–Cheney secrecy deals with activities similar to Nixon's. [It was] a time of unaccountable and imperial presidency.[42]

"Sometimes there needs to be secrecy in government," says Lucy Dalglish of the Reporters Committee for Freedom of the Press, "but this Administration has gone too far."[43] Her voice is echoed throughout the country.

CHAPTER 12

Creating Cutesy Names for
Programs That Reduce Civil Liberties

During the summer of 2002, the acronym-happy federal government publicly disclosed its proposal for Operation TIPS, the Terrorist Information and Prevention System. Dreamed up within the Department of Justice, the nation-wide program would have given "millions of American truckers, letter carriers, train conductors, ship captains, utility employees and others a formal way to report suspicious terrorist activity."[1]

The program involved an 800-number and other ways for citizens to report "any suspicious behavior" about their neighbors. The U.S. Postal Service refused to participate, and House Majority leader Dick Armey (R-Texas), a conservative, strongly argued that "citizens should not be spying on one another."[2] In response, John Ashcroft said the program was merely a "referral service." Together, Armey and Nancy Pelosi (D-Calif.), liberal minority leader, aided by public reaction against Operation TIPS, not only convinced Congress to cancel TIPS (officially Section 771) from the Homeland Security Act of 2002 (H.R. 5005), but inserted language into the Act that specifically prohibited "any and all activities of the Federal Government to implement the proposed component program of the Citizen Corps known as Operation TIPS."

About the same time the Department of Justice was developing TIPS, the Department of Defense was developing TIAP. The Total Information Awareness Program (TIAP), developed within the Defense Advanced Research Projects Agency, was designed to create an "ultra-large-scale" database of databases about individuals, expanding as new information was brought into that database. The director was former Adm. John Poindexter who had been in charge of the illegal Iran-Contra operation under President Ronald Reagan.

Proposed funding was initially about $500 million. When the public, the media, and members of Congress questioned what appeared to be a potential for a massive invasion of their privacy, complete with undocumented information, the Agency kept the acronym but renamed the program the Terrorist Information Awareness Program.

In addition to public fears about misuse and abuse, the Department of Defense's inspector general issued a strong report questioning the possibility of governmental abuse of power, the program's failure to adequately deal with numerous privacy concerns, and for beginning implementation without clear congressional direction.[3] In February 2003, Congress suspended all funding for TIAP until the inspector general's concerns could be addressed; in September, Congress eliminated funding for almost the entire program.

But, the Bush administration wasn't about to be denied. In his State of the Union address on January 2003, probably in preparation for the possibility that Congress would reduce or eliminate TIAP, President Bush announced the creation of the Terrorist Threat Integration Center (TTIC) "to merge and analyze all threat information in a single location."[4] The program, under the Central Intelligence Agency but with the input from several other federal agencies, was designed to "merge and analyze terrorist-related information collected domestically and abroad in order to form the most comprehensive possible threat picture."[5]

Two months after the State of the Union address, the Transportation Security Administration revealed it planned to implement the Computer-Assisted Passenger Profiling System by Fall 2004. CAPPS II (ostensibly to "cap" terrorism) would require airlines to run background checks on all Americans who fly, and to assign each one a "risk score"—"no risk," "elevated or unknown risk," and "high risk." A person with a "high risk" score, even if based upon incorrect data, could be prohibited from flying. A person with a "no risk" score could be a terrorist who meticulously avoided detection and met all requirements to fly. Among data the TSA would enter into the CAPPS II system would be names, phone numbers, addresses, and dates of birth. The TSA also asked airlines to enter into the CAPPS II database how passengers paid for their tickets, their traveling companions, and itineraries, including rental car information and destinations. Other data could include even more personal information, including the passenger's addresses for several years, the kinds of cars the passenger owns—or has owned—and the length of ownership, the names and addresses of businesses the passenger has used, and even newspaper subscriptions.[6] About one hundred million names would be entered into the database. In 2003, the federal government had given Lockheed a five-year grant, with $12.8 million in the first year, to develop the CAPPS II computer system. Much of the data had been mined from airlines which had previously voluntarily provided passenger data to the Army for a program which, at that time, the government denied was part of anything that would lead to CAPPS II.

CAPPS II "is in direct conflict with privacy policies of most major American corporations," according to Nancy Holtzman, executive director of the Association of Corporate Travel Executives.[7] In testimony before the Aviation Subcommittee of the House Transportation and Infrastructure Committee, Holtzman further told the Subcommittee that "distinguished experts on personal freedoms can easily make the case that CAPPS II can be extended into every aspect of American life from the purchase of train tickets to real estate (in an attempt to establish baseline residency)."[8] Implementation of the plan "might run as high as $2 billion" a year just for "costs generated by ticket penalties, missed meetings and canceled support arrangements," Holtzman testified.[9] She did not address the federal cost to taxpayers for implementing the program. The ACLU, Electronic Privacy Information Center, and dozens of other civil liberties organizations argued against the program's apparent invasion of privacy. European airlines and their governments also questioned the scope of CAPPS II and whether it would meet privacy concerns and confine itself to terrorism investigations.

The Government Accounting Office, in a special report to Congress, stated that the CAPPS II plan had only met one of the eight requirements set by Congress for implementation.[10] Congress forbid further development until all eight criteria were met; however, subsequent testimony before the Senate Governmental Affairs Committee, combined with an investigation by *Wired News*, reveals that the TSA apparently continued to mine data without meeting the necessary safeguards.

The Department of Homeland Security modified the program to meet some of the privacy concerns, and announced in Spring 2004 it would begin a review of the system to "evaluate its speed, accuracy, and efficiency."[11] In July 2004, the Department of Homeland Security, under relentless attacks from members of Congress, the public, and civil rights organizations, finally suspended CAPPS II. About $102 million had already been spent on the program; another $60 million had been budgeted for the coming fiscal year.[12] However, within days of acknowledging it was suspending CAPPS II, the Department of Homeland Security also announced it was restructuring it to confine the data to the names of potential terrorism suspects.[13] Within two weeks of President Bush's re-election, the government morphed CAPPS II into "Secure Flight," and required the nation's airlines to turn over personal data on all of its passengers, not just possible terrorism risks.

For more than two years, the federal government's "no-fly" lists, a less ambitious program, were used to single out individuals who may have posed security threats. But, even after the existence of the lists were made public, the Transportation Security Administration refused to state how persons were put onto those lists and what they could do to clear their names.

Testimony on the status of airport security revealed that airport screeners, both government and privately contracted, performed poorly. Evidence presented by the General Accounting Office and the inspector general of the Department of Homeland Security revealed that objects which should never have been cleared were passed through, and that persons who posed no threat were given extensive searches or denied boarding rights. The TSA was presented as "an unresponsive, inflexible bureaucracy that is failing to provide an adequate level of security at airports."[14]

Former Vice President Al Gore and an elderly nun were each subjected to extensive body searches. Five times within a five-week period, U.S. Airlines ticket agents denied Sen. Edward M. Kennedy (D-Mass.), one of the most recognized people in the United States, boarding passes because his name resembled that of a man the government claimed was a "terrorist." Only after extensive delays was Kennedy allowed to board flights originating in Boston, New York, and Washington, D.C. Even then, it took more than three weeks for the government to remove his name from a "no-fly" list.[15]

In Orlando, Florida, privately contracted security screeners, even with the airline verifying the woman's identity, refused to allow a thirty-five-year-old woman to fly from Orlando to her home in Denver. The reason? She didn't look like her driver's license photo. Athena LaPera, a frequent flier, did look different—at the time the photo was taken, she hadn't yet lost weight or her hair due to chemotherapy treatments for cancer.[16] TSA officials were either unavailable or, says LaPera, unable or unwilling to assist. She and her teenage son finally flew two days after her scheduled flight.

Among others detained as potential terrorists were Michelle D. Green, a thirty-six-year-old Air Force master sergeant; and John Shaw, a seventy-four-year-old retired minister. They weren't told why they were on the list; both learned there may have been no way to clear their names. As many others on the list had learned, similar names can trigger the extensive security checks, and persons with common American names are also detained; if a "John Smith" is on the list, then all persons named "John Smith" or even "J. Smith" are likely to be detained. In April 2004, the ACLU, on behalf of Green, Shaw, and five others, filed a class action suit against the TSA, charging that agency with violating Fourth and Fifth Amendment protections of due process and unreasonable search and seizure.[17]

"This case is about innocent people who found out that their government considers them potential terrorists," said ACLU attorney Reginald T. Shulford.[18] "We have a system that doesn't work," declared Rep. John Mica (R-Fla.), chair of the Aviation Subcommittee.[19]

To the system that "doesn't work," the United States lobbied—some say bullied—the European Union to allow detailed data collection of passengers from twenty-five countries. In an agreement signed at the end of May 2004, the Department of Homeland Security would get personal data in thirty-four categories on every passenger, apparently including American citizens, who flies into the United States. Homeland Security had originally wanted to keep all data for fifty years; the EU negotiated that such data would be destroyed forty-two months after each flight.[20] The data collection, while it might be useful, has the same problems as any system that profiles individuals based upon criteria that may or may not be appropriate, and for which verification isn't normally done.

Even private records of citizens of other countries can be compromised. Under the USA PATRIOT Act, if a foreign company, even with no American offices, subcontracts any part of its data collection to an American company, that American company if contacted by a U.S. federal law enforcement agency must surrender that data. Thus, it is not improbable that a manufacturing company in France, a hospital in Nigeria, or a university in Spain that may use an American company—or even a foreign company with an office in the United States—to create, collect, and maintain any computer programs that include personal information, even if bound by secrecy agreements, could be forced to yield that data.

So extensive is the American government's ability to seize private records under the PATRIOT Act that foreign governments have initiated procedures to protect their own citizens against invasions of privacy. Among the most aggressive is British Columbia, which forbids the transmission of sensitive government records to the United States. The province also plans to establish stringent procedures to protect citizen information if any company uses an American company or subsidiary to develop database programs. "The only one foolproof way to keep our personal and confidential information out of the hands of the FBI is to leave it [in Canada] where it belongs," said the British Columbia Government and Service Employees' Union.[21]

Bob Barr opposed President Bush's "special programs." Before the Senate Committee on the Judiciary, Barr testified:

> CAPPS II and its ilk are false security on the cheap. Airports and other terrorist targets will only be made safer with better, more solid, advance intelligence (and better coordination, analysis, evaluation and dissemination of same) on who the specific threats are—not which innocent person looks most suspicious at the gate or in a "black box" database. The arbitrary exercise of power by federal employees now occurring and which would be greatly expanded if CAPPS II goes into effect is of the sort that has never heretofore withstood the test of probable cause or even reasonable suspicion. It ought not to be allowed to do so now. . . .
>
> [T]here are . . . much better ways, much more efficient ways of going about this [protection of Americans] than the route of TIA, CAPPS. . . . If we indeed continue down that road, I think that we will wake up one day in the not-too-distant future where the Fourth Amendment has been effectively rendered meaningless.
>
> We must remain vigilant. TIPS and TIA are being resurrected in part under other names in other departments. For instance, some proponents of blanket surveillance technologies are attempting to circumvent Congress, the agencies or even federal law (such as the Privacy Act) by providing federal taxpayer funds to states or local governments to establish or implement the programs themselves.
>
> The MATRIX Program . . . developed . . . by a private company, to do what Congress has already indicated it did not want done directly through TIA, is an example of this approach.[22]

MATRIX, the government's acronym for the Multistate Anti-Terrorism Information Exchange, was created to give local and state governments a common database that merged government and private records.[23] Seisint,

Inc., of Boca Raton, Florida, a private corporation in charge of MATRIX, acknowledges data includes information of criminal history, driver's license information, FAA pilot licenses and ownership, property ownership, information about motor vehicle, boat, and plane registrations, state sexual offenders lists, federal terrorist watch lists, corporation filings, bankruptcy failings, state-issued professional licenses, and various Uniform Commercial Code filings. It doesn't publicly acknowledge that it also collects data about a person's credit card history, ethnicity, airline flight manifests, or telephone calling records.[24] Interestingly, MATRIX doesn't include any records of gun ownership, which could be a far more important indicator to determine possible terrorism potential than the color of eyes of an individual, based upon driver's license information.

In early 2002, Hank Asher, Seisint's founder, met with Vice President Dick Cheney, Florida Gov. "Jeb" Bush, and homeland security chief Tom Ridge[25] in the White House to outline a massive data tracking proposal. That same year, the Secret Service, FBI, and Immigration and Naturalization Service all issued Asher certificates of commendation.[26] In January 2003, "Jeb" Bush briefed Cheney about the progress of MATRIX, and apparently asked for additional federal funding of about $2 million per participating state; at the time, there were thirteen states.[27] By August, the Department of Justice awarded Seisint $4 million and the Department of Homeland Security awarded the company $8 million for the project that looked suspiciously like a revamped Terrorist Information Awareness Program that Congress had scrapped. In August 2003, Asher resigned from Seisint when it was revealed that in 1987 he was an unindicted coconspirator and given immunity after being arrested for ferrying multiple shipments of cocaine from Columbia. Federal funding continued.

MATRIX publicly claims it is "controlled by the participating states."[28] However, an ACLU investigation and analysis, based upon federal documents, reveals that MATRIX is "under the direct managerial control of the U.S. Department of Homeland Security,"[29] and that Gov. "Jeb" Bush "has personally taken a lead role in selling the program."[30]

Supporters of the program argue that those who are innocent should have nothing to fear. However, the program is designed to profile American citizens and residents, and to target them based upon that profile. The company collects the raw data—by the end of Summer 2004, it had collected more than 20 billion pieces of information—without verifying the accuracy. Persons in the database are not permitted to view their records, nor is there a mechanism to correct errors. MATRIX claims it is concerned about maintaining the privacy of individuals.[31] However, its database, as are all databases, is subject to firewall destruction by hackers.

Seisint claims MATRIX is only a data collection program, not an intelligence operation. However, documents obtained by the ACLU revealed that Seisint officials lied to the public; MATRIX is not just a collection of data, but a program for data mining to establish patterns and profiles of potential terrorists. The company acknowledges its program can link persons to others they know or whom they had contact with, even if there is no criminal act. In 2003, Seisint sent federal authorities a list of 120,000 individuals who received "high terrorist factor scores."[32] Certain criteria could trigger a "profile"—persons who frequently move, for instance. But, the MATRIX web would ensnare students and temporary workers, among others. While the government is involved in a massive violation of the rights of privacy, and focused upon the "profile" and probable surveillance, it is undoubtedly overlooking the work of terrorists who have substantial knowledge of how to accomplish their missions without being detected.

Of sixteen states that were part of MATRIX, eleven had pulled out by March 2004, most of them citing costs, concerns about violating individuals' rights of privacy, and potential abuses of those rights. Remaining states were Pennsylvania (home of Homeland Security secretary Tom Ridge), Florida (home of Gov. "Jeb" Bush), Connecticut, Ohio, and Michigan.

The ACLU of Michigan filed suit against the Michigan State Police in August 2004 for its participation in MATRIX, charging that the police provided information without legislative or citizen oversight authority as required by Michigan law.[33] The State Police claimed the information provided is "public," but Wendy Wagenheim says the ACLU "believes that citizens may be vulnerable to inaccurate data collection under MATRIX, much like they were used to create the 'red squad' files, with even greater risks as a result of 21st century technology."[34]

During the 1960s and 1970s, the Michigan police had created hundreds of files on Michigan citizens who were involved in civil rights and antiwar movements. In 1980, upon discovering the "red files," Michael Milliken, governor from 1969 to 1983, signed the Interstate Law Enforcement Intelligence Organizations Act "in order to protect the privacy of individual citizens and, at the same time, provide law enforcement agencies with the tools they need." Milliken is one of four plaintiffs in the ACLU suit.

By the end of Summer 2004, fifty-two federal departments and agencies were using, or planned to use, data mining programs, according to an audit by the Government Accounting Office (GAO). The GAO identified 199 data-mining programs, including thirty-six purchased from the private sector, used by the federal government.[35] However, the GAO also expressed its concerns about privacy issues:

> Privacy concerns about mined or analyzed personal data also include concerns about the quality and accuracy of the mined data; the use of the data for other than the original purpose for which the data were collected without the consent of the individual; the protection of the data against unauthorized access, modification, or

disclosure; and the right of individuals to know about the collection of personal information, how to access that information, and how to request a correction of inaccurate information.[36]

To TIPS, TIAP, CAPPS, the "No-Fly list," and MATRIX, add a no-name program to peek into hotel registers. Shortly after the Department of Homeland Security declared an "orange alert" in mid-December 2003, the FBI ordered all Las Vegas casinos, hotels, rental car agencies, travel agencies, and airlines flying into and out of McCarran Airport to electronically turn over lists of all of their guests and customers. The casino operators alone may have turned over more than 270,000 names. There is no estimate of the number of additional names the FBI got during its sweep between December 22, 2003, and January 1, 2004. To "capture" all of the information, the FBI chartered airplanes to bring in agents from out of state and had them stay in time-share apartments in the city. There is no estimate of the cost for the "sweep" and for expenses for the fifty to one hundred FBI agents involved.

Rod Smith, who broke the story in the *Las Vegas Review-Journal*, says the FBI was "very open" about demanding the lists—"they even seemed to be proud of what they were doing." The FBI, says Smith, "insisted on receiving information from the casinos on a daily basis." Gary Peck, executive director of the ACLU of Nevada, believes the casinos reluctantly agreed to turn over the lists "because they are heavily regulated by state and federal agencies and are financial institutions that fall under the blanket of the PATRIOT Act." Only the MGM Mirage told the FBI it would not turn over names without a subpoena. The subpoenas for most of the sources came in the form of National Security Letters, which carried no judicial oversight. The airlines, says Smith, "were more than happy to give their passenger lists."

The minimum amount of data on each customer was a name and address. However, both Peck and Smith believe because of the ways the casinos keep data on guests, and the FBI's demands to turn over lists quickly, other data would have been included. "The casinos bundle data and use aggregate information," says Peck, "and within the time frame demanded by the FBI it would have been impossible to extract just the names." Among that data would be credit information, games the customer normally plays, and how much the customer bets, wins, and loses.

Once the FBI had the names of individuals, under Section 314(a) of the PATRIOT Act agents could have gone to the Financial Crimes Enforcement Network (FinCEN) of the Department of the Treasury and demanded that all financial institutions provide further information about individuals. Under the PATRIOT Act and the Intelligence Authorization Act, passed in November 2003 and secretly funded by an estimated $35–40 billion, all persons approached by the FBI to turn over the lists are bound by a gag order not to disclose they were approached for the information. Thus, it isn't entirely impossible to believe that the FBI could have presented a list of more than 300,000 names to every financial institution in the country and demanded full disclosure of financial status and transactions—and even those financial institutions would be forbidden to reveal if they were approached or if they released any financial data.

Persons who were casino guests, came to Las Vegas on an airplane, rented a car, and were certified scuba divers may have fit some kind of a profile. In May 2002, the FBI databases had secured from the Professional Association of Diving Instructors the names of about ten million persons who were certified divers after the Department of Defense learned that some of the 9/11 terrorists may have been trained in scuba techniques.[37]

Smith and Peck both believe that Las Vegas was targeted for the investigation not because there was an "orange alert" during the holidays and the Departments of Justice and Homeland Security had specific information about any plots—even the FBI admits there was no "credible evidence"— but because of three possibilities. First, the city is a tourist attraction; second, it "could" have been a target symbol for militants who wanted to destroy buildings and people's lives to show the world American decadence; and, third, it "might" have been targeted because the casinos, even though heavily regulated, are "financial institutions" in which individuals could easily launder money by placing heavy bets.

There is a fourth possibility. The grab for names and personal information during the 2003 Christmas/New Year season could have been a test of the ability of the federal agencies to collect data whenever and wherever they wished, and to create an alternate database of the discredited TIA, TIAP, CAPPS II, and MATRIX programs, all preliminary steps to the development of a surveillance society in which government officials spend their time not chasing criminals but watching civilians.[38]

Even if the American government could justify the creation and implementation of an extensive database mining system, what happened to a thirty-two-year-old teacher's aide is indicative of the problems of a surveillance society. About 6:30 a.m., June 18, 2004, federal agents at the port of Miami boarded the *Fascination*, a cruise ship returning from Cozumel, Mexico, awakened Hope Clarke in her cabin, handcuffed and shackled her, and turned her over the U.S. marshals who brought her before a federal magistrate after about nine hours in custody. Clarke's "terroristic" offense? She had been cited by the National Park Service more than a year earlier for not putting away hot chocolate and marshmallows while staying at Yellowstone National Park—the park has rules that are designed to reduce interaction between humans and wildlife.

According to the Associated Press, Clarke had paid the $50 fine the same day, but one of the federal databases still had an outstanding warrant on her.

It was that warrant that led federal law enforcement to arrest her. Before Magistrate John O'Sullivan, Assistant U.S. Attorney Peter Outerbridge admitted there may have been some "discrepancies," but still asked that the defendant be returned to a federal court in Wyoming to clear her record. O'Sullivan, who secured a copy of Clarke's citation which indicated the fine had been paid, just as Clarke had stated, refused to accede to the government's request and then apologized to Clarke.[39]

"[T]he American people feel that the government is intent on prying into every nook and cranny of people's private lives," declared Rep. William Delahunt (D-Mass.), "while at the same time doing all it can to block access to government information that would inform the American people about what is being done in their name."[40] It is this invasion of privacy and the refusal to allow the public to see critical public records that has united liberals and conservatives to oppose major sections of the PATRIOT Act.

While the federal government was detaining individuals for more than two years without charging them with any crime or allowing them legal representation, while the government was trying to use whatever powers it believed it had to deny constitutional rights to American citizens, while individual federal agencies were targeting a specific race and religion, some private companies were also doing their part to do what they believed would help the government protect the people against terrorism.

In September 2003, jetBlue Airways confirmed that a year earlier it had provided about five million passenger itineraries, including names, addresses, and phone numbers, to defense contractor Torch Concepts of Huntsville, Alabama, upon a "special request" from the Department of Defense.[41] The contractor added data from Acxiom, a private company that amasses personal data. Both Torch and the Transportation Security Administration, at that time under the Department of Transportation, at first claimed the data was being used to improve security on military bases. That proved to be a lie.

Subsequent investigations revealed that the data was being "massaged" by Torch as a test for a nationwide database of air travelers to be managed by the TSA. In February 2003, Torch presented a report "Homeland Security—Airline Passenger Risk Assessment," to a non-public conference sponsored by the National Defense Industrial Association (NDIA). The existence of the program was first revealed by Edward Hasbrouck, an individual who is active in privacy issues. Subsequent investigations by investigative reporter Ryan Singel for *Wired News* resulted in the NDIA deleting all references to the study, but not before the problem was brought to public attention.[42] In response to public outrage, jetBlue sent an e-mail to those who protested stating that the release of data "was a mistake on our part," that Torch destroyed the data, and that such release would not again occur.[43] It occurred twice more. TSA officials claimed they never received the lists. They did yield to having asked a defense contractor to extract the data from the airline.

JetBlue wasn't the only airline that provided data about their passengers. About nine months after the jetBlue admission, acting TSA director David Stone, in a sworn statement before the Senate Governmental Affairs Committee, testified that America West, Continental, Delta, and Frontier airlines, as well as Galileo International and Sabre, two of the four largest airline reservation centers, all of which previously refused to acknowledge their participation, had in fact provided information to the TSA. New evidence revealed that the data included not only names, addresses, phone numbers, credit card data and health information about passengers, but also meal preferences, a possible clue to identifying Jews and Muslims.[44] In a related incident, Northwest Airlines revealed that it had released several million passenger records between October 1, 2001, through the end of the year to the National Aeronautics and Space Administration, which was also conducting tests into data mining. The airline later said it "acted appropriately and consistent with its own privacy policy and all applicable federal laws." However, it also said its "current policy is to not provide passenger name record data to private contractors or federal government agencies for use in aviation security research projects [and] in light of current privacy concerns . . . believes a data protection protocol addressing privacy concerns should be developed before any further aviation security research with passenger data is conducted."[45] The documents were originally obtained by a Freedom of Information request filed by the Electronic Privacy and Information Center.

An investigation by Nuala O'Connor chief privacy officer of the Department of Homeland Security, concluded:

> TSA employees involved acted without appropriate regard for individual privacy interests or the spirit of the Privacy Act of 1974. In doing so, it appears that their actions were outside normal processes to facilitate a data transfer, with the primary purpose of the transfer being other than transportation security. Such sharing exceeds the principle of the Privacy Act which limits data collection by an agency to such information as is necessary for a federal agency to carry out its own mission. While these actions may have been well intentioned and without malice, the employees arguably misused the oversight capacity of the TSA to encourage this data sharing.[46]

Less than two months after the jetBlue privacy invasion was publicly revealed, two insurance companies also revealed they were assisting the federal government.

Blue Cross and Blue Shield of Michigan, in its November 7, 2003, issue of *Bluesweek*, an internal company newsletter, proudly declared it ran computer checks on the files of six million individuals it insured.[47] Using key words supplied by the federal government, it isolated the names of six thousand individuals. Among the descriptors were the names of passenger ships that had brought immigrants from Arab countries to the United States, as well as whether the individual had an Arab name. Further investigation showed that none of the six thousand had any terrorist ties.

Aetna checked thirteen million records, including about eighteen thousand in Michigan. Aetna, like Blue Cross and Blue Shield, found no connection. Both companies claimed they passed no medical or insurance information to the government, but say they will continue to search their databases and advise the federal government of names of subscribers who may fit certain profiles.[48]

"At what point did Blue Cross/Blue Shield become an arm of the government, as opposed to a service provider for people?" asked Virginia Rezmierski of the Gerald R. Ford School of Public Policy at the University of Michigan. Rezmierski told the *Detroit News* that although the companies claim what they are doing is being a good corporate citizen, people provide information "under the trust and agreement that we are providing information in exchange for services, not for the company's secondary purpose of being a good corporate citizen."[49]

Imad Hamad, director of the Michigan chapter of the American-Arab Anti-Discrimination Committee, acknowledged that governmental agencies "for a legitimate reason" should be able to check on individual records, but "for a well-respected health care provider to try to rush to be considered the most American and run these lists just to play it safe pushes it much too far. It's . . . consistent with the paranoia and fear that we've been dealing with since September 11."[50]

Although the Bush administration and its supporting cast of the Republican-led Congress didn't see any problems with establishing and maintaining massive databases, especially those of private companies tracking persons of Arab descent, it did have problems with one specific database.

Shortly before the 2004 Republican convention, the New York chapter of the Independent Media Center (IMC), a grassroots organization helping persons use the media to promote social and economic justice, put onto its website a database of more than sixteen hundred Republican delegates. Included were their names, home towns, and the hotels where each was staying; for many, also included were their home addresses; for some, there were e-mail, and cellphone, home and work phone numbers. The data was collected from "a variety of sources," most of them public records. "We have verified much of the data, expanded upon it, and republished it more broadly," the IMC told its readers, but pointed out that it may not be 100 percent accurate,[51] an admission the federal government rarely made about its own databases.

A day after the database was published, the U.S. Attorney's Office for the Southern District of New York issued a subpoena to Calyx Internet Access, a web hosting service, to appear before the grand jury to provide the name of the person who provided the information for the database.[52] The cover letter noted the subpoena was issued "in connection with a criminal investigation [undertaken by the Secret Service] of a suspected felony." The suspected felony was a charge of voter intimidation under 17 U.S.C. § 594. "The only intimidation taking place here is the Secret Service intimidating people who speak out against the government," charged Ann Beeson of the ACLU, legal representative for both Calyx and the IMC.[53] The subpoena demanded information and business records of IMC. The Department of Justice further asked that Calyx "voluntarily refrain from disclosing the existence of the subpoena to any third party. . . to preserve the confidentiality of the investigation and because disclosure of the investigation might interfere with and impede the investigation."[54] Calyx, with permission of IMC, revealed the names of four of the New York chapter's leaders. Matt Toups, a student at Carnegie Mellon University, and one of the four leaders, pointed out, "We work to create a safe place for dissenting views [but] the United States is becoming an increasingly repressive and chilling environment for free speech, thanks to government harassment like the recent attempts" by the Secret Service.[55]

The subpoena may even have had a political motive, completely unrelated to federal law. According to Micah Anderson of IMC:

> The Republican Party is also connected to the largest corporate voting interference ever, through the Diebold Corporation, which makes flawed electronic voting systems. In October of 2003, Diebold issued a cease-and-desist notice to Indymedia, because we had links to mirrors of a damning internal Diebold memo that was leaked. As a result of challenges by the Electronic Frontier Foundation (EFF), The Online Policy Group (OPG), and Indymedia, Diebold was forced to back down out of embarrassment.[56]

CHAPTER 13

'The Constitution Is Ours—Not Just His'

With John Ashcroft leading the way, the Bush administration in early 2003 drafted the Domestic Security Enhancement Act, a draconian set of police powers which would allow the government to investigate all credit card purchases, magazine subscriptions, medical prescription records, travel plans, bank deposits, students' records and grades, and even toll road receipts, among numerous other records, all without judicial oversight, all based upon an "administrative subpoena." The proposed Act would also permit wiretaps without a court order and for the federal government to hold individuals, including American citizens, in secret until the filing of criminal charges, which could be indefinite. Americans would have no knowledge the government is investigating their personal files; even should there be a detention or arrest, they wouldn't know where the information came from or if any of it was correct.

Other provisions would authorize secret arrests, would allow the attorney general to be able to deport any legal permanent resident alien whenever he or she determines it is not in the nation's economic or foreign policy interest, would impose gag orders in non-terrorist criminal cases, would allow the government to infiltrate religious organizations even if they are apolitical, and would even place tighter restrictions upon the public's right to know about hazardous wastes. The Department of Justice had even wanted a nationwide DNA database it could search without any court supervision.

The proposed law would also strip citizenship based upon an individual's association, past or present, however remote, with organizations the Department of Justice determined to be legal but which it placed on its list of terrorist organizations, whether or not they truly were terrorist organizations or whether they were merely groups that had different political philosophies than those of the administration. "The framers of our Constitution deliberately omitted mention of such power, because they realized the authority to strip our citizenship is the ability to tailor the electorate to one's advantage," stated Bob Barr before the Senate Committee on the Judiciary.[1] Viet Dinh, a primary writer of the PATRIOT Act, also disagrees with that section. "That policy, vetted, would [not] satisfy legal, constitutional issues," Dinh said after leaving the Department of Justice.[2]

The proposals, heavily promoted by President Bush later in the year, also included expansion of the death penalty from twenty offenses to forty-three,[3] a not unexpected policy since the president, while governor of Texas, oversaw a system that executed more Americans than any other state. In testimony before the Crime, Terrorism, and Homeland Security Subcommittee in the House of Representatives, ACLU legislative counsel Timothy H. Edgar testified:

> The "catch-all" death penalty provision would not only dramatically increase the number of federal capital offenses, but would seriously exacerbate the already considerable chilling effect of the USA PATRIOT Act's "domestic terrorism" definition on political protest groups that use tactics of civil disobedience. This provision would exacerbate the already serious civil liberties problems of the definition of international terrorism and of the similar definition of domestic terrorism enacted by the USA PATRIOT Act.[4]

An interpretation by the Center for American Progress (CAP) suggests that "expanding the number of crimes in which the death penalty is available, the administration's proposal may make it more difficult to obtain evidence and successfully prosecute terrorism cases."[5] CAP cites the reality that all European Union countries "refuse to extradite suspects to the United States unless they are certain the death penalty will not be imposed on the extradited person [and will] refuse to supply evidence if it will be used in obtaining a capital conviction."[6] Most countries also will not extradite their own citizens unless they are sure the charges against them are substantial enough for conviction.

Text of the proposed Act[7] was leaked to the Center for Public Integrity (CPI), which then distributed it to the media in February 2003. "John Ashcroft, with support from President Bush, has increasingly forgotten that the Constitution is ours—not just his," wrote First Amendment scholar Nat Hentoff in the *Washington Times*. The Center for Public Integrity, Hentoff wrote, "has now exposed Ashcroft's sequel to the PATRIOT Act for what it is: an assault on the Bill of Rights drafted without consultation with Congress."[8]

Kay J. Maxwell, president of the nonpartisan League of Women Voters, called upon Congress to "protect our homeland through means that protect our civil liberties rather than chipping away at the basic values for which America stands."[9]

Errol Louis, a columnist for the conservative *New York Sun*, was especially critical of the expanded proposal:

> Staff members in Attorney General John Ashcroft's Justice Department seem to be spending their workdays with the Constitution in one hand and a pair of scissors in the other. . . . [This] 80-page document is a catalog of authoritarianism that runs counter to the basic tenets of modern democracy. . . . [W]ith this latest act of recklessness, Mr. Ashcroft has earned himself a full-blown recall movement. Like most people, I would just as soon not take the time to march in the streets, sit in a jail cell, sign petitions, or organize voters. Mr. Ashcroft, however, has given all of us a reason to think more seriously about our individual rights, and how badly we intend to fight for them—while we can.[10]

Faced by a swelling public outrage, John Ashcroft said he wasn't seeking those sweeping new powers. He didn't fool many. Then, on June 5, 2003, after more than a year of refusing to respond to congressional requests, and having at least once denied he had been seeking additional powers, John Ashcroft asked the House Judiciary Committee for even more powers.[11] Two months later, with congressional and public support for the PATRIOT Act diminishing, Ashcroft went on a month-long thirty city national promotional tour. Each of his ninety-minute stops, all decorated with several American flags, included a carefully prepared thirty-minute speech, including comments about how important the PATRIOT Act was in preventing further terrorist attacks, ten minutes with federal officials, and then a round of media interviews. Possibly believing most print media journalists would ask tough questions, Ashcroft for the first month of his tour allowed only local TV reporters to interview him, and then for only three minutes each. However, following a strong letter of protest by the Society of Professional Journalists, Ashcroft added a five-minute block for questions from print journalists.

Ashcroft's campaign, like the memo sent to U.S. attorneys to direct them to talk with members of Congress about the proposed law, probably violated federal law that prohibits members of the executive department from publicly lobbying for or against proposed legislation. A second Ashcroft directive to the ninety-three U.S. attorneys to meet with community organizations to "dispel emerging misconceptions and misinformation"[12] may have been worded carefully enough to just tread upon, but not violate, federal law.

Opposition to the PATRIOT Act and PATRIOT Act II "has grown so loud that the Bush administration has responded—but not . . . by addressing these concerns in a constructive and open way," Sen. Russell Feingold said on the floor of the Senate. He pointed out that the Bush administration "has initiated what seems to be a public relations campaign in recent weeks to defend the PATRIOT Act in its entirety."[13]

The *New York Times* suggested, "Instead of spin-doctoring the problem, Mr. Ashcroft should work with the critics to develop a law that respects Americans' fundamental rights."[14]

Reiterating his speech before Congress two months earlier, John Ashcroft claimed that even more powers were needed, including the expansion of secret searches, the increased use of administrative subpoenas without judicial oversight, and the detention of individuals for crimes that have no relation to terrorism. Any attempt to weaken the Act, said Ashcroft, could allow further terrorist attacks.[15]

A number of analysts and observers have challenged Ashcroft's assertions. The attorney general "occasionally has blurred fact and fiction in giving the law credit for preventing another terrorist attack on U.S. soil," wrote Toni Locy in *USA Today*.[16]

"Ashcroft clearly played fast and loose with the facts," wrote *Las Vegas Review-Journal* columnist John L. Smith, "when he made it appear the FBI and other federal law enforcement agencies could investigate the Mafia and other complex criminal organizations, but could not investigate suspected terrorists without the PATRIOT Act."[17] However, the already-established Foreign Intelligence Surveillance Act had given the FBI jurisdiction and investigative powers.

During the rest of the year, parts of the proposed PATRIOT Act II began to appear on various bills and presidential executive orders. In September 2003, Sens. Orrin Hatch (R-Utah), John Cornyn (R-Texas), Lindsey Graham (R-S.C.), Jon Kyl (R-Ariz.), and Jeff Sessions (R-Ala.) drafted the Vital Interdiction of Criminal Terrorist Organizations Act, or VICTORY Act, part of it a mask for PATRIOT II, to expand the powers of the federal government. Among its provisions would be those that would make illegal drug possession a terrorist crime if the person gives an illegal drug to anyone later shown to be a terrorist, even if the person giving the illegal drug (which could be one marijuana cigarette) had no knowledge the recipient was a terrorist, or even if given without charge.

The new Act would also give the attorney general administrative subpoena powers, allowing him to bypass the court system. It would also require all telecommunications companies, Internet service providers, and all financial institutions to release consumer records to federal law enforcement if served with a subpoena, including those issued by the Department of Justice not the courts. The legislation would exempt all institutions from civil liability even if the Act was later found to be unconstitutional.

During that same month, Rep. James Sensenbrenner, with the support of the Bush administration, introduced the Anti-Terrorism Intelligence Tools Improvement Act (H.R. 3179), a bill that also included several parts of the PATRIOT Act II. That bill would allow the increased use of National Security Letters by reducing or eliminating judicial review of any kind, as well as a one-year sentence for anyone who discloses that an NSL was issued.

The weekend that Saddam Hussein was captured in December 2003—and overlooked by most major American media, which ran two-inch high banner headlines about the capture—President Bush signed additional legislation that gave the FBI even greater powers. These new powers would include the right to obtain secretly and without a court order, both personal and financial records, including all credit card transactions from all financial institutions. The definition of "financial institution" was expanded beyond that of banks, credit unions, and savings and loan companies to include security and commodities brokers, jewelers, pawnbrokers, casinos, insurance companies, currency exchanges, anyone or any business that sells any vehicle (including car, truck, boat, or airplane), telegraph companies, and any agency that issues travelers' checks. The Congressional authorization had been hidden within an omnibus spending bill, and had not come before public debate. The new law doesn't "come close to protecting the national security, but [it] does obscure government decision-making from the kind of oversight that the public deserves and the kind of oversight that will actually help us win this war," said James Dempsey, executive director for the Center for Democracy and Technology.[18]

CHAPTER 14

'Affirm and Uphold
Civil Rights and Civil Liberties'

A few months after 9/11, Chris Finan, president of the American Booksellers Foundation for Free Expression, said he believed public opinion would eventually shift "from the panic after September 11 to allow a reasonable debate of the dangers of the PATRIOT Act." It's taken longer than he had hoped, but his view is beginning to come true as dozens of politicians who voted for the Act, as well as millions of Americans who once gave the government their unchecked authority, have begun significant protests against both the Act and innumerable civil rights violations.

On the second anniversary of the signing of the PATRIOT Act, several thousand Americans marched through the streets of New York City to protest. In Chelmsford, Massachusetts, Greater Lowell for Peace and Justice, a social activist group, created an eleven-foot float, towed by a minivan, for the city's Fourth of July parade in 2004. On the float was a large rendition of the titles in the Bill of Rights. Next to it was a five-foot cardboard pair of scissors, labeled "USA Patriot Act." Throughout the country, hundreds of civic and nonprofit organizations have presented forums to bring out the issues of the PATRIOT Act. It is the people, with the assistance of several civil liberties organizations, who have spoken out against the PATRIOT Act and who have begun to influence legislation.

Broward County, Florida, with a population of 1.6 million, is the largest county to pass a resolution opposing the PATRIOT Act. The nine Broward County commissioners, most of them politically conservative, were initially opposed to passing the proposed resolution. "One of the commissioners actually said we need to throw out the Bill of Rights to have greater security," says Jennifer Van Bergen, a lawyer/journalist who led the campaign to get the resolution passed. Van Bergen says she didn't think the commissioner "realized what she said, and this pointed out to me exactly what was wrong in sacrificing civil liberties for security." Van Bergen and a coalition of several local organizations conducted a six month information campaign that included a major forum with several distinguished First Amendment attorneys. Teams of two or three persons then met with each of the commissioners to explain the PATRIOT Act, its effects, and to answer their questions. In April 2003, the commissioners voted unanimously to pass a resolution affirming civil rights that may be compromised by execution of the PATRIOT Act. "We were astonished," says Van Bergen. She says she expected more opposition in the final vote. Broward County was the 100th governmental body to oppose the PATRIOT Act.

By the Fall of 2004, more than 350 governmental bodies had passed similar resolutions. Among them are Los Angeles, Chicago, Philadelphia, Baltimore, Detroit, San Francisco, Atlanta, Sacramento, Tucson, and Washington, D.C. The legislatures of Alaska, Maine, Hawaii, and Vermont also declared their opposition to the PATRIOT Act, as have the student governments of more than twenty universities, including the state universities of Texas, California, and Wisconsin.

The National League of Cities, at its annual meeting in December 2003, called for revisions to the PATRIOT Act, and urged the president and his cabinet to "review, revise, and rescind executive orders and policies adopted since the terrorist attacks that limits or compromise the liberties guaranteed by the Constitution and the Bill of Rights," and urged Congress "to restore and protect our nation's fundamental and inalienable rights and liberties."[1]

"[I]f they are coming for you in the morning, they are coming for me at night," said Mayor Rudolph C. McCollum Jr., prior to the Richmond, Virginia, City Council passing a resolution opposing parts of the PATRIOT Act.[2]

In February 2004, the New York City Council, by an overwhelming voice vote, passed Resolution 60 to "affirm and uphold civil rights and civil liberties" and to specifically oppose several sections of the PATRIOT Act. The Council called for the New York congressional delegation to "actively work for the repeal of those sections of the USA PATRIOT Act and related federal actions [that] unduly infringe upon fundamental rights and liberties."[3] More than ninety organizations, and dozens of families of firefighters and police who died in the World Trade Center towers, supported the resolution. The largest American city, the one most identified with the 9/11 murders, became the 250th governing body to urge repeal of many of the PATRIOT Act provisions.

Palo Alto, California, Police Chief Lynne Johnson said her department, following direction of the city council, which had approved a resolution opposing the PATRIOT Act,[4] would not aid the FBI in any searches, surveillance, or interviews conducted under the PATRIOT Act unless there was evidence a crime had been committed. Johnson told the media:

> We take an oath to uphold the Constitution and that's the bottom line for us. We believe we are still able to protect the people of this community, but won't do so by violating people's constitutional and civil rights.[5]

In a resolution calling for a repeal of the Act or at least the provisions that "violate fundamental rights and liberties," the Philadelphia City Council declared it supported the campaign against terrorism, "but also reaffirms that any efforts to end terrorism not be waged at the expense of the fundamental civil liberties of the people of Philadelphia, and all citizens of the United States."[6]

In March 2004, the voters of San Francisco, a contiguous city-county, passed Proposition "E," which amended the City Charter to require that all federal requests for private records, including health and library records, be brought first before the Board of Supervisors to determine if the request was within constitutional guidelines. Previously, federal law enforcement agents, citing the PATRIOT Act, could require department heads to surrender personal information about city-county employees, without telling anyone, including the suspect or senior city-county officials. Department heads would individually have been subject to civil and criminal liability for non-compliance "and we didn't think they should be put into that position," said Jerry Threet, legislative assistant. The proposal, submitted to the voters by a 10–1 vote of the Board of Supervisors, is based upon a similar law passed the previous year by the Arcata, California, City Council which forbids city employees to act upon PATRIOT Act requests.

During the same week that San Francisco passed Proposition "E," the Washington, D.C., City Council unanimously declared:

> [The PATRIOT Act] was enacted . . . without adequate consideration of provisions that undermine our civil liberties. . . .
>
> There is no inherent conflict between the preservation of liberty and the need to protect the public. All security measures taken to enhance public safety can, and must, do so without impairing constitutional rights or infringing upon civil liberties. . . .
>
> It is necessary that the District express its strong support for fundamental constitutional rights and its opposition to federal measures that unnecessarily infringe upon civil liberties, its support for the rights of immigrants and its opposition to measures that single out individuals for scrutiny or enforcement activity based on their country of origin or religion.[7]

The resolution, as were resolutions of many cities opposing the PATRIOT Act, called for all public libraries to post notices to patrons that federal law enforcement may seize records of what they checked out or what they read on the Internet, that public schools shall notify all persons whose records were obtained through PATRIOT Act provisions, and called for Congress to modify the Act.

The Department of Justice's vindictive and highly inaccurate response to local governments which opposed the PATRIOT Act is that half the opposition "are either in cities in Vermont, very small population, or in college towns in California. It's in a lot of the usual enclaves where you might see nuclear free zones, or they probably passed resolutions against the war in Iraq."[8] Once again, the Department of Justice was not just wrong, but substantially wrong.

Resolutions by municipal governments opposing the PATRIOT Act are important not just to establish parameters for local response to possible federal intrusion upon local rights, but also in giving members of Congress a sense of the beliefs of their voting constituents. For two years after 9/11, most of Congress, the public, and the mainstream media essentially accepted the necessity of the PATRIOT Act and the statements of the president, his cabinet, and advisors who vigorously claimed they needed that particular tool to fight the "war on terrorism."

The PATRIOT Act "is a grave threat to freedom of expression, to freedom of association and by extension to freedom of information," says Charles N. Davis of the Freedom of Information Center, "for it ushered in a climate of legislative deference and executive power unmatched in American history."

Slightly more than two years after Congress passed the PATRIOT Act, the *Washington Post* in a major editorial charged:

> Congress has stood by in an alarming silence while a fabric of new law governing the balance between liberty and security has been woven by the other two branches of government. . . . The parties [Democrat and Republican] are united in their desire not to sully their hands by engaging seriously in deciding the shape of the law. They are content not to do their jobs but instead to let the Bush Administration do what it pleases and take the political and judicial heat for it all. . . .
>
> [I]n absenting itself from the policymaking process, Congress does not merely fail to protect American liberty. It also fails to aid the executive branch in fighting terrorism.[9]

"Congress must act now to rein in the PATRIOT Act, limit its use to national security concerns and prevent it from developing 'mission creep' into areas outside of national security," wrote former Speaker of the House Newt Gingrich, a conservative who had developed the strategy that pushed the successful midterm Republican victories in 1994.[10] As the abuses caused by enforcement of the PATRIOT Act became more public, dozens of members of Congress of both major political parties have spoken against the excesses.

There may be hope for the repeal of some of the sections of the PATRIOT Act. During 2003 and 2004, members of Congress submitted more than a dozen bills or amendments to diminish or repeal several sections of the PATRIOT Act.

In the Senate, several bills were introduced to restore personal privacy, increase freedom of information, and prohibit racial profiling. Most of the bills, however, have not moved forward in the Republican-controlled Congress.

The Security and Freedom Ensured Act (SAFE Act), filed on October 2, 2003, in the Senate, and sponsored by both Republican and Democratic senators,[11] would prohibit federal agents from having access to library or bookstore records unless it can show to a court "there are specific and articulable facts giving reason to believe that the person to whom the records pertain is a foreign power or an agent of a foreign power."[12] The Act also called for rollbacks of several sections of the PATRIOT Act, as well as prohibiting increased powers proposed under PATRIOT II. It was presented to Congress only after the Senate's cosponsors had given the attorney general and his staff ninety days to work with them on revising the Act to meet civil rights standards. No one in the Department of Justice responded to the cosponsors' request for input, according to Sen. Dick Durbin (R-Ill.), one of the sponsors.[13]

The proposed legislation did not please John Ashcroft who sent a four-page letter to members of the Senate Committee on the Judiciary. In that letter, Ashcroft told the senators that "The Office of Management and Budget advises that enactment of S.1709 would not be in accord with the president's program," and that if the bill was "presented in its current form to the president, the president's senior advisers will recommend that it be vetoed."[14] The attorney general's response, said Durbin, "is an unfortunate overreaction to a reasoned and measured effort to mend the PATRIOT Act."[15]

In September 2003, Rep. Dennis Kucinich, with twenty-seven cosponsors, introduced the Benjamin Franklin True Patriot Act to repeal ten sections of the bill, among them those that authorized the detention of noncitizens without judicial review, "sneak-and-peek" searches, and personal documents searches without a judicial warrant.

In June 2004, companion bills were introduced in the House and Senate to restore civil liberties for immigrants and to reduce governmental secrecy. Among the bills' provisions are those to assure that all data submitted to the National Crime and Information Center database meets an accuracy requirement; require all federal agencies to report their datamining activities to Congress; require all immigration hearings be public, with few specified exceptions; and to terminate the National Security Entry-Exit Registration System.[16]

The most controversial sections of the controversial Act, Sections 213 and 215, have been hit hardest. In the summer of 2003, Rep. C. L. Otter, a conservative Republican, and Rep. Dennis Kucinich, a liberal Democrat, co-authored an amendment to a budget bill that would stop funding of the PATRIOT Act's "sneak-and-peek" section. On the floor of the House, Otter argued:

> Not only does this provision [of the PATRIOT Act] allow the seizure of personal property and business records without notification, but it also opens the door to nationwide search warrants and allows the CIA and the NSA to operate domestically. . . . American citizens, whom the government has pledged to protect from terrorist activities, now find themselves the victims of the very weapon designed to uproot their enemies.[17]

Otter said he believed the Department of Justice didn't fully understand the concern Americans had against what they believed was an invasion of their privacy. "I don't think [Justice] appreciated what we were hearing in our home districts," Otter told *USA Today*, adding, "Congress made a bad law . . . and needs to fix it."[18] In response, Guy A. Lewis, director of the executive office for United States Attorneys, sent a memo to all U.S. attorneys "to call personally or meet with . . . congressional representatives [to discuss] the potentially deleterious effects" of the amendment. The memo included names of all members of Congress who voted for the amendment.[19] Rep. John Conyers Jr. questioned the propriety of the memo, and charged that any attempt by members of the executive branch to influence legislation was a violation of federal law.

The Electronic Privacy Information Center sent an FOIA request on September 10, 2003, to request a copy of the memo. It also demanded expedited processing, as provided for under the Code of Federal Regulations, for the memo and supporting documents. Twelve days later, two days after the ten-day limit for expedited processing on matters that are of "exceptional media interest" and involve issues of integrity or urgency as defined within the FOIA, the Department of Justice rejected EPIC's request for expedited processing. EPIC then filed suit.[20] Three months after EPIC's FOIA request for public documents, Judge James Robertson of the U.S. District Court for the District of Columbia denied the suit for expedited processing. More than seven months after EPIC's original request, the Department of Justice still had not provided the public documents, none of which threatened national security.

The House passed the bill, written by Otter and Kucinich, 309–118.[21] However, it never moved forward in the Senate. By February 2004, although two-thirds of Americans said they believed the PATRIOT Act either didn't go far enough or was "just right," almost three-fourths of Americans opposed this delayed search provision, according to a *USA Today* poll.[22]

Rep. Bernie Sanders in March 2003 introduced the Freedom to Read Protection Act (H.R. 1157) that would minimize or repeal Section 215. Since then, 149 other representatives added their names as cosponsors. "One of the cornerstones of our democracy is our right of Americans to criticize their government and to read printed materials without fear of government monitoring and intrusion," Sanders said at the time he submitted his bill.[23] More than three dozen of the nation's largest organizations of librarians, booksellers, journalists, and publishers filed a joint statement that not only declared their support for the Freedom to Read Protection Act but also condemned several sections of the PATRIOT Act. Sens. Barbara Boxer (D-Calif.) and Russell Feingold submitted similar legislation in the Senate.

When it appeared that the Freedom to Read bill was stalled in the House of Representatives, Sanders and Reps. John Conyers Jr. (D-Mich.), Jerry Nadler (D-N.Y.), Ron Paul (R-Texas), and Otter tried another way to limit the PATRIOT Act. To the Commerce, Justice, State Appropriations Bill of 2005, they proposed an amendment that would cut off funding to the Department of Justice for searches conducted under Section 215. The amendment didn't diminish the government's capacity to investigate possible terrorism. The federal government could still obtain records, as long as it went into a court of law and showed there was "probable cause" to request such records. Even if the amendment passed, it might have been only a symbolic vote to restore some of the civil liberties lost during the Bush administration's continual harangue about "terrorism." As with the Otter amendment to cut off funding for "sneak-and-peek" searches, it was unlikely the Senate would accept the House amendment. Further, the Department of Justice could use the equally restrictive National Security Letters, which weren't subject of the amendment prohibition, to gain access to records. The Department could also manipulate its own budget in several ways to disguise use of funding to enforce Section 215, especially since it had an obstructionist attitude except when it was politically beneficial to the Bush administration, to release of any data about enforcement of that section.

What the Republican leadership did with the amendment was indicative of the Bush administration's tactics the previous three and one-half years. A day before the vote, the president's budget office sent a memo to House members warning them if they passed anything to weaken the PATRIOT Act, the president would veto the $39.8 billion bill.[24] It would be the first veto in the president's term. By the end of the fifteen-minute voting period, even with the president's assurances of a veto, the amendment had 219 votes for passage, 201 against. But, the Republican leadership at that point held the voting open for an additional twenty-three minutes while Rep. Tom DeLay (R-Texas), House majority leader, and his aides bullied Republicans into changing their votes.[25] Among the tactics, the leadership suddenly produced a letter from the Department of Justice to Rep. James Sensebrenner, chair of the House Judiciary Committee. That letter claimed a member of a terrorist group allied with al-Qaeda used the Internet at a public library. There were no specifics.[26] Since the Department of Justice continually claimed it had "no interest" in going to libraries, how it learned of computer use at a library leads one to question if the Department lied to the people or if it lied to the Congress. The final vote, a 210–210 tie, doomed the amendment.

"You win some, some get stolen," Otter said after the vote. Rep. Nancy Pelosi, the House minority leader, lashed out at "Republican leaders [who] once again undermined democracy, this time so that the Bush administration can threaten our civil liberties. How thoroughly un-American."[27] Sanders called the vote "an outrage" and "an insult to democracy." Rep. Jerry Nadler, whose district includes the site of where the World Trade Center once stood, and is one of the nation's strongest advocates for civil liberties and social justice, was even stronger in condemning the administration's methods:

The shameful tactics used during the vote on the Freedom to Read amendment showed the Republican leadership's alarming desire to deny Americans their civil liberties. Put simply, the vote was rigged to corrupt the democratic process. For all of their talk of patriotism, the Republicans showed something quite different: an abuse of power more likely to be seen in a police state than in a democratic society.

Another representative was even more hostile to the tactics of the House leadership:

[It is] the most heavy-handed, arrogant abuse of power in the 10 years I have been here. . . . [The Speaker of the House is] a heavy-handed son of a bitch and he doesn't know any other way to operate, and he will do anything he can to win at any price. There is no sense of comity left.[28]

However, it wasn't July 2004 but October 1987, and the profane-enhanced tirade was directed not against current Speaker Dennis Hastert (R-Ill.) but against Speaker Jim Wright (D-Texas), who had briefly adjourned the House to allow time to "convince" a couple of Democrats to switch their votes on a pending budget bill. The man who had scoured Wright was Rep. Dick Cheney (R-Wyo.)—the same Dick Cheney who as vice president and president of the Senate told Patrick Leahy in the Senate itself to do something anatomically impossible to himself; the same Dick Cheney who, with George W. Bush, had campaigned four years earlier on a vow to bring "civility" to the Oval Office.

During July, both before the vote in the House and more so after the vote had scared the Republican leadership with how divided the Congress and the nation had become, the president and his cabinet increased their public statements about the necessity for the PATRIOT Act. Because of the use of the PATRIOT Act and the invasion of Iraq and the overthrow of Saddam Hussein, "the nation is safer," they kept repeating.

A year earlier, John Ashcroft had gone on the road to push for additional powers. This time, he was pushing just to keep Congress and the Judiciary from touching any part of the current Act. A year earlier, he limited his media interviews to just TV reporters—and then for only three minutes each. This time, he held press conferences—and, apparently, banned only one reporter.

U.S. Attorney Marcos D. Jimenez, through his press contact, informed WTVJ-TV, an NBC-owned station in Miami, that reporter Ike Seamans would not be allowed to attend a news conference at a federal courthouse. Apparently, Seamans had offended Jimenez for some hard-nosed reporting. Seamans, a former Army officer, had been a TV reporter for about thirty-five years, including several years as the NBC-TV network correspondent for Latin America, and then as a foreign correspondent in the Middle East; in his career, he reported from about eighty countries. Seamans, however, was in Europe at the time of the press conference.

"We always elect to choose the person we feel is most available and most capable," news director Yvette Miley told Kirk Nielsen of the *Miami New Times,* emphasizing, "if Ike had been here, Ike would have been on the story."[29] Had Seamans been there, and been denied the right to cover the news conference and ask questions, it would have been a "cut-and-dried" First Amendment violation, according to the Reporters Committee for Freedom of the Press.[30] Seamans told the *New Times* that only twice in his career was he ever barred from covering a news conference—"That happened in Cuba and the Soviet Union," he said.[31] Ashcroft may not have known of the attempt to bar a reporter, but at the least a U.S. Attorney should be familiar with the basics of constitutional law.

Nevertheless, just two weeks later, after the tie vote in the House of Representatives, the supersecretive, supersensitive attorney general suddenly released for the House Committee on the Judiciary a thirty-one page summary report that gave examples and reasons for keeping all sections of the PATRIOT Act. In prepared comments for the media, John Ashcroft said the report contains a "mountain of evidence that the Patriot Act has saved lives," and that like military weapons, it is "just as vital to targeting the terrorists who would kill our people and destroy our freedom at home."[32] In more than two years, the department claimed the PATRIOT Act was used to bring charges against 310 individuals. However, dozens of those charges were not for terrorism or terrorism-related acts, as the Congress intended when it passed the Act, but for various domestic felonies, all of which could have been investigated without the PATRIOT Act being invoked. The Department of Justice claimed there were 179 convictions or guilty pleas, a conviction rate of only 58 percent.

What the report didn't indicate is even more critical than what it did. Almost half of those convicted or who pled guilty were immigrants charged with relatively minor visa or immigration violations, and their prison sentences, if imposed, were less than a year. Nor did the report indicate if Sections 213 and 215 were used and, if so, the number of times. The report also failed to note if the PATRIOT Act was "central" and "critical" in each of the arrests or how many innocent Americans were detained or arrested under authority of the PATRIOT Act. Most of the nation's mass media reported as fact what the attorney general had stated, even quoting the examples of the kidnapping of an elderly woman and a child molestation arrest; few challenged the data and interpretations why the Act was being used in domestic cases, or whether it was even necessary in order to bring charges.[33]

Although both the judicial and legislative branches have been picking off pieces of the PATRIOT Act, a part of the Act itself may be the most productive way to restore some constitutional liberties.

The PATRIOT Act has a built-in sunset provision (Section 224); sixteen sections will expire unless Congress renews them before December 31, 2005. Among the sections scheduled to sunset are 206 (authority for law enforcement to use roving surveillance of cell phones and hotel rooms without a specific target), 209 (right to seize voice mail), 215 (the controversial seizure of "any tangible things"), 218 (lower standard of proof to obtain a FISA court warrant for covert surveillance), 220 (national search warrants for all computer-based data), 225 (immunity for all persons and law enforcement agencies conducting covert surveillance.) Exempt from the Act's sunset provisions are several sections dealing with civil rights, among them Sections 203 (sharing Grand Jury information with other agencies and without judicial authority), 210 (broadening the scope of subpoenas for electronic communications), 213 (the "sneak-and-peek" section), and 216 (nationwide warrants for electronic surveillance).

Shortly before Congress passed the USA PATRIOT Act, Sen. Patrick Leahy, chair of the Senate's Judiciary Committee, pointed out:

> [The sunset clause is] an enforcement mechanism for adequate oversight [to guarantee] that agencies . . . are going to have to use these powers carefully and in the best way. . . .
>
> [The Sunset clause will] help ensure that law enforcement is fully responsive to Congressional oversight and inquiries on use of these new authorities and that a full record is developed on their efficacy and necessity.[34]

A report prepared by the American Bar Association for its annual meeting in August 2003, reaffirmed and expanded Sen. Leahy's concern:

> The purpose of the sunset provision was to emphasize that new authorities were temporary, enacted quickly in response to a national emergency, and by their nature highly prone to potential use. By placing a time limit on these powers, Congress sought to induce the government to use them with restraint and to assure the American people that lawmakers would conduct a thorough and searching review, in what they hoped would be a calmer and more reflective climate, to determine whether the new powers were being used properly and effectively and whether their further extension was warranted.
>
> Such a review necessarily requires cooperation between congressional oversight committees and the agencies that they oversee to ensure that the committees have timely access to the information they require. To date, however, such cooperation has not been forthcoming. . . .
>
> [E]ffective legislative oversight of executive agencies is critical to maintaining the constitutionally established balance of powers among our branches of government.[35]

The American Bar Association's House of Delegates, in its August 2003 meeting, voted to oppose any attempt to repeal or delay implementation of the sunset clause, and further recommended that Congress "conduct a thorough review of the implementation of the powers granted to the executive branch under the Act before considering legislation that would extend or further expand such powers."[36] The ABA also strongly recommended that the executive branch "cooperate[s] with the congressional committees . . . to ensure that they have timely access to all information they require to fulfill their oversight responsibilities."[37]

Congress, by now hearing more from the public about the PATRIOT Act's excesses, killed in committee a proposal by Sen. Orrin Hatch (R-Utah) to exempt several sections that would have been affected by the sunset clause. But, the administration wasn't about to be denied. In his State of the Union address in January 2004, President Bush specifically called for extension of the Act and to override the sunset provisions that would become effective almost two years later. About a month later, with the president continuing his defense of the PATRIOT Act, Elisabeth Bumiller in the *New York Times* observed, "Mr. Bush has sought to use the renewal of the law to further the perception that he will be far tougher on terrorism than the Democrats, an idea that aides see as his greatest strength going into the November election."[38] In April, with public opposition to the PATRIOT Act increasing, the president began an intense political campaign to emphasize benefits of the PATRIOT ACT and to kill the congressionally imposed sunset provisions:

> The Patriot Act tore down the artificial wall between the FBI and CIA, and enhanced their ability to share the information needed to hunt terrorists. The Patriot Act also marked a major shift in law enforcement priorities. We are no longer emphasizing only the investigation of past crimes, but also the prevention of future attacks. Because we passed the Patriot Act, FBI agents can better conduct electronic surveillance and wiretaps on suspected terrorists. And they now can apply other essential tools—many of which have long been used to investigate white-collar criminals and drug traffickers—to stop terrorist attacks on our homeland.
>
> Our government's first duty is to protect the American people. The Patriot Act fulfills that duty in a way that is fully consistent with constitutional protections. In making America safer, it has helped us defend our liberty. Since I signed the Patriot Act into law, federal investigators have disrupted terror cells in at least six American cities. And since September the 11th, the Department of Justice has charged over 300 persons in terrorism-related investigations. So far, more than half of those individuals have been convicted or pled guilty.
>
> Key elements of the Patriot Act are set to expire next year. Some politicians in Washington act as if the threat to America will also expire on that schedule. Yet we have seen what the terrorists intend for us, in deadly attacks from Bali to Mombasa to Madrid. And we will not forget the lessons of September the 11th. To abandon the Patriot Act would deprive law enforcement and intelligence officers of needed tools in the war on terrorism, and demonstrate willful blindness to a continuing threat.[39]

The president, of course, was wrong on many of his points. Nevertheless, two days after his radio address to the nation, he opened his in-person defense of the PATRIOT Act in Hershey, Pennsylvania, a key state during the 2004 political campaign. In an impassioned speech, in which he affirmed his belief that all provisions of the PATRIOT Act should be permanent, he told his audience, "The Patriot Act defends our liberty. The Patriot Act makes it able for those of us in positions of responsibility to defend the liberty of the American people. It's essential law."[40]

The next day, the president was in Buffalo, New York, again touting the necessity of keeping all sections of the PATRIOT Act.[41] His advisors specifically selected Buffalo since it is the largest city near where the FBI arrested the "Lackawanna Six." The six Yemeni-Americans from suburban Lackawanna had pleaded guilty to aiding al-Qaeda. They acknowledged they had traveled to an al-Qaeda training camp in Afghanistan and had heard a speech by Osama bin Laden. The federal government had no evidence any of the six ever participated in a terroristic threat or attack, or had plans to do so. President Bush repeatedly cited the PATRIOT Act as the legal tool that allowed the arrests since it had broken down the artificial "wall" to permit the sharing of information, and heaped lavish praise upon the FBI agents. The reality is that the FBI, using established FISA laws, could have justified the arrests without use of the PATRIOT Act. Nevertheless, the scene in Buffalo was good campaign trail drama.

In contrast to the local TV stations that gave a positive spin to the president's visit, the *Buffalo News* sarcastically observed:

> The act doesn't need to be renewed until next year, yet Bush and his lieutenants are pushing so hard it seems like it might have expired yesterday. The reason: The law makes good campaign fodder. Bush is able to portray himself as protecting the country not only against terrorists, but from the conservative and liberal bleeding hearts who just don't understand the urgent need for access to every American's library records. In that regard, Bush is also doing a disservice to the act, and the Americans it is meant to protect.[42]

In May, almost six months before the election, the president began running in nineteen key states a series of thirty second TV campaign spots that called for the extension of the PATRIOT Act; as in the president's earlier statements, these ads again incorrectly pointed out that without the Act certain powers to detain potential terrorists were not possible. That same month, Sen. Jon Kyl (R-Ariz.) submitted a bill to repeal the sunset clause. By the end of the month, Vice President Dick Cheney had launched a major political reelection tour that initially focused upon the administration's belief the nation needed the PATRIOT Act, and that those opposed did not have the nation's safety or security at heart.[43] In eight metropolitan cities, police and prosecutors held "information" rallies, promoting both the PATRIOT Act and the Bush–Cheney reelection. Additional TV ads attacked Democrat opponent Sen. John Kerry for opposing the PATRIOT Act, and repeated the president's reasons why the nation should exert pressure to keep the entire Act. In Massachusetts, U.S. Attorney Michael J. Sullivan sent "information packets" to each of the 351 communities in the state; each packet included a four-page letter, a copy of a *Wall Street Journal* editorial defending the Act, and background material. In communities where town meetings were considering resolutions against the Act, Sullivan sent staff members to present the government's side.[44] While the intent may have been commendable—to assure that all sides of an issue were debated—the appearance was that it was electioneering during the presidential campaign.

"The president is using the PATRIOT Act to distract attention from the fact that his administration has done a woefully inadequate job of fixing the intelligence system," said Phil Singer, spokesman for Sen. John Kerry. Singer charged that if President Bush "were truly interested in implementing reforms to improve intelligence sharing, he wouldn't be playing election-year politics with the PATRIOT Act."[45]

Rep. Charlie Gonzales (D-Texas) called for Congress to modify the PATRIOT Act, but said of the president: "[He] has a purely political message. It may be a very effective political message, but it is a disingenuous one and does this nation a great disservice."[46]

Judith Krug of the American Library Association isn't optimistic about the sunset clause being enforced. All sections of the PATRIOT Act "are going to be used as long as they think they can get away with it," says Krug, one of the nation's leading experts in First Amendment rights and civil liberties. "We'll be lucky if we can 'sunset' out any of it," she says.

Even the sunset clause itself was in jeopardy. About five months before the presidential election, Sen. Jon Kyl (R-Ariz.), with nine cosponsors, representing the will of the executive branch, introduced legislation to amend the PATRIOT Act to repeal the sunset section, and to make the PATRIOT Act permanent.

However, the month after that bill was submitted, Sen. Edward M. Kennedy (D-Mass.), with five of the Senate's strongest civil rights advocates, submitted legislation to restore civil liberties lost under enforcement of the PATRIOT Act. The Civil Liberties Restoration Act, if passed, would end secret deportation hearings, establish an independent immigration court, guarantee due process for all persons, including the right to review charges and evidence, terminate the National Security Entry-Exit Registration System, require minimum accuracy requirements for inclusion of information in the National Crime Information Center database, and require the executive branch to provide to Congress detailed and regular reports about its data mining activities. Two weeks after the Senate bill was filed, a similar bill submitted by Rep. Howard L. Berman (D-Calif.) was filed in the House. That bill added an amendment to the PATRIOT Act to limit searches and seizures of individual records and databases to only those cases in which the government establishes a connection to suspected terrorists or terrorist organizations.

Persons on all sides of the political spectrum have questioned the executive branch's encroachment of unrestrained power.

Jim Gilmore—former governor of Virginia, former chair of the Republican National Committee, and appointed by President Bush to look into civil liberties issues—was especially critical of what the Bush administration had done to civil liberties:

> How much are we willing to change in response to [the] 9/11 attack, to tolerate being watched, our information being joined into databases that create a whole new picture of person that didn't exist before, how much should we accept authorities pushing, probing and demanding? . . . If the enemy's going to force us to change what we are as Americans, we should do it with our eyes opened. As a conservative Republican, I'm deeply concerned about this.[47]

Bob Barr pointed out that additional authority under the PATRIOT Act "moves us in the direction of the executive law enforcement power extending to the point where they can do whatever they want, whenever they want, however they want to do it. . . . All in the name of fighting terrorism."[48]

Shirin Ebadi, in her acceptance speech upon receiving the Nobel Peace Prize in December 2003—about nine months after the United States invaded Iraq and six months before "60 Minutes II" aired photos of prisoner abuse— was even more blunt. "In the past two years, some states have violated the universal principles and laws of human rights by using the events of 11 September and the war on international terrorism as a pretext," Ebadi told a world audience. Elaborating, but not specifically identifying the Bush administration, she vigorously noted that "[R]egulations restricting human rights and basic freedoms . . . have been justified and given legitimacy under the cloak of the war on terrorism."[49]

In 1755, in a letter to the governor of Pennsylvania, Benjamin Franklin argued, "They who would give up essential Liberty to purchase a little temporary Safety deserve neither Liberty nor Safety." Several federal court decisions affirmed the constitutional rights decreed by the Founding Fathers. But, every generation, says Sen. Patrick Leahy, "has to protect those rights, and if you succumb, if lawmakers succumb to the temptation to pander to shifting public passions at the expense of the public's everlasting interest in preserving freedom, then you erode freedom."

For four years, the federal government, its influence felt and enhanced in all local and state governments, as well as private business, had been chipping away at constitutional protections. No court or legislative body can completely undo what has been done. Every American has become a suspect in the federal government's callous invasion of individual rights of privacy. While the official word is that the federal government is concerned about maintaining citizen rights, there are still innumerable instances of constitutional violations of reasonable bail, freedom from unreasonable searches, the rights of due process, speedy and fair trials by impartial juries, freedom from cruel and unusual punishment, and equal protection guarantee for both citizens and noncitizens. "Our enemies are ruthless fanatics [but] the solution is not for us to become zealots ourselves so that we remake our society in the image of those that would attack us," said Rep. William Delahunt.[50]

If the PATRIOT Act isn't modified, there will continue to be a government-imposed chill upon First Amendment rights, including both the right of dissent and freedom of religion. Writers may not create the works that a free nation should read; book publishers will take even fewer chances on publishing works that "might" result in a government investigation or be unpopular with the current administration; bookstore owners may not buy as many different titles; the people, fearing that whatever they read might be subject to Big Brother's scrutiny, may not buy controversial books or check books out of the library; individuals may think twice before reading articles and commentaries in alternative publications or logging onto any of millions of sites on the Internet, all easily accessed by government intrusion. How ironic it is that a president who says he wants everyone to read, and whose wife is a former librarian, is the one who may be responsible for giving the people less choice in what they may read.

The repression of constitutional and civil rights under the Bush administration, and the lies it has told about the necessity for the PATRIOT Act and for invading Iraq, have done little to assure our nation's security or to combat terrorism. What they have done is to put far more fear into the American people than any terrorist could.

Congressional Bills to Amend or Repeal Specific Parts of the USA PATRIOT Act

(Current status of congressional bills are available at http://thomas.loc.gov)

United States House of Representatives

Name of Bill: The Detention of Enemy Combatant Act (H.R. 5684)
Sponsor: Rep. Adam Schiff (D-Calif.)
Cosponsor: Rep. Barney Frank (D-Mass.)
Introduced: October. 16, 2002
Purpose: Requires executive branch to establish "clear standards and procedures governing detention" of U.S. citizens and residents, and requires "timely access to judicial review to challenge the basis for a detention, and permit the detainee access to counsel." Restricts who may be called an "enemy combatant."

Name of Bill: Freedom to Read Protection Act (H.R. 1157)
Sponsor: Rep. Bernie Sanders (I-Vt.)
Cosponsors: 144
Introduced: March 6, 2003
Purpose: To amend parts of the Act, including Section 215, to exempt bookstores and libraries from being forced to turn over records of their patrons.

Name of Bill: Surveillance Oversight and Disclosure Act of 2003 (H.R. 2429)
Sponsor: Rep. James Hoeffel (D-Pa.)
Cosponsors: 24
Introduced: June 11, 2003
Purpose: To amend the Foreign Intelligence Surveillance Act of 1978 to improve the administration and oversight of foreign intelligence surveillance, and for other purposes.

Name of Bill: Benjamin Franklin True Patriot Act (H.R. 3171)
Sponsor: Rep. Dennis Kucinich (D-Ohio)
Cosponsors: 27
Introduced: September 24, 2003
Purpose: To repeal Sections 213 and 215 of the PATRIOT Act, and provide for an appropriate constitutional review of the Act.

Name of Bill: Civil Liberties Restoration Act (H.R. 4591)
Sponsor: Rep. Howard L. Berman (D-Calif.)
Cosponsor: Rep. William Delahunt (D-Mass.)
Introduced: June 16, 2004
Purpose: Amends or revokes several sections of FISA and the PATRIOT Act, especially in areas of immigration, data collection, and due process. (Companion bill to S. 2528.)

United States Senate

Name of Bill: Data-Mining Moratorium Act of 2003 (S. 188)
Sponsor: Sen. Russell Feingold (D-Wisc.)
Cosponsors: Sens. John Corzine (D-N.J.), Bill Nelson (D-Fla.), and Ron Wyden (D-Ore.)
Introduced: January 16, 2003
Purpose: To impose a moratorium on implementation of the federal government's Total Information Awareness (TIP) program, which provides significant and substantial access to personnel records

Name of Bill: Domestic Surveillance Oversight Act of 2003 (S. 436)
Sponsor: Sen. Patrick Leahy (D-Vt.)
Cosponsors: Sens. Maria Cantwell (D-Wash.), John Edwards (D-N.C.), Russell Feingold (D-Wisc.), Charles Grassley (R-Iowa), Daniel Inouye (D-Hawaii), and Arlen Specter (R-Pa.)
Introduced: February 25, 2003
Purpose: To improve administration and oversight of the Foreign Intelligence Surveillance Act and courts, and require more accountability of the Department of Justice.

Name of Bill: Restoration of Freedom of Information Act of 2003 (S. 609)
Sponsor: Sen. Patrick Leahy (D-Vt.)
Cosponsors: Sens. Robert Byrd (D-W.Va.), Russell Feingold (D-Wisc.), Bob Graham (D-Fla.), James Jeffords (I-Vt.), John Kerry (D-Mass.), Carl Levin (D-Mich.), and Joseph Lieberman (D-Conn.)
Introduced: March 12, 2003
Purpose: Provides for confidentiality of personal data provided by individuals. Restores FOIA to what it was prior to passage of the PATRIOT Act; reduces the amount of "critical infrastructure" documents that may be classified.

Name of Bill: Library and Bookseller Protection Act (S. 1158)
Sponsor: Sen. Barbara Boxer (D-Calif.)
Introduced: May 23, 2003
Purpose: To amend the Foreign Intelligence Surveillance Act of 1978 to restrict the FBI from obtaining any "tangible" item from a U.S. citizen for the sole purpose of seizing from a bookstore or library information that contains personal information about a patron. Excludes libraries from requirement to comply with FBI requests to provide information on bills or electronic communication records.

Name of Bill: Citizens' Protection in Federal Databases Act (S. 1484)
Sponsor: Sen. Ron Wyden (D-Ore.)
Cosponsors: Sens. Jon Corzine (D-N.J.) and Russell Feingold (D-Wisc.)
Introduced: July 29, 2003
Purpose: Requires the federal government to report to Congress its use of commercial and other databases for national security, intelligence, and law enforcement purposes.

Name of Bill: Data Mining Reporting Act (S. 1544)
Sponsor: Sen. Russell Feingold (D-Wisc.)
Cosponsors: Sens. James Jeffords (D-Vt.) and Patrick Leahy (D-Vt.)
Introduced: July 31, 2003
Purpose: Establishes criteria for use of database searches by government agencies; requires annual reports to Congress.

Name of Bill: The Protecting the Rights of Individuals Act (S. 1552)
Sponsor: Sen. Lisa Murkowski (R-Alaska)
Co-Sponsors: Sen. Ron Wyden (D-Ore.)
Introduced: July 31, 2003
Purpose: To modify and restrict conditions under which the PATRIOT Act may be used to gather information.

Name of Bill: Patriot Oversight Restoration Act of 2003 (S. 1695)
Sponsor: Sen. Patrick Leahy (D-Vt.)
Cosponsors: Sens. Larry Craig (R-Idaho), Richard Durbin (D-Ill.), Russell Feingold (D-Wisc.), John Sununu (R-N.H.), and Harry M. Reid (D-Nev.)
Introduced: October 1, 2003
Purpose: To delete Section 224 and to strengthen the sunset provisions of the Act.

Name of Bill: Reasonable Notice and Search Act of 2003 (S. 1701)
Sponsor: Sen. Russell Feingold (D-Wisc.)
Introduced: October 2, 2003

Purpose: Modifies requirements of issuance of delayed search warrants, time of notification, and requires the attorney general to issue a semiannual report on all warrants.

Name of Bill: Security and Freedom Ensured Act of 2003 (S. 1709)
Sponsors: Sen. Larry Craig (R-Idaho)
Cosponsors: Sens. Daniel Akaka (D-Hawaii), Jeff Bingaman (D-N.Mex.), Maria Cantwell (D-Wash.), Jon Corzine (D-N.J.), Michael D. Crapo (R-Idaho), Christopher J. Dodd (D-Conn.), Richard J. Durbin (D-Ill.), Russell D. Feingold (D-Wisc.), Tom Harkin (D-Iowa), James Jeffords (D-Vt.), Edward M. Kennedy (D-Mass.), John F. Kerry (D-Mass.), Frank Lautenberg (D-N.J.), Blanche Lincoln (D-Ark.), Lisa Murkowski (R-Alaska), Harry M. Reid (D-Nev.), Arlen Specter (R-Pa.), John E. Sununu (R-N.H.), and Ron Wyden (D-Ore.)
Introduced: October 2, 2003
Purpose: To amend parts of the Act, including Section 215, to place reasonable limitations on the use of surveillance techniques and issuance of search warrants without probable cause.

Name of Bill: A Bill to Prohibit Racial Profiling (S. 2132)
(Companion Bill to H.R. 3847)
Sponsor: Sen. Russell Feingold (D-Wisc.)
Cosponsors: 14
Introduced: February 26, 2004
Purpose: Defines and bans racial profiling by state and federal law enforcement agencies.

Name of Bill: Civil Liberties Restoration Act (S. 2528)
Sponsor: Sen. Edward M. Kennedy (D-Mass.)
Cosponsors: Sens. Jon Corzine (D-N.J.), Richard Durbin (D-Ill.), Russell Feingold (D-Wisc.), Patrick Leahy (D-Vt.)
Introduced: June 16, 2004
Purpose: Amends or revokes several sections of FISA and the PATRIOT Act, especially in areas of immigration, data collection, and due process. Opens deportation hearings, ensures due process for immigrants and those detained, establishes an independent immigration court, terminates the National Security Entry-Exit Registration System, requires increased accuracy for the NCIC database, assures those charged under the PATRIOT Act receive same rights as those charged under any criminal statute, including right to review evidence against them, and limits seizure of private databases.

Congressional Bills to Enhance the USA PATRIOT Act

United States House of Representatives

Name of Bill: Intelligence Authorization Act for Fiscal Year 2004 (H.R. 2417)
Sponsor: Rep. Porter J. Goss (R-Fla.)
Introduced: June 11, 2003
Purpose: Fiscal authorization to various agencies concerned with security; establishes the Office of Intelligence and Analysis within the Treasury Dept.; loosens definition of "financial institution" for purpose of provisions governing access to financial records.

Name of Bill: CLEAR ACT (The Clear Law Enforcement for Criminal Alien Removal) (H.R. 2671)
Sponsor: Rep. Charlie Norwood (R-Ga.)
Cosponsors: 120
Introduced: July 9, 2003
Purpose: Authorizes state and local law enforcement to enforce federal immigration; increases criminal and civil penalties for illegal entry into the country and violation of departure orders.

Name of Bill: Terrorist Penalties Enhancement Act (H.R. 2934)
Sponsor: Rep. John R. Carter (R-Tex.)
Cosponsors: 83
Introduced: July 25, 2003
Purpose: Increases and expands death penalty crimes under the PATRIOT Act from 20 to 43.

Name of Bill: Antiterrorism Tools Enhancement Act (H.R. 3037)
Sponsor: Rep. Tom Feeney (R-Fla.)
Introduced: September 9, 2003
Purpose: Authorizes the attorney general, in any investigation concerning a Federal crime of terrorism, to subpoena witnesses, compel the attendance and testimony of witnesses, and require the production of records that he finds relevant or material to the investigation. Establishes a "gag" upon those who are subpoenaed and imposes a prison term of up to five years for those who disclose they were subpoenaed.

Name of Bill: Pretrial Detention and Lifetime Supervision of Terrorists Act (H.R. 3040)
Sponsor: Rep. Bob Goodlatte (R-Va.)
Cosponsors: Reps. John R. Carter (R-Tex.), J. Randy Forbes (R-Va.), Lamar Smith (R-Tex.)
Introduced: September 9, 2003
Purpose: Allows pretrial detention without possibility of bail of persons suspected of terrorist activities, including those believed to be involved in the broad "domestic terrorism" web of Section 802; eliminates a requirement that a terrorist act "must have resulted in, or created a foreseeable risk of death or serious bodily injury to another person in order to qualify for a period of supervised release of any term of years or life."

Name of Bill: Anti-Terrorism Intelligence Tools Improvement Act of 2003 (H.R. 3179)
Sponsor: Rep. F. James Sensebrenner (R-Wisc.)
Cosponsor: Rep. Porter Goss (R-Fla.)
Introduced: September 25, 2003
Purpose: Includes many of the provisions of the PATRIOT Act II bill that was criticized by both liberal and conservative organizations, and was not submitted into Congress after its public disclosure. Increases use of National Security Letters and allows the government to withhold information from defendants. Increases ability of the government to secretly obtain personal records and reduce or eliminate judicial review. Allows imprisonment of one year for disclosure that a National Security Letter was used; restricts rights of judiciary to decide when to restrict classified information.

Name of Bill: Joint Terrorism Task Force Enhancement Act of 2003 (H.R. 3439)
Sponsor: Rep. Carolyn Maloney (D-N.Y.)
Cosponsor: Rep. Martin Frost (D-Tex.)
Introduced: November 4, 2003
Purpose: Promotes the exchange of personnel between federal, state, and local authorities; authorizes the sharing of agents across different agencies.

United States Senate

Name of Bill: To Amend the Foreign Intelligence Surveillance Act of 1978 (S. 113)
Sponsor: Sen. Jon Kyl (R-Ariz.)
Cosponsors: 8

Introduced: January 9, 2003
Passed: May 9, 2003 (referred to House and introduced as H.R. 3552)
Purpose: Amends and loosens FISA rules on wiretaps which required probable cause that the suspect is an agent of a foreign power. Allows individuals who may not be part of any terrorist group to be included in wiretap authorization.

Name of Bill: Terrorist Penalties Enhancement Act (S. 1604)
Sponsor: Sen. Arlen Specter (R-Pa.)
Introduced: September 10, 2003
Purpose: Establishes several new capital crimes for those who commit or assist a terrorist act, even if there is only a remote connection. Denies federal benefits to anyone convicted of terrorist activity.

Name of Bill: Homeland Security Enhancement Act of 2003 (S. 1906)
Sponsor: Sen. Jeff Sessions (R-Ala.)
Cosponsors: Sens. Larry Craig (R-Idaho), Jim Inhofe (R-Okla.), Zell Miller (D-Ga.)
Introduced: November 20, 2003
Purpose: Requires state and local law enforcement to enforce federal immigration laws; establishes criminal penalties and forfeiture for aliens unlawfully present in the United States; increases specified criminal penalties for illegal entry and failure to depart violations.

Name of Bill: A Bill to Amend the USA PATRIOT Act to Repeal the Sunsets (S. 2476)
Sponsor: Sen. Jon Kyl (R-Ariz.)
Cosponsors: Sens. Saxby Chambliss (R-Ga.), John Cornyn (R-Tex.), Lindsey Graham (R-S.C.), Jim Inhofe (R-Okla.), Mitch McConnell (R-Ky.), Zell Miller (D-Ga.), Don Nickles (R-Okla.), Pat Roberts (R-Kans.), and Jeff Sessions (R-Ala.)
Introduced: May 21, 2004
Purpose: Repeal the sunset clause, keeping all sections of the Act.

Major National Organizations Opposing Certain Provisions of the USA PATRIOT Act

American Association of Law
  Libraries
53 W. Jackson, Suite 940
Chicago, Ill. 60604
  Phone: (312) 939-4764
  Fax: (312) 431-1097
  http://www.aallnet.org

American Bar Association
750 N Lake Shore Drive
Chicago, Ill. 60611
  Phone: (312) 988-5000
  http://www.abanet.org

American Booksellers Association
828 South Broadway
Tarrytown, N.Y. 10591
  Phone: (800) 637-0037
  Fax: (914) 591-2720
  http://www.bookweb.org

American Booksellers
  Foundation for Free Expression
139 Fulton Street, Suite 302
New York N.Y. 10038
  Phone: (212) 587-4025
  Fax: (212) 587-2436
  http://www.abffe.org

American Civil Liberties Union
125 Broad Street, 18th Floor,
New York, N.Y. 10004
  Phone: (212) 549-2500
  http://www.aclu.org

American Library Association
50 E. Huron Street
Chicago, Ill. 60611
  Phone: (800) 545-2433
  http://www.ala.org

American Society of Journalists and
  Authors
1501 Broadway, Suite 302,
New York, N.Y. 10036
  Phone: (212) 997-0947
  http://www.asja.org

Association of American
  University Presses
71 West 23rd Street
New York, N.Y. 10010
  Phone: (212) 989-1010
  Fax: (212) 989-0275
  http://aaupnet.org

Association of Booksellers for Children
3900 Sumac Circle
Middleton, Wisc. 53562
  Phone: (608) 836-6050
  Fax: (608) 836-1438

Association of American
  Publishers
71 Fifth Avenue
New York, N.Y. 10003
  Phone: (212) 255-0200
  http://www.publishers.org

Authors Guild
31 E. 28th Street 10th Floor
New York, N.Y. 10016-7923
  Phone: (212) 563-5904
  Fax: (212) 564-5363
  http://www.authorsguild.org

Center for Constitutional Rights
666 Broadway, 7th Floor
New York, N.Y. 10012
  Phone: (212) 614-6464
  Fax: (212) 614-6499
  http://www.ccr-ny.org

Center for National Security Studies
1120 19th Street NW, 8th floor
Washington, D.C. 20036
  Phone: (202) 721-5650
  Fax: (202) 530-0128
  http://www.cnss.org

Electronic Frontier Foundation
454 Shotwell Street
San Francisco, Calif. 94110
  Phone: (415) 436-9333
  Fax: (415) 436-9993
  http://www.eff.org

Free Congress Foundation
717 Second Street NE
Washington, D.C. 20002
  Phone: (202) 546-3000
  Fax: (202) 543-5605
  http://www.freecongress.org

Bill of Rights
  Defense Committee
241 King Street, Suite 216
Northampton, Mass. 01060
  Phone: (413) 582-0110
  http://www.bordc.org

The Center for Democracy
  and Technology
1634 "I" Street NW
Washington, D.C. 20006
  Phone: (202) 637-9800
  Fax: (202) 637-0968
  http://www.cdt.org

The Comic Book
  Legal Defense Fund
P.O. Box 693
Northampton, Mass. 01061
  Phone: (413) 584-7151
  Fax: (413) 582-6955
  http://www.cbldf.org

Electronic Privacy
  Information Center
1718 Connecticut Avenue, N.W.
Suite 200
Washington, D.C. 20009
  Phone: (202) 483-1140
  Fax: (202) 483-1248
  http://www.epic.org

Free Expression Policy
  Project
275 Seventh Avenue
New York, N.Y. 10001
  Phone: (212) 807-6222
  Fax: (212) 807-6245
http://www.fepproject.org

National Association of Independent
Publishers Representatives
111 East 14th Street
New York, N.Y. 10003
  Phone: 888-624-7779
  http://www.naipr.org/

People for the American Way
2000 M. St., NW (suite 400)
Washington, D.C. 20036
  Phone: (202) 467-4999
        (800) 326-7329
  http://www.pfaw.org

Society of Professional Journalists
3909 N. Meridian Street
Indianapolis, Ind. 46208
  Phone: (317) 927-8000
  Fax: (317) 920-4789
  http://www.spj.org

National Coalition to   Repeal
the Patriot Act
22 West Bryan Street
Savannah, Ga. 31401
  http://www.repealnow.com

Society of Childrens Book
  Writers and Illustrators
8271 Beverly Boulevard Los
Angeles, Calif. 90048
  Phone: (323) 782-1010
  http://www.scbwi.org

Notes

(Page numbers in newspaper references refer to the first page of the article.)

INTRODUCTION

[1] Testimony of John Ashcroft before the Senate Committee on the Judiciary; December 6, 2001. [http://www.senate.gov/~judiciary/testimony.cfm?id=121&wit_id=42].

[2] Testimony of John Ashcroft, Senate Committee on the Judiciary; March 4, 2003. [http://www.senate.gov/~judiciary/print_testimony.cfm?id=612&wit_id=42]

[3] "President Bush Speaks at Tsinghua University," news release, White House; February 22, 2002. The president's twenty-one minute speech and response to questions is archived by the Federal Document Clearing House. [http://www.whitehouse.gov/news/releases/2002/02/print/20020222.html]

[4] During the early part of the Civil War, President Lincoln suspended the *writ of habeas corpus*—and was roundly denounced for it by the public and the media.

[5] Although constitutional lawyers, and dozens of major national civil rights organizations, have repeatedly pointed to violations of the Constitution, the final determination of a violation is only through the court system.

[6] Quoted in "These Additional Powers Are Not Necessary," by Arian Campo-Flores, *Newsweek* Web edition; September 12, 2003.

[7] "An Unpatriotic Act," *New York Times*; August 25, 2003; p. A14.

[8] Quoted in "Senators Press for Changes in Patriot Act," Associated Press article distributed October 17, 2003.

[9] "Freedom and Security," speech by Al Gore to MoveOn.Org; November 9, 2003. [http://www.moveon.org/gore/speech2.html]

[10] Quoted in "Kucinich Stresses Civil Liberties," by Juliet Eilperin, *Washington Post*; December 24, 2003; p. A6.

[11] "Americans Generally Comfortable With PATRIOT Act," by Lydia Saad; summary, Gallup Poll News Service; March 2, 2004. [The survey was conducted February 16–17, 2004.]

[12] *Ibid.*

CHAPTER 1 / 'THE SYSTEM WAS BLINKING RED'

[1] See: Bill Clinton, "Remarks on Departure for Washington, DC, from Martha's Vineyard, Massachusetts," *Public Papers of the Presidents*; August 20, 1998; p. 1642; and Bill Clinton, "Address to the Nation on Military Action against Terrorist Sites in Afghanistan and Sudan," *Public Papers of the Presidents*; August 20, 1998; p. 1643.

[2] In July 2004, six Yemeni citizens, all believed to have been part of al-Qaeda, were finally brought before a Yemini court, charged with being involved in planning the attack on the *U.S.S. Cole*.

[3] Testimony by Philip Zelikow, executive director, 9/11 Commission; April 14, 2004. Also see: "Bush Was Warned bin Laden Wanted to Hijack Planes," by David E. Sanger, *New York Times*; May 16, 2002; p. A1; "Bush Briefed on Hijacking Threat Before September 11," by John King, CNN; May 16, 2002; "Bush Knew of Terrorist Plot to Hijack US Planes," by Jason Burke and Ed Vulliamy; *The* [London] *Observer*; May 19, 2002; "Britain Warned US to Expect September 11 al-Qaeda Hijackings," by Torcuil Crichton, *London Sunday Herald*; May 19, 2002; "9/11 Report, Rice Remarks in Conflict: Investigators Say Bush Got Specific

Data on Threats," Associated Press; July 29, 2003; "Ashcroft Flying High," Washington Bureau, CBS-TV News; July 26, 2001; "Traces of Terror: the Intelligence Reports; Egypt Warned U.S. of a Qaeda plot, Mubarak asserts," by Patrick E. Tyler and Neil Macfarquhar. *New York Times*; June 4, 2002; p. A1; "9/11 Probers Say Agencies Failed to Heed Attack Signs," by Dana Priest and Dan Eggen, *Washington Post*; September 19, 2002, p. A1.

[4] Quoted in "9/11 Chair: Attack Was Preventable," CBS News; December 17, 2003. [http://www.cbsnews,com/stories/2003/12/17/eveningnews/printable589137.shtml]

[5] Quoted in "Bush, Cheney Quizzed by September 11 Panel," by Deb Reichmann, Associated Press; April 29, 2004.

[6] In June 2004, Tenet resigned after seven years as the nation's director of Central Intelligence.

[7] See: "To the Minute, Panel Paints a Grim Picture of Day's Terror," by Eric Schmitt and Eric Lichtblau, *New York Times*; June 18, 2004; p. A1; and "9/11 Report Cites Lack of Preparation," by Dan Eggen, *Washington Post*; June 18, 2004; p. A1.

[8] Public Law 107-40, §§1-2, 115 Stat. 224 (2001).

[9] See: *The 9/11 Commission Report* (July 2004); also see: "Bush defends Assertions of Iraq-Al Qaeda Relationship," by Dana Milbank, *Washington Post*; June 18, 2004; p. A9; and "9/11 Report Is Said to Dismiss Iraq-Qaeda Alliance," by Philip Shenon, *New York Times*; July 12, 2004; p. A1.

CHAPTER 2/ DRAFTED UNDER A CLOAK OF SECRECY

[1] *Pro Milone*, by Marcus T. Cicero, Sect. 11, 52 B.C.E.

[2] Quoted in "After: How America Confronted the September 12 Era," by Steven Brill, *Newsweek*; March 10, 2003; p. 66.

[3] See: http://www.lifeandliberty.gov. If we believe the department's official statement, we can only conclude that secondary, less important, responsibilities include investigation and prosecution for racketeering, public corruption, mail fraud, discrimination, and antitrust violations. Further, Justice's mission statement appears to mute the primary function of the Department of Homeland Security.

[4] *The 9/11 Commission Report: Final Report of the National Commission on Terrorist Attacks Upon the United States*, p. 328.

[5] The Act is identified as P.L. 107-056, 115 STAT. 272. [http://frwebgate.access.gpo.gov/cgibin/getdoc.cgi?dbname=107_cong_public_laws&docid=f:publ056.107.pdf.][http://www.eff.org/Privacy/Surveillance/Terrorism/20011025_hr3162_usa_patriot_bill.html][http://www.wpic.org/privacy/terrorism/hr3162.htm]

[6] 50 U.S.C. § 1801

[7] "Hatch Alarms Right Over Anti-Terror Act," *Salt Lake Tribune*; September 15, 2003; p. A1.

[8] Quoted in "GOP Using 9/11 Photographs for Political Gain," by Andrew Miga, *Boston Herald*; May 15, 2002; p. 7.

[9] Quoted in "John Ashcroft's PATRIOT GAMES," by Judy Bachrach, *Vanity Fair*; February 2004; p. 108.

[10] "Congress Should Scrap Flawed Legislation," by Rep. Lynn Woosley, *Roll Call*; March 29, 2004; p. B13.

[11] Quoted in "Terrorizing the Bill of Rights," by Nat Hentoff, *The Village Voice*; November 9, 2001; p. 32 [http://www.villagevoice.com/issues/1046/hentoff.php]

[12] The House bill is available at: http://www.house.gov/judiciary/107-236p1.pdf. Also see: "Congress, Negotiators Back Scaled-Down Bill to Battle Terror," by Neil A. Lewis and Robert Pear, *New York Times*; October 2, 2001; p. A1; "Terror Laws Near Votes in House and Senate," by Neil A. Lewis and Robert Pear, *New York Times*; October 3, 2001; p. B8; and "House Passes Terrorism Bill Much Like Senate's, but With 5-Year Limit," by Robin Toner

and Neil A. Lewis; *New York Times*; October 13, 2001; p. B6. A good overview of the process to get the PATRIOT Act approved is Steven Brill's 2,700-word article, "After: How America Confronted the September 12 Era," in *Newsweek*; March 10, 2003; pp. 66+.

[13] "Terrorizing the Bill of Rights," *op. cit.*

[14] Quoted in "Security Collides with Civil Liberties: Debate Intensifies Over War on Terror," by Sam Stanton and Emily Bazar, *Sacramento Bee*; September 21, 2003 p. A1.

[15] Robert C. Byrd, *Losing America: Confronting a Reckless and Arrogant Presidency.*

[16] Orrin Hatch, *Confessions of a Citizen Senator* (2002), p. 95.

[17] "President Signs Anti-Terrorism Bill," White House news release/transcript; October 26, 2001. [http://www.whitehouse.gov/news/releases/2001/10/200110265. html]. The transcript is also available through the Government Printing Office. [http://frwebgate.access.gpo.gov/cgibin/getdoc.cgi?dbname=2001_presidential_documents&docid=pd29oc01_txt-26]

[18] Earl Blumenauer, *Congressional Record*; October 24, 2001; p. E1922. [http://frwebgate.access.gpo.gov/cgibin/getpage.cgi?position=all&page=E1992&dbname=2001_record]

[19] Carolyn C. Kilpatrick, *Congressional Record*; October 25, 2001; p. E1929 . [http://frwebgate.access.gpo.gov/cgibin/getpage.cgi?position=all&page=E1929&dbname=2001_record]

[20] "Statement of U.S. Senator Russ Feingold," U.S. Senate; October 25, 2001. [http://feingold.senate.gov/~feingold/speeches/01/10/102501at. html]. Also available: "Why I Opposed the Anti-Terrorism Bill," by Senator Russ Feingold, *Counterpunch*; October 26, 2001. [http://www.counterpunch.org/feingold1.html]

[21] "Act Protects U.S. From Terrorism," by Sen. Lindsey Graham, *Roll Call*; March 29, 2004; p. B12.

[22] Testimony, Robert J. Cleary, "America After 9/11: Freedom Preserved or Freedom Lost?" U.S. Senate Committee on the Judiciary; November 18, 2003.

[23] *Ibid.*

[24] See: "Report Scolds Terrorism Prosecutors; U.S. to Drop Convictions Against Trio in Detroit," by Dan Eggen, *Washington Post*; September 2, 2004; p. A3; "Justice Dept. Seeks End to Its Detroit Terror Case," by Danny Hakim, *New York Times*; September 2, 2004; p. A14; "Experts: Terrorism Trial Full of Errors," by David Ashenfelter, *Detroit Free Press*; September 2, 2004; p. B1; and "Judge Reverses Convictions in Detroit Terrorism Case," by Danny Hakim, *New York Times*; September 3, 2004; p. A12.

[25] Several national organizations have written major analyses of the USA PATRIOT Act. Three of the better overviews are "The USA PATRIOT Act: What's So Patriotic About Trampling on the Bill of Rights?" by Nancy Chang, senior litigation attorney for the Center for Constitutional Rights, November 2001. [http://www.ccr-ny.org/v2/reports/docs/USA_PATRIOT_ACT.pdf]; "Summary of Recent Court Rulings on Terrorism-Related Matters Having Civil Liberties Implications," by Nancy Chang of CCR and Alan Kabat of the law firm Bernabei & Katz, Center for Constitutional Rights; February 4, 2004. [http://www.ccrny.org/v2/reports/report.asp?ObjID=n7yKoAObvc&Content=324]; also see: *Unpatriotic Acts: The FBI's Power to Rifle Through Your Records and Personal Belongings Without Telling You*, by Ann Beeson and Jameel Jaffer, American Civil Liberties Union (Washington, D.C.), July 2003. [http://aclu.org/safeandfree/safeandfree.cfm?ID=13246&c=206%E2%80%9D].

[26] Quoted in "Mr. Ashcroft's Smear," editorial, *Washington Post*; April 20, 2004; p. A18. Also see: "Statement of Robert S. Mueller II, director, FBI, before the National Commission on Terrorist Attacks Upon the United States; April 14, 2004. [http://www.fbi.gov/congress/congress04/mueller041404.htm].

[27] "Domestic Intelligence and Civil Liberties," by Kate Martin, *SAIS Review*, Winter-Spring 2004, pp. 8-9.

[28] "The Truth About the 'Wall'," by Jamie S. Gorelick, *Washington Post*; April 18, 2004; p. B7.

[29] *Ibid.*

[30] See: http://www.usdoj.gov/ag/testimony/supplementarymaterial.pdf

[31] "Old Barriers to Fighting Terror," by Viveca Novak, *TIME* web edition; May 1, 2004. [http://www.time.com/time/nation/article/0,8599,631958,00.html].

[32] The PATRIOT Act increased the number of judges from seven to eleven.

[33] Remarks of Rep. Jerrold Nadler (D-N.Y.), *Congressional Record*; October 12, 2001; p. H6764.

[34] *In re All Matters Submitted to the Foreign Intelligence Surveillance Court*, 218 F. Supp. 2nd 611. Also see: "Secret Court Says F.B.I. Aides Misled Judges in 75 Cases," by Philip Shenon; *New York Times*; August 23, 2002; p. A1; and "Congress Criticizes F.B.I. and Justice Department Over Actions Before Secret Wiretap Court," by Philip Shenon; *New York Times*; September 11, 2002; p. A18.

[35] See 18 U.S.C. § 2518(11)(b) and 50 U.S.C. § 1801-1811.

[36] "Domestic Intelligence and Civil Liberties, *op. cit.*, p. 14.

[37] "Ten Myths About the USA PATRIOT Act," by Mary Beth Buchanan, U.S. attorney, Western District of Pennsylvania, May 2003, p. 7.

[38] "The USA Patriot Act: What's So Patriotic About Trampling on the Bill of Rights?" by Nancy Chang, senior litigation attorney for the Center for Constitutional Rights, November 2001. [http://www.ccr-ny.org/v2/reports/docs/USA_PATRIOT_ACT.pdf]

[39] *Electronic Privacy Information Center v. Department of Justice, U.S. District Court for the District of Columbia*, CV 00-1849 (JR), order for compliance filed March 25, 2002.

[40] "Internal Memo Calls Over-Collection of Data Part of 'Pattern' Showing 'Inability of the FBI to Manage' Foreign Intelligence Wiretaps," Electronic Privacy Information Center, with supporting documents; May 28, 2002.

[41] "In the Matter of The United States Department of Justice, Federal Bureau of Information and Drug Enforcement Administration, Joint Petition for Rulemaking to Resolve Various Outstanding Issues Concerning the Implementation of the Communications Assistance for Law Enforcement Act," filed with the Federal Communications Commission; March 10, 2004.

[42] "Keep Big Brother's Hands Off the Internet," by Senator John Ashcroft, *USIA Electronic Journal*; October 1997. [http://usinfo.state.gov/journals/itgic/1097/ijge/gj-7.htm],

[43] Quoted in "Arcada: The Defiant Town Ordinance Penalizes Officials Who Cooperate With PATRIOT Act, But Law May Not Stand Up in Court," by Kevin Fagan, *San Francisco Chronicle*; April 13, 2003; p. 1.

[44] Quoted in "Official Counters PATRIOT Act Critics," by Diana Graettinger, *Bangor* (Maine) *Daily News*; April 4, 2003; p. 1.

[45] Quoted in "Libraries Post PATRIOT Act Warnings: Santa Cruz Branches Tell Patrons That FBI May Spy on Them," by Bob Egelko and Maria Alicia Gaura, *San Francisco Chronicle*; March 10, 2003; p. 1.

[46] "Seeking Truth From Justice," *op. cit.*, pp. 3–4.

[47] Testimony of John Ashcroft before the House Judiciary Committee; June 5, 2003. [http://www.house.gov/judiciary/fulltrans060503.htm].

[48] Quoted in "Mayfield Recalls 'Dark Nights' as FBI Witness," by Noelle Crombie, *The Oregonian*; June 26, 2004; p. C1. Also see: "Madrid Case Leads to Lawyer in Oregon," by Noelle Crombie and Mark Larabee, *The Oregonian*; May 7, 2004; p. A1; "Oregon Attorney Arrested Over Possible Tie to Spain Bombings," by Richard B. Schmitt, *Los Angeles Times*; May 7, 2004; p. A1; "American Held in Madrid Bombings," by Susan Schmidt, *Washington Post*; May 7, 2004; p. A1.; "Brandon Mayfield's Family Waits for Answers," by Rukmini Callimachi, Associated Press; May 16, 2004; "FBI Exonerates Ore. Attorney," by Thomas

Alex Tizon and Richard B. Schmitt, *Los Angeles Times*; May 25, 2004; p. A20; "A Fuzzy Fingerprint Leaves a Lasting Mark," by Thomas Alex Tizon, *Los Angeles Times*; May 29, 2004; p. A1; "Sloppy FBI Investigation Merits More than an Apology," editorial, *News & Record* (Greenville, S.C.); May 31, 2004; p. A10; and "Sensing the Eyes of Big Brother, and Pushing Back," by Timothy Egan, *New York Times*; August 8, 2004; p. A20.

[49] "Report to Congress on Implementation of Section 1001 of the USA PATRIOT Act," U.S. Department of Justice, Office of the Inspector General; September 13, 2004.

[50] *North Jersey Media Group v. Ashcroft*, U.S. District Court for the District of New Jersey, 205 F. Supp. 2nd 288, filed May 28, 2002. [Also 123 S.Ct. 2215 (2003)]

[51] "Dispelling the Myths," Department of Justice.
[http://www.lifeandliberty.gov/subs/u_myths.htm].

[52] "Setting the Record Straight: An Analysis of the Justice Department's PATRIOT Act Website," Center for Democracy & Technology; October 27, 2003.
[http://www.cdt.org/security/usapatriot/031027cdt.shtml].

[53] Bob Barr, testimony before the U.S. Senate Committee on the Judiciary, "America after 9/11: Freedom Preserved or Freedom Lost?"; November 18, 2003.
[http://judiciary.senate.gov/print_testimony.cfm?id=998&wit_id=2874].

[54] Oversight Hearing, House of Representatives Committee on the Judiciary, June 5, 2003.
[http://www.house.gov/judiciary /fulltrans060503.htm]

[55] "ACLU Discloses Documents in Extraordinary Sealed Challenge to Patriot Act Spying Power," news release, ACLU; April 28, 2004.

[56] *[Redacted] and American Civil Liberties Union v. John Ashcroft, Robert Mueller, and Marion E. Bowman*, civil suit Complaint for Declaratory and Injunctive Relief, U.S. District Court for the Southern District of New York; filed April 6, 2004, case 04–2614 (VM). Sealed. Redacted version released on April 28, 2004.

[57] "ACLU Discloses Documents in Extraordinary Sealed Challenge to Patriot Act Spying Power," *op. cit.*

[58] *Ibid.*

[59] Doe v. Ashcroft, U.S. District Court for the Southern District of New York, ruling by Judge Victor Marrero; September 29, 2004.
[http://www.nysd.uscourts.gov/rulings/04CV2614_Opinion_092904.pdf].

[60] *Ibid.*

[61] Quoted in "Several in Sun Cities Say PATRIOT Act Goes Too Far," by Erin Reep, Arizona *Daily News-Sun*; July 26, 2003; part II, pp. A1, A5. [Part I, "PATRIOT Act: Scholars Warn of Loss of Liberties," ran on July 25, 2003; pp. A1 and A5.]

[62] *Ibid.*

[63] CNN transcript 091000CN.V22

[64] Quoted in "Alaska Passes Anti-Patriot Resolution," ABC-TV News; May 23, 2003.
[http://abcnews.go.com/sections/us/DailyNews/Alaska_patriot030523.html].

[65] "Freedom and Security," *op. cit.*

CHAPTER 3 / 'A MONSTROUS FAILURE OF JUSTICE'

[1] "Even a 'Bad Man' Has Rights," by Gary Solis, *Washington Post*; June 25, 2002; p. A19.

[2] "SCV Newsmaker of the Week," by Leon Worden, *Santa Clarita* (Calif.), *Signal*; July 4, 2004; p. 13. [Worden's interview, broadcast on local cable television, is probably the most comprehensive media interview of Janis Karpinski.]
[http://scvhistory.com/scvhistory/signal/iraq/sg070404.htm].

[3] *Ibid.*

[4] See: *Youngstown Sheet & Tube Co., et al. v. Sawyer*, Supreme Court of the United States, 343 U.S. 579; 72 S. Ct. 863; opinion filed June 2, 1952.

[5] "Martial Justice, Full and Fair," by Alberto R. Gonzales, *New York Times*, November 30, 2001; p. A27.

[6] The Geneva Conventions are essentially the doctrine of four separate conventions in 1949, but based upon informal practices dating into the mid-nineteenth century, that relate to treatment of prisoners in war, civilians in occupied countries, and actions of the military. Two protocols, established in 1977, extended the Conventions to civil wars. Countries that signed onto these conventions, including the United States, agree to be bound by its rules. The International Committee of the Red Cross is entrusted with monitoring the Geneva Conventions and reporting abuses to the governments.

[7] *Charles Swift, as next best friend for Salim Ahmed Hamdan v. Donald H. Rumsfeld, et, al.* U.S. District Court for the Western District of Washington, CV04–0777L, filed April 6, 2004. The suit was a petition for a *writ of mandamus*, asking the federal court to order the Department of Defense to comply with federal and international law. In August, the court transferred jurisdiction to the U.S. District Court for the District of Columbia.

[8] *Ibid.*

[9] *Ibid.*

[10] *Ibid.*

[11] *Charles Swift, as next friend for Salim Ahmed Hamdan v. Donald H. Rumsfeld, et al.,* Order Granting Motion to Hold Petition in Abeyance, U.S. District Court for the Western District of Washington, filed May 11, 2004.

[12] Quoted by John Mintz, "Yemeni's Attorney Tries to Halt Tribunals," *Washington Post*, April 8, 2004; p. A15.

[13] See: *Coalition of Clergy, Lawyers, and Professors, et al. v. George Walker Bush, U.S. District Court for the Central District of California, CV 02–570 AHM, 189 F.Supp.2nd 1036,* decided February 21, 2002; *Coalition of Clergy, et al. v. Bush,* U.S. Court of Appeals for the Ninth Circuit, 310 F.3rd 1153, filed November 18, 2002; and *Shafiq Rasul, et al. v. George Walker Bush. U.S. District Court for the District of Columbia, 215 F. Supp. 2nd 55; filed July 30, 2002.*

[14] *Gherebi v. Bush, Rumsfeld,* 352 F.3rd 1278, no. 03-55785 U. S. Court of Appeals for the Ninth Circuit, majority opinion filed by Judge Stephen Reinhardt, filed December 18, 2003.

[15] *Al Odah v. United States,* 321 F. 3rd 1134, U.S. Court of Appeals for the District of Columbia Circuit (2003).

[16] *Brief of Amicus Curiae in Support of petitioners al Odah v. United States, Rasul v. Bush, Hamdi v. Rumsfeld.*

[17] *Shafiq Rasul, et al. v. George W. Bush, et al.,* 03–334; *Fawzi Khalid Abdullah Fahad al Odah, et al. v. United States, et al.,* 03-343, argued April 20, 2004.

[18] Quoted in "High Court Hears Detention Cases," by Charles Lane, *Washington Post*, April 21, 2004; p. A3.

[19] Quoted in "Justices Hear Challenge to War Detentions at Guantánamo," *New York Times*, April 20, 2004; p. A1.

[20] Quoted in "High Court Hears Detention Cases," *op. cit.*

[21] Quoted in "Justices Hear Challenge to War Detentions at Guantánamo," *op. cit.*

[22] *Shafiq Rasul, et al. v. George W. Bush,* Supreme Court of the United States, 03-334; and *Fawzi Khalid Abdullah Fahad Al Odah, et al. v. United States, et al.,* Supreme Court of the United States, 03-343; 542 U.S. (2004).

[23] *United States ex rel. Mezei,* 345 U.S. 206, 218-219 (1953), dissent of Justice Robert Jackson.

[24] "CCR Wins Major Victory for the Rule of Law in Guantanamo Bay," news release, Center for Constitutional Rights; June 29, 2004.

[1] Quoted in "Former Antiterror Advisor Says Bush Ignored 9/11 Warnings," CNN; March 23, 2004. [http://www.cnn.com/2004/ALLPOLITICS/03/22/Clarke.bush/index.html]; "Clarke: White House is Papering Over Facts," interview with Bill Hemmer, CNN; March 23, 2004. [http://www.cnn.com/2004/ALLPOLITICS/03/22/Clarke/index.html]; "Clarke: Bush Didn't See Terrorism as 'Urgent'," CNN; March 25, 2004. [http://www.cnn.com/2004/allpolitics/03/24/911.commission] and "Bush Administration Rejects Clarke Charges," CNN; March 23, 2004. [http://www.CNN.com/2004/allpolitics/03/22/bush.clarke/index/html]

[2] See: "The Times and Iraq," statement from the editors, *New York Times*; May 26, 2004; p. A10; "Weapons of Mass Destruction? Or Mass Distraction?" by Daniel Okrent, *New York Times*; May 30, 2004; and "The Post on WMDs: An Inside Story," by Howard Kurtz, *Washington Post*, August 12, 2004; p. A1.

[3] "The Path to War," by Bryan Burrough, Evgenia Peretz, David Rose, and David Wise, *Vanity Fair*, May 2004; p. 294. Also see: *Hoodwinked: The Documents That Reveal How Bush Sold Us a War*, by John Prados (New Press, 2004).

[4] "White House Officials Went After Me and My Wife, a CIA Operative, After I Questioned Their Claim That Saddam Was Pursuing Nuclear Weapons. Here's How They Did It, and Why It Was So Important to Them," by Joseph C. Wilson IV, *San Jose Mercury News*; May 2, 2004; p. 1P. Also see: *The Politics of Truth: Inside the Lies that Led to War and Betrayed My Wife's CIA Identity: A Diplomat's Memoir*, by Joseph C. Wilson (2004.)

[5] Memorandum, Alberto Gonzales to George W. Bush; January 25, 2002.

[6] "With 'All Necessary and Appropriate Force'; In Interrogations, U.S. Actions Align With Treaties and Congress' Wishes," Op-Ed commentary, by John C. Yoo, *Los Angeles Times*; June 11, 2004; p. B13.

[7] "U.S. Said to Overstate Value of Guantanamo Detainees," by Tim Golden and Don Van Natta Jr., *New York Times*; June 21, 2004; p. A1.

[8] *Ibid.*

[9] Quoted in "Chain of Command: How Department of Defense Mishandled the Disaster at Abu Ghraib," by Seymour Hersh, *New Yorker*, May 17, 2004; p. 41.

[10] Quoted in "USA: Pattern of Brutality and Cruelty," news release, Amnesty International; May 7, 2004.

[11] News briefing, Donald Rumsfeld; January 22, 2002. [http://www.defenselink.mil/news/Jan2002/t01222002_t0122sd.html].

[12] "Join Task Force Guantanamo," U.S. Department of Defense. [http://www.nsgtmo.Navy.mil/jtfgtmo/mission.html].

[13] Quoted in "U.S. Pledges to Avoid Torture," by Peter Slevin, *Washington Post*; June 27, 2003; p. A11.

[14] Quoted in "Top UK Judge Slams Camp Delta," BBC News; November 26, 2003 [http://news.bbc.co.uk/2/hi/uk_news/politics/3238624.stm].

[15] *Ibid.*

[16] "United States: ICRC President Urges Progress on Detention-Related Issues," news release, International Committee of the Red Cross; January 16, 2004.

[17] "A Look Behind the 'Wire' at Guantanamo," by Scott Higham, *Washington Post*; June 13, 2004; p. A1.

[18] "Britain Frees 5 Citizens Sent Home From U.S. Jail," Reuters; March 11, 2004.

[19] Quoted in "British Police Release all Guantanamo Returnees," by Peter Kononczuk, Agence France Presse; March 11, 2004.

[20] Quoted in "US Abuse Could Be War Crime," by Vikram Dodd and Tania Branigan, *The Guardian* (Manchester, England); August 5, 2004.

[21] See: "U.S. Hands Over First French Terror Suspects at Guantanamo," by Piere-Antoine Souchard, Associated Press; July 27, 2004; and "4 Detainees Are Returned to France After 2 Years at Guantánamo," by Elaine Sciolino, *New York Times*; July 28, 2004; p. A5.

[22] "U.S. Said to Overstate Value of Guantanamo Detainees," *op. cit.*

[23] *"Enduring Freedom": Abuses by U.S. Forces in Afghanistan*, Human Rights Watch, March 2004.

[24] "Prisoners Released From Bagram Forced to Strip Naked, Deprived of Sleep, Ordered to Stand for Hours," by Kathy Gannon, Associated Press, March 14, 2003.

[25] Quoted in "Red Cross: Iraqi Abuse Widespread and Routine, Most Detained by Mistake," by Alexander G. Higgins, Associated Press; May 10, 2004.

[26] "Army Investigates Wider Iraq Offenses," by Bradley Graham, *Washington Post*, June 1, 2004; p. A1.

[27] "Red Cross: Iraqi Abuse Widespread and Routine, Most Detained by Mistake," *op. cit.*

[28] "What Is the IRC's Position on the Reported Abuse of Iraqi Prisoners by US and UK Forces," information fact sheet; May 6, 2004.
[http://www.icrc.org/Web/eng/siteeng0.nsf/iwpList74/40A0CDE4C698440BC1256E8A004B42AA].

[29] "Red Cross Cited Detainee Abuse Over a Year Ago," by David S. Cloud, *Wall Street Journal*; May 10, 2004; p. A1.

[30] Brig. Gen. Janis Karpinski, quoted in "Officer Says Army Tried to Curb Red Cross Visits to Prison in Iraq," by Douglas Jehl and Eric Schmitt, *New York Times*; May 19, 2004; p. A1.

[31] Quoted in "Rumsfeld Issues an Order to Hide Detainee in Iraq," by Eric Schmitt and Thom Shanker, *New York Times*; June 17, 2004; and "Officer Says Army Tried to Curb Red Cross Visits to Prison in Iraq," *op. cit.*

[32] "SCV Newsmaker of the Week," *op. cit.*, p. 30.

[33] "Red Cross Fears US Is Hiding Suspects," by Naomi Koppel, Associated Press; July 13, 2004.

[34] "Army Says C.I.A. His More Iraqis Than It Claimed," by Eric Schmitt and Douglas Jehl, *New York Times*; September 10, 2004; p. A1.

[35] "Memo Lets CIA Take Detainnees Out of Iraq," by Dana Priest, *Washington Post*; October 24, 2004; p. A1.

[36] "Red Cross Cited Detainee Abuse Over a Year Ago," *op. cit.*

[37] *Ibid.*

[38] Quoted in "With Iraq Strategy Under Fire, Bush Faces Some Stark Choices," by Carla Anne Robbins, Jackie Calmes, and Greg Jaffe, *Wall Street Journal*; May 7, 2004; p. A1; and in "Red Cross Cited Detainee Abuse Over a Year Ago," *op. cit.*

[39] Statement of Pierre Kraehenbuehl, operations director, International Committee of the Red Cross; May 7, 2004.

[40] "An open letter to President George W. Bush on the question of torture and cruel, inhuman or degrading treatment," letter from Irene Kahn, Amnesty International, to President George W. Bush; April 7, 2004.
[http://news.amnesty.org/library/print/ENGAMR510752004].
[The letter is at: http://web.amnesty.org/library/Index/ENGAMR510532002].

[41] Quoted in "Their Pleas Ignored; Human Rights Monitors Say That for Nearly a Year They Have Pressed Coalition to Investigate Reports of Abuse," by James Rupert, *Newsday*; May 8, 2004; p. A5.

[42] "Pentagon Was Warned of Abuse Months Ago; U.S. Officials, Rights Groups Sought Changes," by Peter Slevin and Robin Wright, *Washington Post*; May 8, 2004; p. A12.

[43] "Bush Privately Chides Rumsfeld," by Robin Wright and Bradley Graham, *Washington Post*; May 6, 2004; p. A1.

[44] "Red Cross Cited Detainee Abuse Over a Year Ago," *op. cit.*

[45] "The Gray Zone," by Seymour Hersh, *The New Yorker*, May 24, 2004; p. 42

[46] "SCV Newsmaker of the Week," *op. cit.*, p. 24

[47] More than 6,000 pages of documents, interviews, and investigations made up the bulk of that report.

[48] The final report was April 4, 2004.

[49] Quoted in "Torture at Abu Ghraib," by Seymour M. Hersh, *The New Yorker*, May 10, 2004; p. 43.

[50] *Ibid.* The report was subsequently published on the website of the *Army Times*, an influential but civilian-run publication. Specific instances of abuse are documented at pp. 16–17 and annexes 25, 26, and 53 of "Article 15–6 Investigation of the 800th Military Police Brigade," prepared by Maj. Gen. Antonio Taguba.
See: http://www.armytimes.com/content/editorial/pdf/050604dodprisonabusereport.pdf

[51] Statement, U.S. Department of the Army; May 21, 2004.

[52] "Pentagon Approved Tougher Interrogations," by Dana Priest and Joe Stephens, *Washington Post*; May 9, 2004; p. A1.

[53] "Brutal Interrogation in Iraq; Five Detainees' Deaths Probed," by Miles Moffeit, *Denver Post*; May 19, 2004; p. A1; and "Skipped Autopsies in Iraq," by Miles Moffeit, *Denver Post*; May 21, 2004; p. A1.

[54] "Soldiers Charged in Drowning," by Thomas E. Ricks, *Washington Post*; July 3, 2004; p. A1.

[55] "Fort Carson Soldiers Charged," by Miles Moffeit and Eileen Kelley, *Denver Post*; July 2, 2004; p. A1.

[56] See: "Commanders get Immunity in Case of Iraqi Civilians Forced to Jump Off Bridge," by Robert Weller, Associated Press; July 30, 2004; "Hearing for Tree GIs Ends," by Arthur Kane and Eileen Kelley, *Denver Post*; August 1, 2004; p. C5; and "Officers Urged Lies in Abuse of Iraqis," *Los Angeles Times*; July 31, 2004; p. A17.

[57] Quoted in "Soldier: Unit's Role Was to Break Down Prisoners," by Jackie Spinner, *Washington Post*; May 8, 2004; p. A1.

[58] "Soldier: Unit's Role Was to Break Down Prisoners," *op. cit.*

[59] Quoted in "In Abuse, a Portrayal of Ill-Prepared, Overwhelmed G.I.'s," by Douglas Jehl and Eric Schmitt, *New York Times*; May 9, 2004; p. A1.

[60] Quoted in "Prison Visits by General Reported in Hearing," by Scott Higham, Joe Stephens, and Josh White, *Washington Post*; May 23, 2004; p. A1.

[61] Quoted in "Torture at Abu Ghraib, *op. cit.*, p. 44.

[62] "Pentagon Probes Why Photos Were Ever Taken," by Christopher Cooper, *Wall Street Journal*; May 7, 2004; p. A8.

[63] Quoted in "New Details of Prison Abuse Emerge," by Scott Higham and Joe Stephens, *Washington Post*; May 21, 2004; p. A1.

[64] *Ibid.*

[65] "Article 15–6 Investigation of the 800th Military Police Brigade," *op. cit.*; and "The Struggle for Iraq: Prisoners; Command Errors Aided Iraq Abuse, Army Has Found," by James Risen; *New York Times;* May 3, 2004; p. A1.

[66] *Ibid.*

[67] "Article 15-6 Investigation of the 800th Military Police Brigade." *op. cit.*; also see: "Punishment and Abuse," by Scott Higham and Joe Stephens, *Washington Post*; May 22, 2004; p. A1.

[68] "General Granted Latitude at Prison," by R. Jeffrey Smith and Josh White, *Washington Post*; June 12, 2004; p. A1.

[69] "Scant Evidence Cited in Long Detention of Iraqis," by Douglas Jehl and Kate Zernike, *New York Times*; May 30, 2004; p. A1.

[70] "Army's Report Faults General in Prison Abuse," by Douglas Jehl and Eric Schmitt, *New York Times*; August 27, 2004; p. A1.

[71] "Iraq Abuse 'Ordered From the Top'," BBC News; June 15, 2004.

[72] "Enemy Prisoners of War, Retained Personnel, Civilian Internees and Other Detainees," Army regulation 190–8; October 1, 1997; Chapter 2–1(d). [Also: OPNAVINST 3461.6 (Navy), AFJI 31–304 (Air Force), MCO 3461.1 (Marine Corps)]

[73] *Ibid.*

[74] "SCV Newsmaker of the Week," *op. cit.*, pp. 11–12.

[75] See: *Detainee Operations Inspection* report, Department of the Army, Office of the Inspector General; July 21, 2004. However, unlike the Taguba report, the Mikolashek report did not conclude there was a "systemic" failure in the command structure, but the prisoner abuse was isolated and conducted by "unauthorized actions taken by a few individuals." Mikolashek's report brought condemnation from several members of Congress who believed he, and the Army, were trying to "whitewash" the problem. His report's major conclusion was also in conflict with reports from the International Committee of the Red Cross.

[76] "Abu Ghraib: Its Legacy for Military Medicine," by Steven H. Miles, *Lancet*, August 21, 2004; p. 725+.

[77] Quoted in "Prison Visits by General Reported in Hearing," *op. cit.*

[78] *Ibid.*

[79] Quoted in "Perspectives," *Newsweek*, June 28, 2004; p. 21.

[80] "Pentagon Approved Tougher Interrogations," *op. cit.*

[81] "Article 15-6 Investigation of the 800th Military Police Brigade," *op. cit.*

[82] Quoted in "Article 15-6 Investigation of the 800th Military Police Brigade," *op. cit.*; and "Chain of Command: How the Department of Defense Mishandled the Disaster at Abu Ghraib," *op. cit.*, pp. 38–39.

[83] See: "Use of Dogs to Scare Prisoners Was Authorized," by Josh White and Scott Higham, *Washington Post*, June 11, 2004; p. A1.

[84] "General Granted Latitude at Prison," *op. cit.*

[85] "Use of Dogs to Scare Prisoners Was Authorized," *op. cit.* "Army's Report Faults General in Prison Abuse," *op. cit.*

[86] "Chain of Command: How the Department of Defense Mishandled the Disaster at Abu Ghraib," *op. cit.*, p. 39.

[87] "Lawyers Decided Bans on Torture Didn't Bind Bush," by Neil A. Lewis and Eric Schmitt, *New York Times*, June 8, 2004; p. A1.

[88] "Standards of Conduct for Interrogation under 18 U.S.C. §§ 2340–2304A," memorandum for Alberto R. Gonzales, counsel to the president; August 1, 2002; p. 1. Also see: "Memo Offered Justification for Use of Torture," by Dana Priest and R. Jeffrey Smith, *Washington Post*, June 8, 2004; p. A1.

[89] "Standards of Conduct for Interrogation under 18 U.S.C. §§ 2340–2304A," *op. cit.*, p. 13.

[90] See: Standards of Conduct for Interrogation under 18 U.S.C. §§ 2340–2304A," *op. cit.*, pp. 31–35.

[91] See: Standards of Conduct for Interrogation under 18 U.S.C. §§ 2340-2304A," *op. cit.*, pp. 39–41.

[92] "Pentagon Report Set Framework for Use of Torture; Security or Legal Factors Could Trump Restrictions, Memo to Rumsfeld Argued," by Jess Bravin, *Wall Street Journal*, June 7, 2004; p. A1.

[93] "Lawyers Decided Bans on Torture Didn't Bind Bush," by Neil A. Lewis and Eric Schmitt, *New York Times*, June 8, 2004.

[94] "Memo Offered Justification for Use of Torture," *op. cit.*

[95] "Lawyers Decided Bans on Torture Didn't Bind Bush," *op. cit.*

[96] Quoted in "U.S. Missed Chances to Stop Prison Abuse," by Dave Moniz, *USA Today*, May 14, 2004; p. 4A.

[97] Quoted in "The Gray Zone," *op. cit.*, p. 42.

[98] Quoted in "Rumsfeld Defends Rules for Prison," by Dana Priest and Dan Morgan, *Washington Post*, May 13, 2004; p. A1.

[99] "U.S. Missed Chances to Stop Prison Abuse," op. cit.

[100] *Ibid.*

[101] Quoted in "Administration Lawyers Concluded President Has Legal Authority to Order Torture," by John J. Lumpkin, Associated Press; June 8, 2004.

[102] "White House Says Prisoner Policy Set Humane Tone," by Richard W. Stevenson, Associated Press; June 23, 2004.

[103] "SCV Newsmaker of the Week," *op. cit.*, p. 33.

[104] Testimony, Donald Rumsfeld, *op. cit.*

[105] *Ibid.*

[106] See: "Chain of Command: How the Department of Defense Mishandled the Disaster at Abu Ghraib," *op. cit.*

[107] "SCV Newsmaker of the Week," *op. cit.*, p. 9.

[108] Quoted in "In Abuse, a Portrayal of Ill-Prepared, Overwhelmed G.I.'s," *op. cit.*

[109] *Ibid.*

[110] Geneva Convention for the Amelioration of the Condition of the Wounded and Sick in Armed Forces in the Field, 75 U.N.T.S. 31; October 21, 1950. Chapter 1, article 3.

[111] "Abuse of Iraqi POWS by GIs Probed," CBS News; April 29, 2004. (Report broadcast April 28, 2004.) [http://www.cbsnews.com/stories/2004/04/27/60II/main614063.shtml].

[112] "Soldier: Unit's Role Was to Break Down Prisoners," *op. cit.*

[113] "SCV Newsmaker of the Week," *op. cit.*, p. 14.

[114] *Detainee Operations Inspection* report, *op. cit.*

[115] See: "Rough Justice in Iraq," by Rod Nordland and John Barry, *Newsweek*; May 10, 2004; p. 28; and "SCV Newsmaker of the Week," *op. cit.*

[116] Statement of Sgt. Javal S. Davis, as quoted in "Punishment and Abuse," *op. cit.*

[117] "Abuse of Iraqi POWS by GIs Probed," *op. cit.*

[118] "Torture at Abu Ghraib," *op. cit.*, p. 44.

[119] Statement, Rep. Gene Taylor, before the Senate and House Armed Forces Committees; May 7, 2004.

[120] Quoted in "Officials Grapple With How and When to Release Images," by Thom Shanker, *New York Times*; May 10, 2004; p. A1.

[121] Testimony, Donald Rumsfeld, Senate Armed Forces Committee; May 7, 2004.

[122] "Homesick for Texas," by Daniel Klaidman, *Newsweek*; July 12, 2004; p. 32.

[123] "The Rule of Law and the Rules of War," by Alberto R. Gonzales, *New York Times*; May 15, 2004; p. A17.

[124] President Bush, Jordanian King Discuss Iraq, Middle East," news release, The White House; May 6, 2004. [http://www.whitehouse.gov/news/releases/2004/05/20040506-9.html].

[125] See: "Bush Privately Chides Rumsfeld," *op. cit.*

[126] Statement, Donald Rumsfeld, before the Senate and House Armed Forces Committees; May 7, 2004. [http://armed-services.senate.gov/statemnt/2004/May/Rumsfeld.pdf].

[127] *Ibid.*

[128] Sen. Lindsey O. Clark, comments on "Meet the Press," NBC-TV; May 9, 2004. [http://www.msnbc.msn.com/id/4938258/]

[129] "President Outlines Steps to Help Iraq Achieve Democracy and Freedom: Remarks by the President on Iraq and the War on Terror," speech at Army War College (Carlisle, Pa.); May 24, 2004.

[130] "Abuse of Captives More Widespread, Says Army Survey," by Douglas Jehl, Steven Lee Myers, and Eric Schmitt, *New York Times*; May 26, 2004; p. A1.

[131] "The Gray Zone," *op. cit.*, p. 38.

[132] *Ibid.*

[133] See: "Pentagon Denies Secret Interrogation Deal," by Lisa Miller, Reuters; May 17, 2004; and "Pentagon Seeks to Quash Rumsfeld Report," by Jim Wolf, Reuters; May 17, 2004.

[134] See: "Warner Bucks GOP Right on Probe of Prison Abuse," by Helen Dewar and Spencer S. Hsu, *Washington Post*; May 28, 2004; p. A1.

[135] Quoted in "Bush Lauds Rumsfeld for Doing 'Superb Job'," by Mike Allen and Bradley Graham, *Washington Post*, May 11, 2004; p. A15.

[136] Quoted in "Bush Sorry for Abuse of Iraqi Prisoners, but Backs Rumsfeld," by Elisabeth Bumiller and Eric Schmitt, *New York Times*, May 6, 2004; p. A1.

[137] Quoted in "Leadership Failure Is Blamed in Abuse," by Bradley Graham and Thomas E. Ricks, *Washington Post*, May 12, 2004; p. A1.

[138] "A Failure of Leadership at the Highest Levels," editorial, *Army Times*, May 17, 2004.

[139] Letter from Kenneth Roth to Donald Rumsfeld on mistreatment of prisoners; May 6, 2004. [http://hrw.org/english/docs/2004/05/06/usint8548.htm].

[140] "All Red Cross Reports Now to Go Through Miller," by Kathleen T. Rhem, American Forces Press Service [Department of Defense]; May 20, 2004.

[141] "Torture at Abu Ghraib," *op. cit.*

[142] "Red Cross: Iraqi Abuse Widespread and Routine, Most Detained by Mistake," *op. cit.*

[143] Report of Army Provost Marshal Maj. Gen. Donald J. Ryder, in "Scant Evidence Cited in Long Detention of Iraqis," by Douglas Jehl and Kate Zernike, *New York Times*, May 30, 2004; p. A1.

[144] See: "Prison Interrogations in Iraq Seen as Yielding Little Data on Rebels," by Douglas Jehl and Eric Schmitt, *New York Times*, May 26, 2004; p. A1.

[145] Quoted in "Congress Disputes Bush Pledge," by Jonathan Weisman, *Washington Post*, May 26, 2004; p. A17.

[146] "Military Judge Declares Abu Ghraib Prison a Crime Scene and Orders It Not to Be Destroyed," by Fisnik Abrashi and Jim Krane, Associated Press; June 21, 2004.

[147] "A Failure in Leadership, All the Way Up the Ranks," by Bradley Graham, *Washington Post*, August 26, 2004; p. A1.

[148] Quoted in "A Trail of 'Major Failures' Leads to Defense Secretary's Office," by Douglas Jehl, *New York Times*, August 25, 2004; p. A1.

[149] Quoted in "Abuses at Prison Tied to Officers in Intelligence," by Eric Schmitt, *New York Times*, August 26, 2004; p. A1.

CHAPTER 5/ 'A PERILOUS NEW COURSE'

[1] *Ex parte Milligan*, Supreme Court of the United States, 71 U.S. 2, 120-121 (1866).

[2] *Home Building & Land Association v. Baisdell, et al.*, Supreme Court of the United States, 290 U.S. 398; 54 S. Ct. 231, decided January 8, 1934.

[3] *Duncan v. Kahanamoku*, Supreme Court of the United States, 327 U.S. 304; 66 S. Ct. 606; decided February 25, 1946.

[4] "Liberty, Security, and the Courtds," speech by Associate Justice Stephen G. Breyer, Association of the Bar of the City of New York; April 14, 2003.

[5] *Yaser Esam Hamdi v. Donald H. Rumsfeld*, 294 F. 3d 598 (2002); also see: 243 F. Supp. 2nd 527.

[6] *Ibid.*

[7] *Yaser Esam Hamdi v. Donald H. Rumsfeld*, 316 F.3rd 450, U.S. Court of Appeals for the Fourth Circuit. Also see: 337 F.3rd 335 (2003) and 243 F.Supp 2nd 527 (2002).

[8] *Hamdi v. Rumsfeld*, 337 F.3rd 371.

[9] "Military to Watch Prisoner Interview," by Jerry Markon, *Washington Post*, January 31, 2004; p. B3.

[10] Quoted in "John Ashcroft's PATRIOT GAMES," *op. cit.*, p. 160.

[11] "Even a 'Bad Man' Has Rights," *op. cit.*

[12] *José Padilla v. Donald Rumsfeld*, 233 F. Supp. 2nd 564, U.S. District Court for the Southern District of New York; also see: 243 F. Supp. 2nd 42, decided March 11, 2004; and 256 F. Supp 2nd 218, decided April 9, 2003.

[13] "Report," Task Force on Treatment of Enemy Combatants (Neal R. Sonnett, chair), American Bar Association (Washington, D.C.), February 10, 2003. This report is probably the definitive legal and historical analysis of the issue of "enemy combatants" and the Bush administration's policies and procedures to detain U.S. citizens.

[14] *Ibid.*

[15] Resolution/Recommendation No. 109, House of Delegates, American Bar Association; February 10, 2003. [http://www.abanet.org/leadership/recommendations03/109.pdf].

[16] *Padilla v. Rumsfeld*, 352 F. 3rd 699, docket Nos. 03-2235 (L); 03-2438, U.S. Court of Appeals for the Second Circuit; December 18, 2003. Majority opinion written by Judges Barrington Parker and Rosemary Pooler. [http://www.ca2.uscourts.gov:81/isysnative/RDpcT3BpbnNcT1BOXDAzLTIyMzVfb3BuLnB kZg==/03-2235_opn.pdf].

[17] See: *Hamdi v. Rumsfeld*, 03-6696 and *Rumsfeld v. Padilla*, 03–1027, Supreme Court of the United States, oral arguments of April 28, 2004.

[18] *Ibid.*

[19] *Ibid.*

[20] Quoted in "Supreme Court Takes Closest Look Yet at Security and Terrorism," by Anne Gearan, Associated Press; April 28, 2004.

[21] Quoted in "Court Hears Case on U. S. Detainees," by Linda Greenhouse, *New York Times*; April 29, 2004; p. A1.

[22] "Supreme Court Takes Closest Look Yet at Security and Terrorism," *op. cit.*

[23] Quoted in "Justices Question Denial of Hearings for Detainees," by David G. Savage, *Los Angeles Times*; April 29, 2004; p. 1.

[24] "Court Hears Case on U. S. Detainees," *op. cit.*

[25] "Deputy Attorney General James Comey Holds a Justice Department News Conference Concerning Jose Padilla," transcript of conference, Federal Document Clearing House; June 1, 2004.

[26] *Ibid.*

[27] Quoted in "'Dirty Bomb' Suspect Jose Padilla Planned to Blow Up Buildings, Government Says," by Larry Margasak, Associated Press; June 1, 2004.

[28] "Deputy Attorney General James Comey Holds a Justice Department News Conference Concerning Jose Padilla," *op. cit.*

[29] Quoted in "DOJ and Padilla," by Nat Hentoff, Op-Ed column, *Washington Times*; June 14, 2004; p. A19.

[30] "Trial by News Conference? No Justice in That," by Scott Turow, *Washington Post*; June 13, 2004; p. B1.

[31] Quoted in "High Court Hears Detention Cases," *op. cit.*

[32] *Yaser Esam Hamdi v. Donald H. Rumsfeld*, Supreme Court of the United States, case 03-6696, opinion June 28, 2004; 542 U.S. (2004).

[33] *Donald H. Rumsfeld v. Jose Padilla*, Supreme Court of the United States, case 03-1027, dissent by Justice John Paul Stevens; June 28, 2004; 542 U.S. (2004).

[34] See: "Military Commission Media Rules Released," Reporters Committee for Freedom of the Press; August 19, 2004.

[35] "Two Military Lawyers Appointed to Represent the First Two Guantanamo Detainees Ordered to face a Military Tribunal," reported by Jackie Northrop, "Morning Edition," National Public Radio; June 8, 2004; and "Lawyer Pleads for Help to Defend Al-Qaeda Accountant at US Tribunal," Agence France Presse; August 27, 2004.

[36] Quoted in "Guantanamo Defense Team Taking on System," by John Hendren, *New York Times*; July 3, 2004; p. A29.

[37] Quoted in "Military Tribunals Uphold Detentions of 4," by Adam Liptak, *New York Times*; August 14, 2004; p. A1.

[38] Quoted in "Detainee Will Challenge U.S. Tribunals," by Bob Franken, CNN; July 7, 2004.

CHAPTER 6/ 'ROUNDED UP SECRETLY, JAILED SECRETLY, DEPORTED SECRETLY'

[1] Quoted in "Memo Warns Against Use of Profiling as Defense," by Bill Dedman, *Boston Globe*; October 12, 2001; p. A27.

[2] *Ibid.*

[3] *Ibid.*

[4] *Ibid.*

[5] Quoted in "Corzine, Other Dems Sponsor Law to Address Patriot Act 'Abuses'," by Wayne Parry, Associated Press; June 16, 2004.

[6] Quoted in "Jailed Without Cause," *Newsweek* Web edition; January 18, 2002. [Record Number: 011802_barrett_QAromero].

[7] FBI directive of February 3, 2003, reported by the California Senate Office of Research, April 2004.

[8] *The PATRIOT Act: Other Post-9/11 Enforcement Powers and the Impact on California's Muslim Communities*, California Senate Office of Research; May 2004, p. i.

[9] Report to the Congress, Department of Justice; May 21, 2003.

[10] "PATRIOT Act Fears Are Stifling Free Speech, ACLU Says in Challenge to Law," *op. cit.*

[11] *Muslim Community Association of Ann Arbor, et al. v. Ashcroft and Mueller*, U.S. District Court, Eastern District of Michigan, Southern Division, civil action 03-72913, Plaintiffs' Response to Defendants' Motion to Dismiss.

[12] "Muslims Hesitating on Gifts as U.S. Scrutinizes Charities," by Laurie Goldstein, *New York Times*; April 17, 2003; p. B1.

[13] "Domestic Intelligence and Civil Liberties," *op. cit.*, p. 15.

[14] "Seeking Truth From Justice," *op. cit.*, p. 8.

[15] See 8 U.S.C. § 1101and 8 U.S.C. § 1226a(a)(1); USA PATRIOT Act, Section 236.

[16] See: Transcript of the Hearing Before the Subcommittee on the Constitution of the Committee on the Judiciary, U.S. House of Representatives; May 20, 2003. [http://www.house.gov/judiciary/87238.PDF].

[17] See: *Report to Congress on Implementation of Section 1001 of the USA PATRIOT Act*, U.S. Department of Justice; July 7, 2003. [http://www.usdoj.gov/oig/special/03-07/index.htm].

[18] Quoted in "Report on USA PATRIOT Act Alleges Civil Rights Violations," by Philip Shenon; *New York Times*; July 20, 2003; p. A1.

[19] Remarks of Attorney General John Ashcroft to the International Association of Chiefs of Police (Philadelphia); October 24, 2003. [http://www.usdoj.gov/ag/speeches/2003/102403iacp.htm].

[20] *Report to Congress on Implementation of Section 1001 of the USA PATRIOT Act, op. cit.*

[21] Testimony of Attorney General John Ashcroft before the Senate Committee on the Judiciary; December 6, 2001. [http://www.usdoj.gov/ag/testimony.2001/1206/transcriptsenate judiciarycommittee.htm].

[22] David Cole, "A Matter of Rights," *The Nation*; September 20, 2001; p. 6. [http://www.thenation.com/doc.mhtml?i=20011008&s=cole].

[23] Wetzel was warden at the Federal Correctional Institution in South Miami-Dade County.

[24] "Secrecy Within," by Dan Christensen, *Miami Daily Business Review*; March 12, 2003; p. A11.

[25] "4 Iranians Challenge Detention," by H. G. Reza, *Los Angeles Times*; June 7, 2004; p. B1.

[26] *Ibid.*

[27] *Ibid.*

[28] *Ibid.*

[29] See: "U.S. Sees No Basis to Prosecute Iranian Opposition 'Terror' Group Being Held in Iraq," by Douglas Jehl, *New York Times*; July 27, 2004; p. A1.

[30] Letter from Colleen Rowley to Robert Mueller; February 26, 2003. [http://www.startribune.com/stories/484/3738192.html].

[31] See: Associated Press article written by Anne Gearan, distributed January 12, 2004.

[32] *Center for National Security Studies, et al. v. U.S. Department of Justice*; civil action No. 01-2500, 217 F. Supp. 2d 58.

[33] See: *CNSS v. Department of Justice* 215 F. Supp 2nd 94, 2002, decided August 15, 2002; and 331 F. 3rd 918, 1003, decided June 17, 2003.

[34] See United States Code § 552(b)(7)(A)

[35] *Center for National Security Studies v. U.S. Department of Justice*, 356 U.S. App. D.C. 333; 331 F.3rd 937, U.S. Court of Appeals for the District of Columbia, dissent filed by Judge David S. Tate.

[36] *CNSS v. Department of Justice*, cert. Denied, 124 S.Ct. 1041 (2004).

[37] The INS was transferred from the Department of Justice to the Department of Homeland Security on March 1, 2003. At that time, four separate bureaus, most from INS, were created: the U.S. Citizenship and Immigration Services, Bureau of Customs and Border Protection, Bureau of Immigration and Customs Enforcement (BICE), and Office of Immigration Statistics.

[38] Quoted in "Homeland Security Versus Right to Information," by Cynthia Price; *NFPW Agenda*; Summer 2003; p. 1. Also see: *Homefront Confidential: How the War on Terror Affects Access to Information and the Public's Right to Know*, available from the Reporters Committee on Freedom of the Press and online at http://www.rcfp.org/homefront-confidential.

[39] Michael Creppy, memo, "Re: Cases Requiring Certain Procedures," U.S. Immigration and Naturalization Service; September 21, 2001.

[40] *Detroit Free Press, et al., v. John Ashcroft, et al.*, U. S. Court of Appeals for the Sixth Circuit, case 02-1437, 303 F. 3rd 68, decision filed August 26, 2002.

[41] *North Jersey Media Group v. Ashcroft*, U.S. Court of Appeals for the Third Circuit, 308 F. 3rd 198, decision filed October 8, 2002.

[42] *North Jersey Media Group v. Ashcroft*, 205 F. Supp. 2nd 288.

[43] "Hundreds Are Detained After Visits to INS," by Megan Garvey, Martha Groves, and Henry Weinstein, *Los Angeles Times*; December 19, 2002; p. A1.

[44] "Supreme Court Rejects Appeal Over Secret September 11 Detentions," by Anne Gearan, Associated Press, published in *USA Today*; January 12, 2004.

[45] Quoted in "Ashcroft Refuses to Release '02 Memo," by Susan Schmidt, *Washington Post*; June 9, 2004; p. A01

[46] Memorandum for all United States Attorneys, from Deputy Attorney General, U.S. Dept. of Justice; November 9, 2001.

[47] See: *Assessing the New Normal*, Lawyers Committee for Human Rights, September 2003. Also see: "Immigration Crackdown Shatters' Muslims' Lives," by Cam Simpson, Flynn McRoberts, and Liz Sly, *Chicago Tribune*; three-part series (November 16, 2003; November 23, 2003; December 1, 2003).

[48] See: *American-Arab Anti-Discrimination Committee, et al. v. John Ashcroft, et al.*, brief filed December 24, 2002; ruling filed in U. S. District Court for the Central District of California, CV 02–1200, 241 F. Supp. 2nd 1111, filed January 15, 2003.

[49] "What's Next: Concentration Camps?" by Maria Tomchick, *Eat the State*; January 1, 2003. [http://eatthestate.org/07-09/whatsnextconcentration.htm].

[50] Center for Democracy & Technology, Center for American Progress, and Center for National Security Studies, *Strengthening America by Defending Our Liberties*; October 31, 2003; p. 9.

[51] Letter from Bob McDonnell, president, California Police Chiefs Association, to Attorney General John Ashcroft; April 10, 2002.

[52] "Special Report: Patriot Act Blurred in Public Mind," by Toni Locy, *USA Today*, February 26, 2004; p. A5.

[53] Testimony of Dr. James Zogby, Senate Committee on the Judiciary; November 18, 2003. [http://www.senate.gov/~judiciary/testimony.cfm?id=998&wit_id=2873].

[54] "Uprooted Again: Fearful Muslims Find Refuge in Canada," by Sam Stanton and Emily Bazar, *Sacramento Bee*; September 23, 2003' p. A1.

[55] Quoted in "Jailed Without Cause," *op. cit.*

[56] "ACLU Files Complaint with United Nations in Geneva Seeking Justice for Immigrants Detained and Deported After 9/11," news release, American Civil Liberties Union; January 27, 2004. [http://www.aclu.org/SafeandFree/SafeandFree.cfm?ID=14802&c=206]. For the ACLU report, *America's Disappeared: Seeking International Justice for Immigrants Detained After September 11.*
[http://www.aclu.org/SafeandFree/SafeandFree.cfm? ID=14800&c=206].

[57] Privacy Act of 1974, as amended in 28 C.F.R. § 16 (2003).

[58] Quoted in "Deportation Sweep Targets Middle Easterners," by Jonathan Peterson, *New York Times*; January 9, 2002; p. A5.

[59] Quoted in "Big Brother Takes a Grip on America," by Paul Harris; *Observer*; September 7, 2003, p. 20.

[60] See the FBI Uniform Crime Reports for hate crimes.
[http://www.fbi.gov/ucr/hatecrimes2002.pdf].

[61] *The Status of Muslim Civil Rights in the United States: Guilt by Association*, Council on American-Islamic Relations, 2004 [Report for 2003].

[62] "Uprooted Again: Fearful Muslims Find Refuge in Canada," *op. cit.*

[63] "Security Checks Strand Doctors From Abroad," by Gaiutra Bahadur, *Philadelphia Inquirer*; June 6, 2004; p. A3.

[64] *Ibid.*

[65] "Global View," by George Melloan, *Wall Street Journal*; March 2, 2004; p. 1.

[66] Speech by Anthony Romero to the National Press Club "Newsmaker Luncheon"; March 9, 2004. [http://www.aclu.org/news/NewsPrint.cfm?ID=15216&c=207].

[67] "Profiling Charged on 'Nightmare' Flight," by Thomas Ginsberg, *Philadelphia Inquirer*, September 19, 2002; p. A1.

[68] Quoted in "Second Passenger Detained by Federal Marshals Last Month May Sue," Associated Press; September 19, 2002.

[69] "Profiling Charged on 'Nightmare' Flight," *op. cit.*

[70] "Physician Treated as Terrorist Settles Suit," by Bill Douthat, *Palm Beach* (Fla.) *Post*; August 1, 2003; p. A1.

CHAPTER 7/ A NEED TO RAID NUDIE BARS

[1] Quoted in "FBI Can Request Library Logs," by Zenaida A. Gonzalez; *Florida Today*; September 23, 2002; p. A1.

[2] Quoted in "Official Counters PATRIOT Act Critics," *op. cit.*

[3] Speech by Viet Dinh, National Press Club (Washington, D.C.); April 24, 2003.

[4] Testimony of Timothy Burgess before Alaska Senate State Affairs Committee; May 13, 2003.

[5] "Seeking Truth from Justice," American Civil Liberties Union, pp. 2–3.
[http://www.aclu.org/safeandfree/safeandfree.cfm?ID=13099&c=207].

[6] Testimony of John Ashcroft before the Senate Committee on the Judiciary; December 6, 2001. [http://www.senate.gov/~judiciary/testimony.cfm?id=121&wit_id=42].

[7] Quoted in "Stretching PATRIOT Act," *Las Vegas Review-Journal*; September 16, 2003; p. 8B.

[8] *In re All Matters Submitted to the Foreign Intelligence Surveillance Court*, 218 F. Supp. 2nd 611, filed May 17, 2002. Also see: "Secret Court Rebuffs Ashcroft," by Dan Eggen and Susan Schmidt, *Washington Post*; August 23, 2002; p. A1; and "Doesn't Anyone Notice the Erosion of Our Freedoms?" by Robyn E. Blumner, *St. Petersburg* (Fla.) *Times*; October 20, 2002; p. 3D.

[9] *In re: Sealed Case 02–001*, F.I.S. Ct. Rev., filed November 18, 2002.

[10] Mark D. Agrast, *et al.*, "Report to the House of Delegates," Section of Individual Rights and Responsibilities, American Bar Association, February 2003, p. 3. [http://www.abanet.org/leadership/recommendations03/118.pdf]

[11] Recommendation/Resolution, House of Delegates, American Bar Association; February 2003. [http://www.abanet.org/leadership/recommendations03/118.pdf].

[12] See: *Report to the House Judiciary Committee on the USA PATRIOT Act and Related Measure*, Department of Justice; May 13, 2003.

[13] *Ibid.*

[14] Statement by Sen. Patrick Leahy, Senate Committee on the Judiciary, September 10, 2002.

[15] Bob Barr, testimony before the U.S. Senate Committee on the Judiciary, *op. cit.*

[16] *Ibid.*

[17] Quoted in "Corruption Investigation: LV FBI Used Anti-terrorism Law," by J. M. Kalil; *Las Vegas Review-Journal*; November 4, 2003; p. 1A.

[18] Quoted in "PATRIOT Act Knows No Limits," editorial, *Las Vegas Review-Journal*; November 5, 2003; p. 11B.

[19] "ACLU Says PATRIOT Act Use Against Las Vegas Stripclub Window into Law's Abuse Since 9/11," news release, American Civil Liberties Union; November 5, 2003. [http://www.aclu.org/news/NewsPrint.cfm?ID=14338&c=206].

[20] Quoted in "PATRIOT Act: Law's Use Causing Concerns," by J. M. Kalil and Steve Tetreault, *Las Vegas Review-Journal*; November 5, 2003; p. 1A.

[21] *Ibid.*

[22] "Patriot Act's Broad Brush: Aimed at Terrorists, the Landmark Legislation Affects Average Citizens," by Sam Stanton and Emily Bazar, *Sacramento Bee*; December 21, 2003; p. A1.

[23] "Liberty in the Balance: Patriot Act's Broad Brush," by Sam Stanton and Emily Bazar, *Sacramento Bee*; December 21, 2003.

[24] "ACLU Says PATRIOT Act Use Against Las Vegas Stripclub Window Into Law's Abuse Since 9/11," news release, American Civil Liberties Union; November 5, 2003.

[25] Quoted in "PATRIOT Act Knows No Limits," *op. cit.*

[26] Quoted in "U.S. Uses Terror Law to Pursue Crimes," by Eric Lichtblau, *New York Times*; September 28, 2003; p. A1.

[27] "Show Me the Money," by Michael Isikoff, *Newsweek*; December 1, 2003; p. 36.

[28] *Ibid.*

[29] "Wiretap Authorizations Increase in 2003," news release, Administrative Office of U.S. Courts; April 30, 2004. [http://www.uscourts.gov/Press_Releases/03wtreport.pdf].

[30] Quoted in "Data Show Different Spy Game Since 9/11," by Dan Eggen and Susan Schmidt, *Washington Post*; May 1, 2004; p. A1.

[31] "ACLU Says Rare Veto Threat Shows Viability of PATRIOT Act Fix, Assails Justice Department's Deaf Ear to Bipartisan, Popular Criticism," news release, American Civil Liberties Union; January 29, 2004.

CHAPTER 8 / 'IT'S NOT THE GOVERNMENT'S JOB'

[1] See: Testimony of Attorney General A. Mitchell Palmer, Committee on Rules, U. S. House of Representatives, 1920.

[2] A. Mitchell Palmer, *The Case Against the Reds* (1920), Vol. II.

[3] See: *Schenk v. U.S.*, 249 U.S. 47 (1919); *Abrams v. U.S.*, 250 U.S. 616 (1919); *Debs v. United States*, 249 U.S. 211 (1919); and *Gitlow v. New York*, 268 U.S. 652 (1925).

[4] See: Koramatsu v. United States [323 U.S. 214 (1944).

[5] See: *United States v. Rumely*, Supreme Court of the United States, 345 U.S. 41; 73 S. Ct. 543, decided March 9, 1953, opinion by Justice Felix Frankfurter.

[6] Other cases occurred in Denver and Kansas City (2000), and Cleveland and New Jersey (2001). The American Booksellers Foundation for Free Expression [www.abffe.org] tracks all cases of attempts by law enforcement to seize bookstore records.

[7] "Dispelling the Myths," Department of Justice. [www.lifeandliberty.gov/subs/u_myths.htm]

[8] http://www.ala.org/Template.cfm?Section=IF_ resolutions&Template=/ContentManagement/ContentDisplay.cfm&ContentID=1189; resolution adopted January 29, 2003.

[9] "Resolution on the USA PATRIOT Act and Related Measures That Infringe on the Rights of Library Users," South Carolina Library Association; March 13, 2003. [http://www.scla.org/docs/patriotactresolution.html].

[10] The full resolution is available at: http://www.santacruzpl.org/libraryadmin/ljpb/patres.shtml.

[11] See: "Librarians Step Up: They Prepare for 'Knock on the Door'," by Sam Stanton and Emily Bazar, *Sacramento Bee*; September 22, 2003; p. A1.

[12] *Ibid.*

[13] Quoted in "Several in Sun Cities Say PATRIOT Act Goes Too Far," *op. cit.*

[14] Quoted in "Librarians Step Up: They Prepare for 'Knock on the Door'," *op. cit.*

[15] "Spies in the Stacks," by Dan Malow, *Fort Worth Weekly*; April 17, 2003.

[16] "Rights and the New Reality: Book Snoopers' Open Door," editorial, *Los Angeles Times*; March 2, 2003; p. M4.

[17] See: *Muslim Community Association of Ann Arbor, et al. v. Ashcroft and Mueller, op. cit.*

[18] For a list of organizations filing briefs, see: http://www.aclu.org/SafeandFree.cfm?ID=13255&c=207.

[19] "Free Speech Groups Support PATRIOT Act Change, news release, American Booksellers Foundation for Free Expression; November 3, 2003. [http://www.abffe.org/11-3-03pressrelease.html]. The *amicus curiae* brief is accessible at: http://www.abffe.com/amicus_brief.pdf

[20] Brief of *Amicus Curiae*, First Amendment Organizations in Support of Plaintiffs' Opposition to Defendants' Motion to Dismiss, civil action 03–72913, U. S. District Court for the Eastern District of Michigan, Southern Division. [see: http://www.abffe.com/amicus_brief.pdf].

[21] "Book, Library Groups Launch Petition Drive to Restore Privacy Safeguards to USA PATRIOT Act," news release, American Booksellers Foundation for Free Expression; February 17, 2004.

[22] Quoted in "Booksellers Respond to PATRIOT Act," by Elizabeth Fakazis, *Wisconsin State Journal*; June 28, 2004; p. B1.

[23] "PATRIOT Act Petition Campaign Gathering Steam," news release, American Booksellers Association; February 4, 2004. [Also see: http://www.readerprivacy.org]

[24] *Ibid.*

[25] "Librarians Protest Potential Snooping; PATRIOT Act Makes Access to Records too Easy, They Say," by Judith Graham, *Chicago Tribune*; April 4, 2003; p. 18.

[26] "Dispelling the Myths," *op. cit.*

[27] Transcript of the Hearing Before the Subcommittee on the Constitution of the Committee on the Judiciary, U.S. House of Representatives; May 20, 2003 .

[http://www.house.gov/judiciary/87238.PDF].

[28] *Public Libraries and Civil Liberties: A Profession Divided*, The Library Research Center, University of Illinois at Urbana-Champaign (Leigh S. Estabrook, director). Also see: "Legality of Patriot Act Questioned: Some Worry the Law Infringes on Civil Liberties," by Dianne Struzzi, *Hartford* (Conn.) *Courant*, March 23, 2003; p. B1.

[29] "Statement of Barbara Comstock, director of public affairs, on DOJ Testimony Regarding Libraries," news release, U.S. Department of Justice; June 2, 2003.

[30] Library Group Wants to Know When Agents Have Obtained Records," by Mike Schneider, Associated Press; June 25, 2004.

[31] Quoted in "Justice Dept. Lists Use of New Power to Fight Terror," by Eric Lichtblau, *New York Times*; May 21, 2003; p. A1.

[32] Quoted in "Kucinich Stresses Civil Liberties," *op. cit.*

[33] See: "Ashcroft Mocks Librarians and Others Who Oppose Parts of Counterterrorism Law," by Eric Lichtblau, *New York Times*; September 16, 2003; p. 23.

[34] Quoted in "Ashcroft Mocks Librarians and Others Who Oppose Parts of Counterterrorism Law," by Eric Lichtblau, *New York Times*; September 26, 2003; p. A23.

[35] See: *American Civil Liberties Union, et al. v. United States Department of Justice*, U.S. District Court for the District of Columbia, CV 03-2522 (ESH).

[36] "Government Says It Has Yet to Use Power to Check Library Records," by Eric Lichtblau, *New York Times*; September 19, 2003; p. A16.

[37] Memorandum, heavily redacted, FBI, October 15, 2003. Also see: "New Records Show That FBI Invoked Controversial Surveillance Powers After Attorney General Declared that Power Had Never Been Used," news release, ACLU; June 17, 2004; and "Patriot Act Provision Invoked, Memo Says," by Amy Goldstein, *Washington Post*; June 18, 2004; p. A11.

[38] See: *American Civil Liberties Union, et al. v. United States Department of Justice*, *op. cit.*

CHAPTER 9 / 'THE MOST DANGEROUS OF ALL SUBVERSIONS'

[1] "President Bush Speaks at Tsingua University," *op. cit.*

[2] http://www.lifeandliberty.gov/subs/u_myths.htm

[3] "Cheney Warns Democrats," CBS News; May 17, 2002; "Cheney's 'Irresponsible' Speech," by Ray McGovern, AlterNet; July 31, 2003.

[4] Testimony of Attorney General John Ashcroft to U.S. Senate Committee on the Judiciary; December 6, 2001.
[See: http://wwww,usdoj.gov/ag/testimony/2001/1206transcriptsenatejudiciarycommittee.htm]

[5] "The Patriot War," by Kris W. Kobach, *New York Post*; March 1, 2004; p. 26.

[6] Quoted in "John Ashcroft's PATRIOT GAMES," *op. cit.*, p. 160.

[7] "Freedom to Dissent Is Crucial for Nation," by Jack P. Calareso, *Columbus Dispatch*; January 25, 2003; p. 6A.

[8] Theodore Roosevelt, "Sedition, a Free Press and Personal Rule," *Kansas City Star*; May 7, 1918; p. 2.

[9] Quoted in "A Word With Gen. Wesley Clark," *Arizona Republic*; January 23, 2004; p. B11.

[10] "Ashcroft's Endless Attacks Diminish Office," editorial, *Dayton* (Ohio) *Daily News*; August 11, 2003.

[11] "Protesters Kept at a Distance; Three Arrested," by Kevin Graham and Angela Moore, *St. Petersburg Times*; June 5, 2001.

[12] See: "Protests Not Seen or Heard: How Polite," column by Howard Troxler, *St. Petersburg Times*; June 6, 2001; "Anti-Bush Protesters May Sue Over Arrests," by William March, *Tampa Tribune*; June 15, 2001; p. 1; and '3 Protesters Sue Tampa Police," by Graham Brink, *St. Petersburg Times*; November 2, 2002.

[13] See: *Sonja Haught, Janis Lentz, and Mauricio Rosas v. The City of Tampa, Fla., et., al.,* U.S. District Court for the Middle District of Florida, Tampa Division, Complaint for Declaratory and Injunctive Relief, Damages, Attorney's Fees, and a Demand for a Jury Trial,. 8:02CV2021-T-27EAJ.

[14] "Protestors Kept at a Distance; Three Arrested," *op. cit.* Also see: "Take This Constitution and . . ." by Daniel Ruth, *Tampa Tribune*, June 8, 2002; p. 2.

[15] "Take This Constitution and . . ." *op. cit.*

[16] *Ibid.*

[17] *Sonja Haught, Janis Lentz, and Mauricio Rosas v. The City of Tampa, Fla., et al., op. cit.*

[18] "Bush Rally Protesters Plan to Sue City, Police," by Graham Brink, *St. Petersburg Times*, October 20, 2001.

[19] *Haught, et al. v. Tampa, et al.,* U.S. District Court for the Middle District of Florida, Tampa Division, order of Judge James D. Whittemore, January 30, 2004.

[20] See: "7 Protesters Arrested; Ticketholders Kept Out," by John Balz and Mike Brassfield, *St. Petersburg Times*, November 3, 2002; p. 11A; and "7 Arrested for Protest of President, Brother," *Tampa Tribune*, November 3, 2002; p. 10.

[21] "Charges Against Protestors Dismissed," by Christopher Goffard, *St. Petersburg Times*, May 2, 2003; p. 3B.

[22] "7 Protesters Arrested; Ticketholders Kept Out," *op. cit.*

[23] *Adam Elend, Jeff Marks, and Joe Redner v. Sun Dome et al.,* U.S. District Court for the Middle District of Florida, civil case 8:03-CV-1657-T-23TGW, Verified Complaint for Declaratory and Injunctive Relief, Damages, Attorney's Fees, and a Demand for Jury Trial; filed August 2, 2003.

[24] "Bush Protester Ordered to Pay $500," by Cliff LeBlanc, *The State* (Columbia, S.C.); January 7, 2004; p. B1; "Anti-Bush Protester Found Guilty, Fined $500," Associated Press; January 7, 2004; "Critics Say Ruling Threatens Free Speech," by Cliff LeBlanc, *The State* (Columbia, S.C.); January 11, 2004; p. B1; "Bursey Arrest Part of Administration's Suppression of Free Speech," editorial, *The State* (Columbia, S.C.); p. A8. Also see: letter from Rep. Barney Frank, *et al.* to John Ashcroft, May 27, 2003. [http://www.house.gov/frank/scprotester2003.html].

[25] See: "One of Largest Demonstrations Ever in Stockton Invisible to Bush," by Dana M. Nichols and Audrey Cooper, *Stockton* (Calif.) *Record*, August 24, 2002; p. A8.

[26] *People of the State of Michigan v. Antoine Jennings,* Eighth District Court for the County of Kalamazoo, case 01-05340, order August 17, 2001.

[27] "Criticize Cheney, Go to Jail," by John Blair, *Counterpunch*; February 8, 2002; "Free Speech a Victim of 'Security'," by Mike Finch, *American Free Press.* [http://www.americanfreepress.net/Censored/12_02%20Free%20Speech%20a%20Victim%20of%20.htm]. Also see: *John Blair v. City of Evansville, Indiana, et al.,* U.S. District Court for the Southern District of Indiana, CV 3:03–CV–003 RLY/WGH, filed February 20, 2003.

[28] Interviewed on "American Morning," CNN; January 9, 2004. [http://www.cnn.com/TRANSCRIPTS/0401/09/ltm.12.html].

[29] Quoted in "Judge Acquits Bush Protestor, Scolds Police," Associated Press; November 1, 2002.

[30] "5 Suing Over Crawford's Protest Ordinance," Associated Press; June 18, 2003.

[31] "Trial Begins for 5 Accused of Violating Crawford's Parade Ordinance," by Miguel Liscano, *Waco* (Texas) *Tribune-Herald*, February 8, 2004; p. A1; and "Antiwar Protestors Convicted for Demonstrating Near Bush's Ranch," Reporters Committee for Freedom of the Press; February 18, 2004.

[32] "Texas Jury Convicts Activists of Violating Protest Ordinance," Associated Press; February 17, 2004.

[33] Quoted in "Charges Dismissed Against Texas Antiwar Demonstrators," Associated Press; July 14, 2004.

[34] *ACORN, et al. v. City of Philadelphia et al.*, U.S. District Court for the Eastern District of Pennsylvania, filed amended complaint filed September 23, 2003; civil case 03–4312.

[35] See: *Acorn, et al. v. Philadelphia, et al., op. cit.*, Memorandum and Order; May 5, 2004.

[36] Marvin Miller, quoted in "George W. Bush's T-Shirt Police Got Their Family," by Joe Snapper, *Saginaw News*; August 6, 2004; p. A2.

[37] "NARAL Turns T-Shirt Fracas Into Money," by Emily Piece, *Roll Call*; August 16, 2004; p. 3. Also see: "T-Shirt Going National," by Joe Snapper, *Saginaw News*; August 11, 2004; p. B1.

[38] See: "Some Democrats Seeking Cheney Tickets Had to Sign Loyalty Oaths," by Richard Benke, Associated Press; July 29, 2004; "Obtaining Cheney Rally Ticket Requires Signing Bush Endorsement," by Jeff Jones, *Albuquerque Journal*; July 30, 2004; p. A1; "Cheney Visit Brings Partisan Barbs," by Shea Andersen, *Albuquerque Tribune*; July 30, 2004; p. A2; "Cheney: 'I Really Like This Crowd,'" by Leslie Linthicum, *Albuquerque Journal*; August 1, 2004; p. A1; and "High-Profile Profile Protest Greets Cheney on Way to Rally," by Jeff Jones, *Albuquerque Journal*; August 1, 2004; p. A1.

[39] See: "Bush Visit Cost $53,000," by Paul J. Nyden, *Charleston Gazette*; July 14, 2004.

[40] "Kerry Will Allow Protesters; Bush Policy Not Clear," by Chris Wetterich, *Charleston Gazette*; July 15, 2004; p. A1.

[41] See: "FEMA Worker Ordered Home," by Paul J. Nyden, *Charleston Gazette*; July 8, 2004; p. A1; "Free Speech? Critics Clobbered," editorial, *Charleston Gazette*; July 9, 2004; p. A4; We Weren't Doing Anything Wrong,' Couple in Anti-Bush T-Shirts Were Arrested at President's Speech," by Tara Tuckwiller, *Charlesion Gazette*; July 14, 2004; p. A1.

[42] "Trespass Charges Dropped Against Bush Protesters," Associated Press; July 15, 2004.

[43] Quoted in "T-Shirt Charges Dismissed," by Tara Tuckwiller, *Charleston Gazette*; July 16, 2004.

[44] *Ibid.*

[45] Quoted in "Kerry Will Allow Protesters; Bush Policy Not Clear," *op. cit.*

[46] *Ibid.*

[47] "Secret Service Not Coddling Hecklers," by Dana Milbank, *Washington Post*; September 10, 2004; p. A8.

[48] "Bush Camp Solicits Race of Star Staffer," by C. J. Karamargin, *Arizona Daily Star*, July 31, 2004; p. A7.

[49] *Ibid.*

[50] "Photog's Race Is Just 'Personal Identifier," by C. J. Karamargin, *Arizona Daily Star*, August 3, 2004; p. A8.

[51] *Ibid.*

[52] The forty to fifty protestors actually chose that site at the extreme end of the campus more than two hours before the vice president's speech, so as "not to cause a confrontation." Later, they moved closer to the basketball court where the vice president would speak.

[53] For further information, see: "Credentialed Columnist Denied Access to Cheney Speech," Reporters Committee for Freedom of the Press; August 27, 2004. [http://www.rcfp.org/news/2004/0827/syndic.html].

[54] "Vice President to Visit BU," news release, Bloomsburg University; August 23, 2004.

[55] *Coalition to Protest the Democratic National Convention, et al. v. City of Boston*, U.S. District Court for the District of Massachusetts, CA-04-11608-DPW and CA-04-11620; July 22, 2004.

[56] Quoted in "GOP Zinged for Meeting in N.Y.," by Anna Badkhen, *San Francisco Chronicle*; July 19, 2004; p. A10.

[57] *Ann Stauber v. City of New York*, U.S. District Court for the Southern District of New York; civil case 03-9162, ruling July 20, 2004. The city announced it would appeal the decision, then dropped the appeal about two weeks later.

[58] Quoted in "'First Amendment Furor," by Glenn Thrush, *Newsday*; August 17, 2004; p. A16.

[59] About fifteen thousand persons were accredited to report the Republican National Convention, with stories from all forms of media. Perhaps the best firsthand reporting about the arrests and detention of protestors was written by two students on the staff of the *Daily Kent Stater*. See separate stories under one headline: "'It's Not Club Med': New York City Mayor Michael Bloomberg Said Conditions at a Detention Facility Weren't Supposed to be Perfect," by Beth Rankin and Nick Gehrig, *Daily Kent Stater*, September 7, 2004; p. 1. Also see: "Demonstrators Eager to Greet Republicans," by Patty Reinert, *Houston Chronicle*; August 29, 2004; p. A17; "'Send Him Back to Texas': Tens of Thousands March Against Bush," by Sara Kugler, Associated Press; August 29, 2004; "More than 100,000 in New York March Against Bush," by Sara Kugler, Associated Press; August 29, 2004; "'No More Years!' Chant Bush Foes," MSNBC News; August 29, 2004; "25,000 Abortion-Rights Advocates March to City Hall," by Michael Slackman and Ann Farmer, *New York Times*; August 29, 2004; p. A27; "'Demonstrators Held at Pier 57 Complain of Conditions and Long Waits," by Patrick Healy and Susan Saulny, *New York Times;* August 29, 2004; p. A12; "The G.O.P. Arrives, Putting September 11 into August," by Adam Nagourney and Robin Toner, *New York Times*; August 30, 2004; p. A1; "Upstaging Before the Show," by Todd S. Purdum, *New York Times*; August 30, 2004; p. A1; "Bush's Leadership Style Another Key Question," by Mike Allen and David Broder, *Washington Post*; August 30, 2004; p. A1; "At Least 900 Arrested in City as Protesters Clash With Police," by Diane Cardwell and Marc Santora, *New York Times*; September 1, 2004; "20,000 Keep Anti-GOP Rallies Going," by Michael Powell and Michelle Garcia, *Washington Post*; August 31, 2004; p. A9; "Police Tactics Mute Protesters and Messages," by Michael Slackman and Diane Cardwell, *New York Times*; September 2, 2004; p. A1; "Judge Orders Protesters Released, Rallies Carry On," by M. E. Sprengelmeyer, Scripps Howard News Service; September 2, 2004; "Convention Detainees Describe Long Stays in Grimy Conditions," by Larry Neumeister, Associated Press; September 2, 2004. Also see: "NYCLU Grades Policing of Protesters at the RNC," news statement, New York Civil Liberties Union; September 3, 2004.

[60] Quoted in "Protesters Disrupt RNC Youth Event Inside Madison Square Garden," by Bryan Bender and Tatsha Robertson, *Boston Globe*; September 2, 2004; p. A26. Also see: "Scuffle and Arrests as Activists Get Onto Floor," by Jonathan E. Kaplan, *The Hill*; September 2, 2004; and "Crashing the Party Was Surprisingly Easy, Activists Say," by Anna Badkhen, *San Francisco Chronicle*; September 4, 2004; p. A1. Also see: WABC-TV coverage of the protest and subsequent beating of a young woman; September 2, 2004;

[61] See: "Facing Fine, City Frees Hundreds of Detainees," by Susan Saulny and Diane Cardwell, *New York Times*; September 3, 2004; p. P1; "Metro Briefing," *New York Times*; September 9, 2004; p. B4; "Judge Keeps City on Notice Over Convention Protest Arrests," by Julia Preston, *New York Times*; September 10, 2004; "City Faces Penalty Hearing in Protester Arrests," by Diane Cardwell, *New York Times*; September 11, 2004.

[62] See: "30 Seconds," *Press Enterprise* (Bloomsburg, Pennsylvania); September 10–14, 2004.

[63] See: news release, "Convention Ends With Numerous and Lengthy Journalist Detainments," Reporters Committee for Freedom of the Press; September 3, 2004.

[64] "Member of Student Youth Group Gets Swept Up in Arrests on Convention Floor," by Joie Tyrell, *Newsday*; September 4, 2004.

[65] *United States v. United States District Court*, 407 U.S. 313–315 (1972).

[66] See: *Select Committee to Study Governmental Operations with Respect to Intelligence Activities, Intelligence Activities and the Rights of Americans, Final Report of the Senate Select Committee to Study Governmental Operations with Respect to Intelligence Activities*, 94th Cong., 2nd Sess. (1976), better known as the *Church Report*. Also see: *War at Home: Covert Action Against U.S. Activists and What We Can Do About It*, by Brian Glick, 1990;

Snitch Culture: How Citizens Are Turned Into the Eyes and Ears of the State, by Jim Redden, 2000; *COINTEL-PRO: The FBI's Secret War on Political Freedom*, by Nelson Blackstock, 2000; *COINTELPRO Papers: Documents From the FBI's Secret Wars Against Domestic Dissent*, by Ward Churchill and Jim Vander Wall, 2002.

[67] News Release, Reporters Committee for Freedom of the Press; August 20, 2003. [Also see: http://www.rcfp.org/news/documents/20030820ashcroft.html].

[68] "PATRIOT Act Fears Are Stifling Free Speech, ACLU Says in Challenge to Law," news release, American Civil Liberties Union; November 3, 2003.

[69] "Lawyers Take Aim at Patriot Act," by Steve Terrell, *Santa Fe New Mexican;* February 18, 2003; p. A1; and "Man Detained at NM College Library," *Library Journal* web edition; March 3, 2003. [http://www.libraryjournal.com/article/CA280571].

[70] "Gym Debate Led to Agents' Visit," *Sacramento Bee*; September 21, 2003; p. A20.

[71] "City Must Balance Freedom, Security," by Michael Powell and Michelle Garcia, *New York Times*; August 17, 2004; p. A1.

[72] "Liberty in the Balance: More Scrutiny of Peace Groups," by Sam Stanton and Emily Bazar, *Sacramento Bee*; November 9, 2003; p. A1; and "F.B.I. Scrutinizes Antiwar Rallies," by Eric Lichtblau, *New York Times*; November 23, 2003; p. A1. (Lichtblau's reporting upset the FBI; Cassandra Chandler, an FBI spokesman, sent a memo to senior FBI officials attacking Lichtblau's reporting and suggested "each of you to please avoid providing information to this reporter." About the same time, the Department of Justice revoked Lichtblau's press credentials.) Also see: "Video Surveillance—FOIA Documents," Electronic Privacy Information Center. [http://www.epic.org/privacy/surveillance/foia.html].

[73] See: "Big Brother Takes a Grip on America," *op. cit.*

[74] "Why Were We on No-Fly List?" *Sacramento Bee*; September 21, 2003; p. A18; and "Detained, Questioned and Branded," *Modesto* (Calif.) *Bee*; September 28, 2003; p. A19.

[75] Interview, Bill Whitaker with Rebecca Gordon, CBS-TV Evening News; October 6, 2002.

[76] See: "ACLU Calls for Denver Police to Stop Keeping Files on Peaceful Protesters," news release, ACLU of Colorado; March 11, 2002. Also see: "Cops Have 'Spy Files'," by Sarah Huntley, *Rocky Mountain News*; March 12, 2002; p. 1; and "Police 'Spy Files' Assailed ACLU Criticism Spurs City Review of Log on Protesters," by Sean Kelly, *Denver Post;* March 12, 2002; p. A1. During the next few months, the city's two major local dailies, the wire services, and other news media published dozens of stories about the police department and its intelligence files.

[77] The discovery of file sharing was made by Citizens for Peace and the Pikes Peak Justice and Peace Commission.

[78] Wellington E. Webb, news statement; March 13, 2002.

[79] *Ibid.*

[80] "Expressing the Commitment if the City and County of Denver to Civil Rights and Liberties," Resolution 13–2002; March 18, 2002.

[81] "Hundreds File Requests to See Cops' 'Spy files': Records Contain Some Surprises," by Carol Kreck, *Denver Post;* September 4, 2002; p. B1; and "'Spy File' Backlog Has Police Hopping," by Sarah Huntley; *Rocky Mountain News*; September 5, 2002; p. 1.

[82] "People Named in 'Spy Files' Feel Left in Dark: Police Blacked Out Many Pages," by Carol Kreck, *Denver Post;* September 8, 2002; p. B2.

[83] "Zavaras: Spy File Abuse a Surprise," by Owen S. Good, *Rocky Mountain News*; December 23, 2003.

[84] "Police Could Take Home 'Spy Files'," by Kevin Vaughn, *Rocky Mountain News*; January 4, 2003; p. 3A.

[85] *American Friends Service Committee, et al. v. City and County of Denver*, U.S. District Court for the District of Colorado, CV 02–N–0740 (CBS)

[86] "City Must Pay $470,000 in Lawsuit Over 'Spy Files,'" by Karen Abbott, *Rocky Mountain News*; August 7, 2004.

[87] "Nuns Sentenced to Prison for Colorado Nuclear Protest," by Keith Coffman, Reuters; July 26, 2003.

[88] Memo to Chief of Police from Director, Civil Rights and Force Investigation Division, Metropolitan (D.C.) Police Department; January 25, 2003.
[http://www.dcd.uscourts.gov/02-2010.pdf].

[89] *Ibid.* Also see: "Doubt Cast on Arrests of IMF Protestors," by David A. Fahrenthold and David Nakamura, *Washington Post*; February 27, 2003; p. B1.

[90] See: Rayming *Chang, et al. v. United States, et al. civil action* 02–2010; *Jeffrey Barham, et al. v. Charles H. Ramsey, et al.,* civil action 02–2283; and *Franklin Jones, et al. v. District of Columbia, et al.,* civil action 02–2310; and *Julie Abbate, et al. v. Charles H. Ramsey, et al.,* civil action 03–767; 203 F.R.D. 262, District Court for the District of Columbia.

[91] "ACLU Official Sues Officers, Phoenix," *Arizona Republic*; March 26, 2003.

[92] Quoted in "CCR Sues the NYPD for Protestor Arrests," information bulletin, Center for Constitutional Rights; February 12, 2003.

[93] *Sarah Kunstler, et al. v. The City of New York, et al.,* U.S. District Court for the Southern District of New York; filed February 11, 2004.

[94] "Presence of Army Agents Stirs Furor," by Jane Elliott, *Houston Chronicle*; February 14, 2004; p. A33.

[95] *Ibid.*

[96] "Students Protest Army Probe Into Campus Islam Conference," Associated Press; February 16, 2004.

[97] At that protest, eleven persons were arrested for trespassing for stepping over a line painted in the grass; none had entered the armory. One person was charged with resisting arrest and assault for going limp. Three of those arrested were in their 70s and 80s.

[97] "An Antiwar Forum in Iowa Brings Federal Subpoenas," by Monica Davey, *New York Times*; February 10, 2004; p. A14.

[98] *Ibid.*

[99] Quoted in "Protecting and Defending the US Constitution," by Chris Trotter, *The Daily News* (New Plymouth, New Zealand); February 13, 2004; p. 6.

[100] Quoted in "Campus Reacts to Government Sanction," by Liz Owens, *Times-Delphic* (Drake University); February 9, 2004; p. 1.

[101] "Subpoenas Issued to Drake University," Statement of the American Association of University Professors Special Committee on Academic Freedom and National Security in a Time of Crisis; February 11, 2004.
[http://www.aaup.org/statements/SpchState/subpoenas.htm].

[102] "Campus Reacts to Government Sanction," *op. cit.*

[103] *Ibid.*

[104] Quoted in "Federal Officials Clearing Abusing Their Power," editorial, *Telegraph-Herald* (Dubuque, Iowa); February 13, 2004; p. A4. Harkin's letter was sent, February 9, 2004, the day the abuse came to light.

[105] "Statement of Drake University President David Maxwell," news release, Drake University; February 10, 2004. [For further discussion, see: "National Lawyers Guild Claims Victory; Government Withdraws Subpoena," news release, National Law Guild; February 10, 2004; "U.S. Officials Drop Activist Subpoenas," by Jeff Eckhoff and Mark Siebert, *Des Moines Register*; February 11, 2004; p. A1; "Prosecutors Withdraw Subpoena Against University, Protestors," Associated Press; distributed February 11, 2004; "Stepping on the Constitution," editorial, *St. Louis Post-Dispatch*; February 11, 2004; p. C12; "Drake Group Amused by Probe," by Jeff Eckhoff and Mark Siebert, *Des Moines Register*; February 12, 2004; p. B1; "Tactics of Intimidation?" editorial, *San Francisco Chronicle*; February 12, 2004; p. A22; "Four Fight for Peace," by Mike Kilen, *Des Moines Register*; February 14, 2004; p. E1.

[106] "Mosque Raid Shakes Community," by Thomas Ginsberg, *Philadelphia Inquirer*, May 29, 2004; p. A1.

[107] *Ibid.*

[108] *Ibid.*

[109] Also see: "ACLU Denounced FBI Tactics Targeting Political Protesters," news release, ACLU of Eastern Missouri; August 16, 2004; "F.B.I. Goes Knocking for Political Troublemakers," by Eric Lichtblau," *New York Times*; August 16, 2004; p. A1; and " FBI Surveillance Intimidated Missouri Protesters, ACLU Says," by Peter Shinkle, *St. Louis Post-Dispatch*; August 19, 2004.

[110] "Warnings Precede Party Conventions," by Karen Abbott, *Rocky Mountain News*; July 24, 2004.

[111] Statement of Cassandra M. Chandler, assistant director, FBI; August 16, 2004.

[112] "Warnings Precede Party Conventions," *op. cit.*; Also see: "FBI Goes Knocking for Political Troublemakers," *op. cit.*

[113] Joe Parris, FBI spokesman, quoted in "F.B.I. Goes Knocking for Political Troublemakers," *op. cit.*

[114] "Teaching the Silent Treatment," by Amy Herdy, *Denver Post*; August 8, 2004.

[115] "FBI Tactics Erode Public Trust," editorial, *Denver Post*; August 19, 2004.

[116] "Interrogating the Protesters," editorial, *New York Times*; August 17, 2004; p. A20.

[117] "Liberty vs. Security: The Knock at the Door," editorial, *St. Louis Post-Dispatch;* August 18, 2004; p. B6.

[118] Letter from John Conyers Jr., Jerrold Nadler, and Robert C. Scott to Glenn Fine, FBI inspector general; August 17, 2004.

[119] 18 U.S.C.§ 2331.

[120] Bob Barr, testimony before the U.S. Senate Committee on the Judiciary, *op. cit.*

[121] Quoted in "Paige Calls Teachers Union a Terrorist Organization," by Nick Anderson, *Los Angeles Times*; February 24, 2004; p. A15.

[122] Letter from Jane Buck to Rod Paige; February 24, 2004.
[See: http://www,aaup.org/newsroom/News-Archive.htm].

[123] U.S.C. 18 § 2279.

[124] See: *United States of America v. Greenpeace*, U.S. District Court for the Southern District of Florida, case 03-20577-CR-JORDAN.

[125] "Silencing Greenpeace," editorial, Daytona Beach *News-Journal*; May 20, 2004; p. 4A

[126] "Greenpeace Prosecuted Under Antiquated Law," editorial, *Miami Herald*; October 30, 2003; p. 20.

[127] "Order on Pending Motions," *United States of America v. Greenpeace*, U.S. District Court for the Southern District of Florida, ruling by Judge Adalberto Jordan; April 15, 2004.

[128] *Ibid.*

[129] "Judge Dismisses Ashcroft Attempt to Shut Down Greenpeace," news release, Greenpeace USA; May 19, 2004.

[130] Carlos B. Castillo, quoted in "Judge Dismisses Greenpeace Charges," by Manuel Roig-Franzia, *Washington Post*; May 20, 2004; p. A14.

[131] *National Council of Resistance of Iran v. Department of State*, U.S. Court of Appeals for the District of Columbia Circuit, 251 F. 3rd 192-197 (2001).

[132] *United States of America v. Roya Rahmani, et al.*, U. S. District Court for the Central District of California, CR01-209-RMT, 209 F. Supp 2nd 1045.

[133] See: "8 Groups in U.S. Protest Bush Move Against Foundation," by Laurie Goldstein, *New York Times*; December 5, 2001; p. A8.

[134] See: "Islamic Charity Says F.B.I. Falsified Evidence Against It," by Eric Lichtblau, *New York Times*; July 27, 2004; p. A1

[135] See: "Indictment Accuses Muslim Charity of Aiding Hamas," by Toni Heinzl, *Fort Worth Star-Telegram*; July 28, 2004; p. A1; "U.S. Charity Charged With Funding Hamas

Terror Group," by Curt Anderson, Associated Press; July 27, 2004; "Muslim Charity Indicted, Accused of Dealing With Terrorists," by David Koenig, Associated Press; July 28, 2004; "Texas Charity, Leaders Are Charges With Aiding Hamas," by Stephen Braun, *Los Angeles Times*; July 28, 2004; p. A8; "Muslim Charity, Officials Indicted," by John Mintz, *Washington Post*; July 28, 2004; p. A1.

[136] Quoted in "Indictment Accuses Muslim Charity of Aiding Hamas," *op. cit.*

[137] See: "F.B.I. Raids 2 of the Biggest Muslim Charities; Assets of One Are Seized," by Philip Shenon, *New York Times*; December 15, 2001; p. B 6.

[138] Quoted in "Part of PATRIOT Act Is Struck Down," by John Mintz; *Washington Post*; January 27, 2004; p. A15.

[139] *Humanitarian Law Project, et al. v. John Ashcroft, et al.,* case CV 03–6107 ABC (MCx), United States District Court for the Central District of California, 309 F. Supp. 2nd 1185; opinion by Judge Audrey Collins; filed January 22, 2004. Also See: *Humanitarian Law Project v. United States*, U.S. Court of Appeals for the Ninth Circuit, 351 F. 3rd 282; filed December 3, 2003.

[140] Quoted in "Bank Worker's Tip Led to Terror Trial," by Betsy Z. Russell, *Spokesman-Review* (Seattle); April 15, 2004; p. A1.

[141] *Ibid.*

[142] Quoted in "Attorneys in Terrorism Trial Spar Over Constitution," Associated Press article in *Spokesman-Review* (Seattle); May 29, 2004.

[143] Quoted in "Jury Gets Case in Trial of Saudi Grad Student Accused of Helping Terrorists," by Bob Fick, Associated Press; June 2, 2004.

[144] Resolution 2004-13, City of Moscow, Idaho; passed June 7, 2004.

[145] "Al-Hussayen acquitted of Using Internet to Support Terrorism," by Bob Fick, Associated Press; June 10, 2004.

[146] *Ibid.*

[147] Quoted in "Acquittal in Internet Terrorism Case is a Defeat for Patriot Act," by Richard B. Schmitt, *Los Angeles Times*; June 11, 2004; p. A20.

[148] "Acquittal Welcomed by University Community," Associated Press; June 11, 2004.

[149] *Ibid.*

[150] Quoted in "Government Drops Immigration Charges, Al-Hussayen Drops Deportation appeal," by Bob Fick, Associated Press; June 30, 2004.

[151] "Al-Hussayen Still in Jail as Immigration Wheels Grind Slowly," by Bob Fick, Associated Press; July 16, 2004.

[152] "Jury Opens Second Week of Deliberations," Associated Press; June 7, 2004.

[153] "F.B.I. Scrutinizes Antiwar Rallies," *op. cit.*

[154] "We lose sight of our rights when freedom and fear collide: Inside the First Amendment," statement by Ken Paulson, executive director, Freedom of Information Center (Arlington, Va.); September 8, 2002. The survey was conducted on behalf of the Center by the Center for Survey Research & Analysis, University of Connecticut. [http://www.fac.org/commentary.aspx?id=2225&].

[155] "Support of First Freedoms Back to pre-9/11 Levels, New Survey Shows," news release, First Amendment Center; June 30, 2004.

[156] "The One Un-American Act," by William O. Douglas, *Nieman Reports*; January 1953; p. 20.

CHAPTER 10/ 'AN ALLERGY TO ANY KIND OF LEGAL RESTRAINT'

[1] "President Bush Speaks at Tsinghua University," *op. cit.*

[2] Quoted in "Prisoner Abuse Could Undercut U.S. Credibility," by Greg Jaffe, Carla Anne Robbins, and Roger Thurow, *Wall Street Journal*; May 10, 2004; p. A10.

[3] "The Impact of the USA PATRIOT Act: An Update," by Nancy Kranich; Free Expression Policy Project, 2003.

[4] "Silence on the Hill," editorial, *Washington Post*, January 5, 2004; p. A16.

[5] "Ashcroft's Endless Attacks Diminish Office," *op. cit.*

[6] "Reaction of Senate Judiciary Chairman Patrick Leahy to the Decision of the U.S. District Court for the District of Columbia Directing the Department of Justice to Comply With the Freedom of Information Act to Release Information on Detainees," news release, Office of Sen. Patrick Leahy; August 2, 2002. [http://leahy.senate.gov/press200208/080202b.html].

[7] Opening Statement of Sen. Patrick Leahy, Hearing on Protecting Our National Security From Terrorist Attacks; U. S. Senate, Committee on the Judiciary; October 21, 2003.

[8] "The USA PATRIOT Act and Beyond," Reporters Committee for Freedom of the Press, p. 6. [http://rcfp.org/homefrontconfidential/usapatriot.html].

[9] *Ibid.*

[10] "Freedom of Information Under Siege," general session, American Society of Newspaper Editors/ Newspaper Association of America; April 22, 2004.

[11] Opening Remarks, Sen. Patrick Leahy, U.S. Senate Committee on the Judiciary; June 8, 2004. [http://www.judiciary.senate.gov/member_statement.cfm?id=1212&wit_id=2629].

[12] See: 5 U.S.C. app § 7.2(1).

[13] *Judicial Watch v. National Energy Policy Development Group* and *Sierra Club v. Vice President Richard Cheney, et al.*, U.S. District Court for the District of Columbia, civil suit 02-631, 219 3rd Fed. 2nd 20, filed July 11, 2002.

[14] *Judicial Watch v. National Energy Policy Development Group* and *Sierra Club v. Vice President Richard Cheney, et al.*, U.S. Court of Appeals for the District of Columbia Circuit, civil suit 02-631, 334 Fed 3rd 1096.

[15] *Judicial Watch v. National Energy Policy Development Group* and *Sierra Club v. Vice President Richard Cheney, et al.*, U.S. Court of Appeals for the District of Columbia Circuit.

[16] Quoted in "Supreme Court Hears Cheney Case," by Joan Biskupic, *USA Today*, April 28, 2004; p. 3A.

[17] Quoted in "Justices Appear to Support Cheney Task Force Secrecy," by David G. Savage, *Los Angeles Times*, April 28, 2004; p. 1. The case is *Richard B. Cheney, et al. v. U.S. District Court for the District of Columbia, et al.*, 03-475, Supreme Court of the United States, oral arguments April 27, 2004 [Decided June 24, 2004].

[18] For further information, see: "Bush Administration Defends Secrecy of Energy Task Force," by Stephen Henderson, Knight Ridder/Tribune News Service; April 28, 2004; "Court Hears Argument in Complex Cheney Case," by Michael McGough, Pittsburgh *Post-Gazette*; April 28, 2004; p. A1; "High Court Hears Case on Cheney Energy Panel; White House Argues for Confidentiality," by Charles Lane; *Washington Post*, April 28, 2004; p. A1; "Supreme Court Expresses Concern in Cheney Case About Piercing Presidential Secrecy," by Gina Holland, Associated Press; April 27, 2004; "Supreme Court Hears Secrecy Case," Associated Press; April 27, 2004;

[19] "Bush Administration Holds on to Cheney Secrets," news release, The Sierra Club; September 16, 2003.

[20] *Ibid.*

[21] See: "Bush and Cheney to Face 9/11 Commission Today," by Dan Eggen and Walter Pincus, *Washington Post*, April 29, 2004; p. A2; and "9/11 Panel Questions Bush and Cheney," by Dan Eggen and Dana Milbank, *Washington Post*, April 30, 2004; p. A1.

CHAPTER 11/ THE 'AMBIGUOUS' ADMINISTRATION

[1] Patrick Henry, "The Debates in the Convention of the Commonwealth of Virginia on the Adoption of the Federal Constitution," session of June 9, 1788. [http://www.constitution.org/rc/ratt_va.07.htm].

[2] *United States v. Reynolds*, 345 U.S. 1 (1953), decided March 9, 1953, majority opinion filed by Chief Justice Fred M. Vinson.

[3] See: "Victim's Daughter Says US Lied About Crash; Ruling From 1948 Accident Shapes National Security Law," by Marcella Bombardieri, *Boston Globe*; March 18, 2001; p. B1; and "Government in Security," by L. Stuart Ditzen, *Philadelphia Inquirer*, May 23, 2004; p. M1.

[4] "An Injustice Wrapped in a Pretense; In '48 Crash, the U.S. Hid Behind National Security," by Timothy Lynch, Op-Ed, *Washington Post*; June 22, 2003; p. B3.

[5] *Ellen Mariani v. United Air Lines, Inc.*, U.S. District Court for the Southern District of New York, CV 01-1162, filed December 20, 2001; *Ellen Mariani v. George W. Bush, et al.*, U.S. District Court for the Eastern District of Pennsylvania; March 3, 2003, CV 03–5273.

[6] *Ellen Mariani v. George W. Bush, et al.*, U.S. District Court for the Eastern District of Pennsylvania; September 12, 2003, CV 03–5273. In May 2004, the case was transferred to the U.S. District Court for the Southern District of New York.

[7] "911 Victim's Wife Files RICO Case Against GW Bush," news release from Philip J. Berg; November 27, 2003.

[8] "Freedom of Information Under Siege," *op. cit.*

[9] "Funding, Framework for National Animal Identification System Announced," *Journal of the American Veterinary Medical Association*; June 15, 2004.

[10] Quoted in "Government Puts Nuclear Info Under Wraps," Associated Press; August 6, 2004.

[11] *Ibid.*

[12] "Vital Health, Safety Information Endangered by Transportation Bill Secrecy Provision," news release, BushGreenwatch; July 21, 2004.

[13] See: Amendment to Executive Order 12958, Classified National Security Information; March 25, 2003. [http://www.whitehouse.gov/news/releases/2003/03/20030325-11.html].

[14] Memorandum, "The Freedom of Information Act," under authority of John Ashcroft; October 12, 2001.

[15] See: "Government Openness at Issue as Bush Holds on to Records," by Adam Clymer, *New York Times*; January 3, 2003; p. A1.

[16] "Agency Views on Changes Resulting from New Administration Policy," Government Accounting Office; September 2, 2003. [http://www.gao.gov/new.items/d03981.pdf].

[17] Letter to Marie A. O'Rourke, assistant director, FOIA/Privacy Unit, Executive Office for United States Attorneys, Department of Justice; April 13, 2004.

[18] Response, Marie A. O'Rourke, assistant director, FOIA/Privacy Unit, Executive Office for United States Attorneys, Department of Justice; May 18, 2004. [Public existence of the Department's refusal first published, "New From D.C.: Secret Press Releases," by William P. Barrett, *Forbes*; July 26, 2004; p. 44.

[19] "Freedom of Information Under Siege," *op. cit.*

[20] "Freedom and Security," *op. cit.*

[21] "Secrecy Report Card: Quantitative Indicators of Secrecy in the Federal Government," by Rick Blum, OpentheGovernment.org (Washington, D.C.); report of August 26, 2004.

[22] See: *American Civil Liberties Union v. Department of Justice*, November 2002, 265 F. Supp.2nd 20.

[23] "ACLU Presses for Full Disclosure," news release; January 17, 2003. [http://www.aclu.org/news/NewsPrint.cfm?ID=11638&c=206].

[24] "The Government's Response," American Civil Liberties Union," ACLU. [http://www.aclu.org/patriot_foia/foia3.html].

[25] FOIA request, Electronic Privacy Information Center to Office of Homeland Security; March 20, 2002. Also see: *EPIC v. Homeland Security*, U.S. District Court for the District of Columbia; April 2, 2002.

[26] *Electronic Privacy Information Center v. Office of Homeland Security and Tom Ridge*, U. S. District Court for the District of Columbia, civil action 02–620; opinion by Colleen Kollar-Kotelly; filed December 26, 2002.

[27] See: http://www.epic.org/privacy/litigation/default.html.

[28] "Fugitives Remain a Step Ahead of the INS," by Marisa Taylor, *San Diego Union-Tribune*; January 9, 2003. p. A1; "Foreign Lobbyist Database Could Vanish," by Kevin Bogardus, Center for Public Integrity; June 28, 2004.

[29] "Foreign Lobbyist Database Could Vanish," by Kevin Bogardus, Center for Public Integrity; June 28, 2004.

[30] *Center for Public Integrity v. U.S. Department of Justice*, U.S. District Court for the District of Columbia, filed July 29, 2004.

[31] The organizations filing the request were the American Civil Liberties Union, Center for Constitutional Rights, Physicians for Human Rights, Veterans for Common Sense, and Veterans for Peace.

[32] *American Civil Liberties Union, et al. v. Department of Defense, et al.*, complaint for injunctive relief, U.S. District Court for the Southern District of New York, filed June 2, 2004. Also see: "ACLU Requested Information on Prisoner Abuse in October," news release, American Civil Liberties Union; May 13, 2004.

[33] *American Civil Liberties Union, et al. v. Department of Defense, et al.*, U.S. District Court for the Southern District of New York; 04 Civ. 4151 (AKH), filed August 17, 2004.

[34] Quoted in "'Secrets' Perplex Panel," by Michael J. Sniffen, Associated Press; September 3, 2004.

[35] *Ibid.*

[36] "From the White House, With Silence," by Dana Milbank, *Washington Post*; April 20, 2004; p. A17.

[37] Quoted in "A Word With Gen. Wesley Clark," *op. cit.*

[38] Bill Moyers, speech, Society of Professional Journalists national convention; September 11, 2004.

[39] Walter Cronkite, "Perspective: Secrecy and Lies," syndicated column (King Features Syndicate); April 4, 2004.

[40] *Ibid.*

[41] "Freedom of Information Under Siege, *op. cit.*

[42] John W. Dean, *Worse Than Watergate*, Little, Brown (New York, N.Y.), 2004.

[43] Quoted in "Homeland Security Versus Right to Information," *op. cit.*

CHAPTER 12 /
CREATING CUTESY NAMES FOR PROGRAMS THAT REDUCE CIVIL LIBERTIES

[1] Originally posted on www.citizencorps.gov/tips.html and White House and Department of Justice websites, and then removed several months later. One of the first articles in the mass media to expose this program was a commentary by Peter Sussman, "Your Neighbor Is Watching," *San Francisco Chronicle*; July 18, 2002.

[2] Quoted in "Homeland Security Plan Spurs Civil Liberties Concerns," by David Westphal, *Sacramento Bee*; August 9, 2002; p. A12.

[3] See: http://www.dodig.osd.mil/audit/reports/FY04/04-033.pdf.

[4] George W. Bush, "State of the Union," January 28, 2003. [http://www.whitehouse.gov/news/releases/2003/01/20030128-19.html].

[5] "Fact Sheet: Strengthening Intelligence to Better Protect America," Office of the Press Secretary, the White House; January 28, 2003. [http://www.whitehouse.gov/news/releases/2003/01/20030128-12.html].

[6] See: "New Screening Tool Draws Fire; Test of Air Traveler Database Ignites Concerns About Privacy," by Eunice Moscoso, *Atlanta Journal-Constitution*; April 25, 2004; p. 5B.

[7] Statement of Nancy Holtzman, "Hearings on the Status of the Computer-Assisted Passenger Prescreening System, Aviation Subcommittee," House Transportation and Infrastructure Committee; March 15, 2004.
[http://www.acte.org/resources/press_release/testimony_to_congress.shtml].

[8] *Ibid.*

[9] *Ibid.*

[10] *Aviation Security: Computer-Assisted Passenger Prescreening System Faces Significant Implementation Challenges,* Report to Congress, General Accounting Office; February 2004; GAO–04–385.

[11] "New Notice Outlines Changes in CAPPS II System," posting in Federal Register, U.S. Department of Homeland Security. [http://www.dhs.gov/dhspublic/display?content=1135].

[12] See: "Plan to Collect Flier Data Cancelled," by Mimi Hall and Barbara DeLollis, *USA Today;* July 15, 2004; p. 1A; "Privacy Worries Doom Screening Plan for Airlines," by Audrey Hudson, *Washington Times;* July 16, 2004; p. A7; "U.S. Rethinks Air Travel Screening," by Ricardo Alonso-Zaldivar, *Los Angeles Times;* July 16, 2004; p. A20; and "New Airline Screening System Postponed," by Sara Kehaulani Goo and Robert O'Harrow Jr., *Washington Post;* July 16, 2004; p. A2;

[13] See: "Revised Flier-Screening Plan in Works," by Mimi Hall and Alan Levin, *USA Today;* July 16, 2004; p. 3A; "CAPPS II to be Redesignated but Critics Remain Skeptical," by Harvey Simon, *Homeland Security & Defense;* July 21, 2004; p. 7; and "U.S. Rethinks Air Travel Screening, *op. cit.*

[14] See: Statement of Clark Kent Ervin, inspector general, U.S. Department of Homeland Security; and "Aviation Security," statement of Norman J. Rabkin, managing director, Homeland Security and Justice, Government Accounting Office. Testimonies presented to the Aviation Subcommittee, U.S. House of Representatives; April 22, 2004.

[15] Comments by Sen. Edward M. Kennedy, hearings, "The 9/11 Commission and Recommendations for the Future of Federal Law Enforcement and Border Security, U.S. Senate, Committee on the Judiciary; August 17, 2004. Also see: "Sen. Kennedy Flagged by No-Fly List," by Sarah Kehaulani Goo, *Washington Post;* August 20, 2004; p. A1; and "Senator? Terrorist? A Watch List Stops Kennedy at Airport," by Rachel L. Swarns, *New York Times;* August 20, 2004; p. A1.

[16] "Airport Security Bars Cancer Patient," by Henry Pierson Curtis, *Orlando* (Fla.) *Sentinel;* April 22, 2004; p. A1.

[17] *Michelle D. Green, et al. v. Transportation Security Administration, et al.,* United States District Court for the Western District of Washington; filed April 6, 2004. [Also see: "Cleric, Air Force Sergeant Are on 'No-fly' List," by Emily Bazar, *Sacramento Bee;* April 7, 2004, p. A3.]

[18] Quoted in "ACLU Files First Nationwide Challenge to 'No-Fly' List, Saying Government List Violates Passengers' Rights," ACLU news release; April 6, 2004.

[19] "Report: Airport Screeners Perform Poorly," Associated Press; April 22, 2004.

[20] See: "DHS and EU Sign Agreement to Allow Collection of Passenger Data," news release, Department of Homeland Security; May 28, 2004; and "U.S., EU Sign Agreement on Transfer of Airline Passenger Data," United States Mission to the European Union, news release; May 28, 2004.

[21] Quoted in "MP Vows to Campaign Against Patriot Act," by Cindy E. Harnett, *Times Colonist* (Victoria, B.C.); August 12, 2004; p. A4.

[22] Bob Barr, Testimony, *op. cit.*

[23] Interestingly, MATRIX does not include any records of gun ownership. MATRIX acknowledges data includes information of criminal history, driver's license information, FAA pilot licenses and ownership, property ownership, information about motor vehicle registration and Coast Guard registered vessels, state sexual offenders lists, federal terrorist watch lists, corporation filings, bankruptcy failings, state-issued professional licenses, and various Uni-

form Commercial Code filings. It claims it does not include birth and marriage licenses, divorce decrees, airline reservations or travel records, utility bill payments, or mortgage payments.

[24] "MATRIX: First Responder Support," Seisint, Inc., presentation for State of Utah on January 24, 2004. [See: http://www.aclu.org/Files/OpenFile.cfm?id=15813].

[25] At the time, Ridge was a special assistant to the president and not yet a cabinet secretary.

[26] "U.S. Backs Florida's New Counterterrorism Database," by Robert O'Harrow Jr., *Washington Post*, August 6, 2003; p. A1.

[27] "Briefing Points for the Vice President of the United States," January 2003. [http://www.aclu.org/privacy/privacy.cfm?ID=15821&c=130].

[28] "MATRIX Misconceptions," at http://www,matrix-at.org/misconceptions.htm.

[29] "ACLU Unveils Disturbing New Revelations About MATRIX Surveillance Program," news release, American Civil Liberties Union; May 20, 2004.

[30] "New Documents Obtained by ACLU Raise Troubling Questions About Matrix Program," ACLU Issue Brief No. 2; May 20, 2004.

[31] See: http://www.matrix-at.org/privacy_policy.pdf.

[32] "ACLU Unveils Disturbing New Revelations About MATRIX Surveillance Program," *op. cit.*

[33] *William Milliken, Sister Elizabeth LaForest, Al Fishman, and the American Civil Liberties Union Fund of Michigan v. Tadarial J. Sturdivant*, Circuit Court for the County of Wayne (Michigan); filed August 2, 2004. [Sturdivant is director of the Michigan State Police.]

[34] "Lawsuit Filed Against Michigan State Police," news release, ACLU of Michigan; August 3, 2004.

[35] "Data Mining: Federal Efforts Cover a Wide Range of Uses," Government Accounting Office, May 2004, GAO–04–548.

[36] *Ibid.*

[37] "Security Collides With Civil Liberties: Debate Intensifies Over War on terror," *op. cit.*

[38] For additional information, see: "Fed Role Feared After Breaches," by Rod Smith, *Las Vegas Review-Journal*; May 5, 2003; p. D1; "New Law Concerns Gaming Industry," by Rod Smith, *Las Vegas Review-Journal;* December 16, 2003; p. D1; "Airlines, Hotels Ordered to Give FBI Information," by Rod Smith, *Las Vegas Review-Journal*; December 31, 2003; p. A1; "Sources: FBI Gathered Visitor Information Only in Las Vegas," by Rod Smith, *Las Vegas Review-Journal*; January 7, 2004; p. A1; and "'Surveillance City'," editorial, *Las Vegas Review-Journal*; January 11, 2004; p. E2.

[39] See: "Wyoming Vacationer Gets 9-Hour Jail Detour From Cruise," by Catherine Wilson, Associated Press; June 18, 2004.

[40] Quoted in "Ashcroft Wants Stronger PATRIOT Act," by Susan Schmidt, *Washington Post*; June 6, 2003; p. A11.

[41] "JetBlue retains Deloitte & Touche to Assist the Airline in Its Analysis of Its Privacy Policy," news release; September 22, 2003.

[42] See: "JetBlue Shared Passenger Data," *Wired News*; September 18, 2003. [http://www.wired.com/news/privacy/0,1848,62373,00.html]; and "No Law Broken in JetBlue Scandal," by Ryan Singel, *Wired News*; February 21, 2004. [http://www.wired.com/news/privacy/0,1848,62373,00.html].

[43] Quoted in "No Law Broken," *op. cit.*

[44] See: "Nomination Hearing for David M. Stone to be Assistant Secretary of Homeland Security, Transportation Security Administration," U.S. Senate, Governmental Affairs Committee; June 23, 2004. [http://govt-aff.senate.gov/audio_video/062304video.ram][http://govt-aff.senate.gov/_files/062304stone1005.pdf]; also see: "More False Information From TSA," by Ryan Singel, *Wired News*; June 23, 2004. [www.wired.com/news/0,1294,63958,00.html].

[45] "Northwest Airlines Statement on Media Reports Regarding NASA Aviation Security Research Study," news release, Northwest Airlines; January 18, 2004.

[46] "Report to the Public on Events Surrounding jetBlue Data Transfer," by Nuala O'Connor Kelly, Department of Homeland Security Privacy Office; February 20, 2004. [http://www.dhs.gov/interweb/assetlibrary/PrivacyOffice_jetBlueFINAL.pdf].

[47] See: "Blues Do Part for National Homeland Security," *Bluesweek*; November 7, 2003; p. 1.

[48] See: "Blues, Aetna Help Hunt Terrorists," by Amy Lee; *Detroit News*; November 16, 2003; p. A1.

[49] *Ibid.*

[50] *Ibid.*

[51] www.nyc.indymedia.org/newswire/display_any/101494.

[52] Subpoena, United States District Court for the Southern District of New York, issued to Calyx Internet Access; August 19, 2004.

[53] "ACLU Criticizes Secret Service Investigation of News Website That Posted RNC Delegates' Names," news release, ACLU; August 30, 2004.

[54] Letter from Timothy J. Treanor, Assistant U.S. Attorney to Calyx Internet Access; August 19, 2004.

[55] "ACLU Criticizes Secret Service Investigation of News Website That Posted RNC Delegates' Names," *op. cit.*

[56] Statement, Micah Anderson; August 30, 2004. [http://www.aclu.org/news/NewsPrint.cfm?ID=16337&c=86].

CHAPTER 13/ 'THE CONSTITUTION IS OURS—NOT JUST HIS'

[1] Bob Barr, Testimony, *op. cit.*

[2] Quoted in "John Ashcroft's PATRIOT GAMES," *op. cit.*

[3] A specific bill (H.R. 2934) was introduced into the House in July 2003. The forty-three "federal crimes of terrorism," only twenty of which carried the death penalty, is 18 U.S.C. § 2332(b)(g)(5).

[4] Testimony of Timothy H. Edgar, before House Judiciary Committee, Subcommittee on Crime, Terrorism, and Homeland Security; April 21, 2004. [http://www.house.gov/judiciary/edgar042104.pdf].

[5] *Strengthening America by Defending Our Liberties*, *op. cit.*, p. 24.

[6] *Ibid.*

[7] A copy of the confidential draft memo of January 9, 2003, is available at: http://www.publicintegrity.org/dtaweb/downloads/Story_01_020703_Doc_1.pdf. For a discussion of the impact of the Act, see: "ACLU Fact Sheet on PATRIOT Act II," American Civil Liberties Union; March 28, 2003. [http://www.aclu.org/SafeandFree.cfm?ID=11835&c=206].

[8] "Sweet Land of Liberty," by Nat Hentoff, *Washington Times*; February 24, 2003; p. A23.

[9] Kay Maxwell, "Civil Liberties Are Cornerstone of American Values," September 11, 2003.

[10] "Ashcroft and the Constitution," by Errol Lewis, *New York Sun*; February 10, 2003; p. 6.

[11] See: "Justice Dept. Balks at Effort to Study Antiterror Powers," by Adam Clymer, *New York Times*; August 15, 2003; p. A21.

[12] Quoted by U.S. Attorney Jim Lenton, "Patriot Act Aids Police; Acting U.S. Attorney Says Rights Protected, " *Times-Picayune* (New Orleans); March 11, 2004; p. 1.

[13] Russell Feingold, *Congressional Record*; October 22, 2003; p. S12990.

[14] "An Unpatriotic Act," editorial, *New York Times*; August 25, 2003; p. A14.

[15] "Ashcroft Says Efforts to Weaken Terrorism Law Will Place Americans at Greater Risk," by Eric Lichtblau, *New York Times*; August 20, 2003; p. A14.

[16] "Special Report: Patriot Act Blurred in Public Mind," by Toni Locy, *op. cit.*

[17] "The Attorney General and the PATRIOT Act," by John L. Smith, *Las Vegas Review-Journal*; August 31, 2003; p. 1E.

[18] Interview with James Dempsey by Bob Garfield, "Snooping in the Dark," *On the Media*, WNYC-AM/National Public Radio; January 9, 2004.

CHAPTER 14 / 'AFFIRM AND UPHOLD CIVIL RIGHTS AND CIVIL LIBERTIES'

[1] "Resolution Affirming Principles of Federalism and Civil Liberties," Resolution 2004–37, National League of Cities.

[2] Quoted in "PATRIOT Act Gets 'NO' Vote," *Richmond* (Va.) *Times Dispatch*; March 9, 2004; p. B1.

[3] "Resolution Calling Upon Federal, State and Local Officials, and Upon New York City Agencies and Institutions, to Affirm and Uphold Civil Rights and Civil Lliberties," Resolution 60–2004 (February 4, 2004), New York City Council.
[http://www.nycbordc.org/resolution0909-2003.html].

[4] "Resolution of the City of Palo Alto Directing Enhanced Efforts to Assure the Protection of Civil Liberties That are Threatened by the U.S.A. Patriot Act," resolution 8301, Palo Alto (Calif.) City Council; passed June 9, 2003.

[5] Quoted in "Palo Alto Librarians, Police Protest Patriot Act," by Beth Fouhy, Associated Press; May 28, 2003.

[6] "Resolution Against the USA PATRIOT ACT and Other Executive Orders for the City of Philadelphia, Pennsylvania," Resolution 020394; May 28, 2003.
[http://www.philly peace.org/patriotact/resolution.html].

[7] "Sense of the Council in Support of Protection of Civil Liberties Resolution of 2004," Resolution 15-468; March 2004.
[http://www.dccouncil.washington.dc.us/images/00001/20040205164119.pdf]

[8] Quoted by Sen. Patrick Leahy, Hearing on Protecting Our National Security From Terrorist Attacks; U. S. Senate, Committee on the Judiciary; October 21, 2003.

[9] "Silence on the Hill," *op. cit.*

[10] "The Politics of War Refocus the Mission," by Newt Gingrich, *San Francisco Chronicle*; November 11, 2003; p. A17.

[11] Primary sponsors were Sens. Larry Craig (R-Idaho), Richard Durbin (D-Ill.), John Sununu (R-N.H.), and Russell Feingold (D-Wisc.).
The bill is available at: http://thomas.loc.gov/cgi-bin/quiery/z?c108:s.1709.

[12] Security and Freedom Ensured Act of 2003; S. 1709; filed October 2, 2003.
[http://Thomas.loc.gov/cgi-bin/query/z?c108:5.1709].

[13] "Durbin Responds to Veto Threat Against the SAFE Act," news release, Sen. Dick Durbin; January 28, 2004.

[14] Letter from John D. Ashcroft to Sen. Orrin Hatch, chair, Senate Committee on the Judiciary; January 28, 2004. [http://bordc.org/dojresponse.pdf].
For a complete list of pending legislation, see Appendix 1.

[15] "Durbin Responds to Veto Threat Against the SAFE Act," *op. cit.*

[16] See: S. 2528 and H.R. 4591, both submitted June 16, 2004.

[17] C. L. Otter, "Remarks Upon Introducing an Amendment to the Departments of Commerce, Justice, and State, the Judiciary, and Related Agencies Appropriations Act, 2004," *Congressional Record*; July 22, 2003; p. H7290.

[18] "Special Report: Patriot Act Blurred in Public Mind," by Toni Locy, *op. cit.*

[19] The memo was sent August 14, 2003. See: "Prosecutors Are Urged to Press Congress," by Don Eggen, *Washington Post*; August 22, 2003; p. A19.

[20] See: *Electronic Privacy Information Center v. U.S. Department of Justice*, civil action 03-2078 (JR), U.S. District Court for the District of Columbia.

[21] Voting for the bill were 195 Democrats, 113 Republicans, and one Independent; voting against the bill were 114 Republicans and 4 Democrats. Seven representatives did not vote.

[22] *Ibid.*

[23] Bernie Sanders, introduction to "Freedom to Read Protection Act," *Congressional Record* (extensions); March 12, 2003; pp. E441–E442.

[24] "White House Threatens Spending Bill Veto If Patriot Act Is Weakened," by Alan Fram, Associated Press; July 7, 2004.

[25] Twelve Republicans changed their votes: Reps. Doug Bereuter (Nebraska), Michael Billirakis (Florida), Rob Bishop (Utah), Barbara Cubin (Wyoming), Tom Davis (Virginia), Wayne Gilchrest (Maryland), Katherine Harris (Florida), Jack Kingston (Georgia), Marilyn Musgrave (Colorado), Nick Smith (Michigan), Thomas Tancredo (Utah), and Zach Wamp (Tennessee). Democrats switching from "nay" to "yea" were Robert Cramer (Alabama), Rodney Alexander (Louisiana), and Brad Sherman (California). Voting "present" was Rep. Zoe Lofgren (D-Calif.)

[26] See: "Effort to Curb Patriot Act Fails in House," by Alan Fram, Associated Press; July 8, 2004; "Bush Prevails as House Refuses to Curb Patriot Act," by Alan Fram, Associated Press; July 8, 2004.

[27] Quoted in "Effort to Curb Scope of Antiterrorism Law Falls Short," by Eric Lichtblau, *New York Times*; July 9, 2004; p. A16.

[28] Quoted in "Majority Rules," *Congressional Daily*, November 25, 2003; and comments by Rep. Steny Hoyer (D-Md.), discussion of H.R. 4754; *Congressional Record*; July 8, 2004; p. 5348+. Originally quoted by James A. Barnes in *National Journal*, October 1987.

[29] "High and Mighty," by Kirk Nielsen, *Miami New Times*; July 15, 2004.

[30] *Ibid.*

[31] *Ibid.*

[32] "Prepared Remarks of Attorney General John Ashcroft," July 13, 2003. [http://www.justice.gov/ag/speeches/2004/071304_patriot_report_remarks.htm].

[33] See: "Report from the Field: The USA PATRIOT Act at Work," Department of Justice, report prepared for the House of Representatives Committee on the Judiciary, July 2004.

[34] Sen. Patrick Leahy, remarks, *Congressional Record*, vol. 147, S11015, S1015 (October 25, 2001).

[35] Mark D. Agrast, *et al.*, "Report," Section of Individual Rights and Responsibilities, Report to the House of Delegate, American Bar Association, August 2003, p. 2.

[36] Resolution, House of Delegates, American Bar Association; August 2003.

[37] *Ibid.*

[38] "President Urges Renewal of the Antiterrorism Law," by Elisabeth Bumiller, *New York Times*; March 2, 2004; p. A12.

[39] George W. Bush, "Radio Address to the Nation," April 17, 2004. [http://www.whitehouse.gov/news/releases/2004/04/20040417.html].

[40] George W. Bush, "President Bush Calls for Renewing the USA PATRIOT Act," news release; April 19, 2004. [http://www.whitehouse.gov/news/releases/2004/04/20040419-4.html].

[41] See: "Freedom vs. Security at Issue," by Dan Herbeck, *Buffalo News*; April 21, 2003; p. A1; "Bush Decries Bail for Terror Suspects," by Bill Sammon, *Washington Times*; April 21, 2004; p. A3; and "Bush Promotes Patriot Act in Buffalo, Raises Funds in New York City," Bulletin News Network; April 21, 2004.

[42] "Patriot Act Games," editorial, *Buffalo News*; April 21, 2004; p. B10.

[43] See: "Vice President Cheney Remarks at the KCI Expo Center," Federal News Service; June 1, 2004.

[44] Letter Michael J., Sullivan to Boards of Selectmen, Commonwealth of Massachusetts; May 28, 2004. Also see: "PATRIOT Act Is Praised in Mailing; US Attorney Steps Up Advocacy of 2001 Law," by Connie Paige, *Boston Globe*; June 12, 2004; p. B1.

[45] Quoted in "Bush to Tout Patriot Act, Stump for Senator Facing Primary Challenge," by Deb Reichmann, Associated Press; April 19, 2004.

[46] Quoted in "Permanent Patriot Act Urged," by Gary Martin, *San Antonio Express-News*; April 21, 2004; p. 9A.

[47] Quoted in "Domestic Spying vs. Secret Police: FBI Walking Tough, Thin Line on Domestic Surveillance," by Michael Moran, MSNBC; September 2, 2003. [http://www.msnbc.msn.com/id/3071395/]. Also see: "Panel: FBI Should Lose Terror Role in U.S.," by Michael Kilian, *Chicago Tribune*; December 17, 2002; p. 24.

[48] "Subpoena Plans Stirs Alarm," by Rebecca Carr, *Atlanta Journal-Constitution;* September 26, 2003, p. A1.

[49] "In the Name of the God of Creation and Wisdom," Nobel Peace Prize acceptance speech by Shirin Ebadi; December 10, 2003. [http://nobel.no/eng_lect_2003b.html].

[50] Quoted in "Patriot Act Redux," by Sara-Ellen Amster, *Intelligence Report* (Southern Poverty Law Center), Summer 2003.

For Further Information

American Civil Liberties Union, *Civil Liberties After 9/11*, ACLU (New York, N.Y.), 2003.
———, *Freedom Under Fire: Dissent in Post-9/11 America*, ACLU (New York, N.Y.), 2003.
———, *Seeking Truth From Justice: PATRIOT Propaganda: The Justice Department's Campaign to Mislead the Public About the USA Patriot Act*, ACLU (New York, N.Y.), 2003.
———, *The ACLU in the Courts Since 9/11*, ACLU (New York, N.Y.), 2004.
———, *The FBI's Power to Rifle Through Your Records and Personal Belongings Without Telling You*, ACLU (New York, N.Y.), 2003.
Anderson, Shannon R., *Total Information Awareness and Beyond: The Dangers of Using Mining Technology to Prevent Terrorism*, Bill of Rights Defense Committee (Northampton, Mass.), 2004.
Ball, Howard, *The USA Patriot Act: A Reference Handbook*, ABC-CLIO, 2004.
Barrett, Jerry, ed., *Big Bush Lies*, RiverWood Books (Ashland, Ore.), 2004.
Bazar, Emily, Sam Stanton, and Paul Kitagaki Jr., "Liberty in the Balance," *Sacramento Bee*; September 21–24, 2003.
Brasch, Walter, *Sex and the Single Beer Can: Probing the Media and American Culture*, Lighthouse Press (Deerfield Beach, Fla.), 2004.
Brown, Cynthia, ed., *Lost Liberties: Ashcroft and the Assault on Personal Freedom*, The New Press (New York, N.Y.), 2003.
Byrd, Robert C. *Losing America: Confronting a Reckless and Arrogant Presidency*, W.W. Norton (New York, N.Y.), 2004.
Chang, Nancy, *The USA Patriot Act*, Center for Constitutional Rights (New York, N.Y.), 2003.
Chang, Nancy and Alan Kabat, *Summary of Recent Court Rulings on Terrorism-Related Matters Having Civil Liberties Implications*, Center for Constitutional Rights (New York, N.Y.), 2004.
Cole, David, *Enemy Aliens: Double Standards and Constitutional Freedoms in the War on Terrorism*, The New Press (New York, N.Y.), 2003.
Cole, David and James Dempsey, *Terrorism and the Constitution: Sacrificing Civil Liberties in the Name of National Security*, The New Press (New York, N.Y.), 2002.
Dadge, David, *Casualty of War: The Bush Administration's Assault on a Free Press* Prometheus Books (Amherst, N.Y.), 2004.
Dalglish, Lucy A., Jennifer LaFleur, and Gregg P. Lesie, *Homefront Confidential: How the War on Terrorism Affects Access to Information and the Public's Right to Know*, Reporters Committee on Freedom of the Press (Arlington, Va.), 4th edition, September 2003.

221

Electronic Frontier Foundation, *EFF Analysis of the Provisions of the USA PATRIOT Act That Relate to Online Activities*; Electronic Frontier Foundation (San Francisco, Calif.), October 31, 2001.

Fahrenheit 9/11, written, directed, and produced by Michael Moore, Dog Eat Dog Films; released June 25, 2004.

Foerstel, Herbert N., *Refuge of a Scoundrel: The Patriot Act in Libraries*, Greenwood Publishing (Westport, Conn.), 2004.

Goldberg, Danny, Victor Goldberg, and Robert Goldberg, eds., *It's a Free Country: Personal Freedom in America After September 11*, Nation Books (New York, N.Y.), 2003.

Hentoff, Nat, *The War on the Bill of Rights and the Gathering Resistance*, Seven Stories Press (New York, N.Y.), 2003.

Heymann, Philip B., *Terrorism, Freedom, and Security: Winning Without War*, MIT Press (Cambridge, Mass.), 2003.

Human Rights Watch, *"Enduring Freedom": Abuses by U.S. Forces in Afghanistan*, Human Rights Watch (New York, N.Y.), 2004.

Institute for Social Policy and Understanding, *The USA Patriot Act: Impact on the Arab and Muslim American Community*, Institute for Social Policy and Understanding (Clinton Twp., Mich.), September 2003.

Kiss, Terry, "Media Coverage of 9/11 and Its Aftermath, Air University Library, Maxwell Air Force Base, U.S. Air Force, June 2003.

Kranich, Nancy, *Update on the USA Patriot Act,* Free Expression Policy Project (New York, N.Y.), 2003.

Leone, Richard C. and Gregh Anrig Jr., eds., *The War on Our Freedoms: Civil Liberties in an Age of Terrorism*, Century Foundation (New York, N.Y.), 2003.

Martin, Kate, "Domestic Intelligence and Civil Liberties," *SAIS Review*; Vol. 24, No. 1 (Winter–Spring 2004), pp. 7-021.

Parenti, Christian, *The Soft Cage: Surveillance in America From Slavery to the War on Terror,* Basic Books (New York, N.Y.), 2003.

Rosen, Jeffrey, *The Naked Crowd: Reclaiming Security and Freedom in an Anxious Age*, Random House (New York, N.Y.), 2004.

Schulhofer, Stephen J. *The Enemy Within: Intelligence Gathering, Law Enforcement, and Civil Liberties in the Wake of September 11*, Century Foundation (New York, N.Y.), 2002.

Schultz, William, *Tainted Legacy: 9/11 and the Ruin of Human Rights*, Nation Books (New York, N.Y.), 2003.

Strengthening America by Defending Our Liberties: An Agenda for Reform, Center for Democracy and Technology, Center for American Progress and Center for National Security Studies; October 31, 2003.

The Cost of Freedom—Civil Liberties, Security and the USA PATRIOT Act, television documentary, Duncan Entertainment and Iowa Public Television, 2004.

Van Bergen, Jennifer, *The Twilight of Democracy: The Bush Plan for America*, Common Courage Press (Monroe, Maine), 2004.

Vanzi, Max, *The Patriot Act: Other Post-9/11 Enforcement Powers and the Impact on California's Muslim Communities*, Senate Office of Research (Sacramento, Calif.), May 2004.

Index

OTHER BOOKS BY THE AUTHOR

A Comprehensive Annotated Bibliography of
American Black English (with Ila Wales Brasch)

A ZIM Autobiography

Betrayed: Death of an American Newspaper

Black English and the Mass Media

Cartoon Monickers:
An Insight Into the Animation Industry

Brer Rabbit, Uncle Remus, and the 'Cornfield Journalist':
The Tale of Joel Chandler Harris

Columbia County Place Names

Enquiring Minds and Space Aliens
Wandering Through the Mass Media and American Culture

Forerunners of Revolution:
Muckrakers and the American Social Conscience

Sex and the Single Beer Can:
Probing the Media and American Culture

Social Foundations of the Mass Media
(coauthor)

The Joy of Sax:
America During the Bill Clinton Era

The Press and the State:
Sociohistorical and Contemporary Issues
(coauthor)

With Just Cause:
Unionization of the American Journalist

About the Author

Long before the PATRIOT Act became law, Walter Brasch was actively writing about civil rights, social issues, and the First Amendment.

He is a university professor of journalism and a syndicated newspaper columnist. Previously, he was a newspaper reporter and editor, a multimedia writer-producer, and magazine writer and editor. He was president of the Society of Professional Journalists Keystone State Professional Chapter that won the national Freedom of Information Award, and was founding coordinator of Pennsylvania Journalism Educators.

He is also the author of fifteen books, most of them focusing upon the fusion of historical and contemporary social issues, including *Black English and the Mass Media* (1981); *Forerunners of Revolution: Muckrakers and the American Social Conscience* (1991); *With Just Cause: The Unionization of the American Journalist* (1991); *Brer Rabbit, Uncle Remus, and the 'Cornfield Journalist': The Tale of Joel Chandler Harris* (2000); *The Joy of Sax: America During the Bill Clinton Era* (2001); and *Sex and the Single Beer Can: Probing the Media and American Culture* (2004). He is also senior author of *The Press and the State* (1986), recognized as an Outstanding Academic Book by *Choice* magazine, published by the American Library Association.

During the past decade, he has won more than one hundred regional and national media awards from the Society of Professional Journalists, National Society of Newspaper Columnists, National Federation of Press Women, Pennsylvania Press Club, Pennsylvania Women's Press Association, PennWriters, and other organizations.

He was honored by San Diego State University as a Points of Excellence winner in 1997. At Bloomsburg University, he earned the Creative Arts Award, the Creative Teaching Award, and was named an Outstanding Student Advisor. He was honored with the Martin Luther King Jr. Humanitarian Service Award, and is the first recipient of the Dean's Award for Excellence, recognizing superior teaching and research/writing. For the Pennsylvania Humanities Council, he was a Commonwealth Speaker.

He is listed in *Who's Who in America, Contemporary Authors*, and *Who's Who in the Media*. Dr. Brasch earned an A.B. in sociology from San Diego State College, an M.A. in journalism from Ball State University, and a Ph.D. in mass communication/journalism, with cognate areas in American government and language and culture studies from The Ohio University.

Visit Dr. Brasch's website at
http://www.walterbrasch.com